Envisioning Asia

Envisioning Asia

On Location, Travel, and the Cinematic Geography of U.S. Orientalism

Jeanette Roan

THE UNIVERSITY OF MICHIGAN PRESS

Ann Arbor

Copyright © by the University of Michigan 2010
All rights reserved
Published in the United States of America by
The University of Michigan Press
Manufactured in the United States of America
♾ Printed on acid-free paper

2013   2012   2011   2010   4   3   2   1

A CIP catalog record for this book is available from the British Library.

Library of Congress Cataloging-in-Publication Data

Roan, Jeanette, 1970–
     Envisioning Asia : on location, travel, and the cinematic
     geography of U.S. orientalism / Jeanette Roan.
          p.   cm.
     Includes bibliographical references and index.
     ISBN 978-0-472-07083-1 (cloth : alk. paper) —
     ISBN 978-0-472-05083-3 (pbk. : alk. paper)
     1. Asians in motion pictures.   2. Asia—In motion pictures.
3. Culture in motion pictures.   4. Motion pictures—United States—
History—20th century.   5. Documentary films—United States—
History—20th century.   I. Title.

PN1995.9.A78R63   2010
791.43'65851—dc22   2009047780

ISBN13 978-0-472-02706-4 (electronic)

To my parents
Yeai and Mei-Sha Roan

Acknowledgments

This journey has been a long one, and I have incurred many debts along the way. Leslie Bostrum, my undergraduate adviser in the Department of Visual Art at Brown University, mentioned one day that she could imagine me obtaining a doctoral degree. Although I no longer recall the context of that conversation, I do know that pursuing a Ph.D. had not occurred to me prior to it. I first began thinking through the issues at the center of this book while a student in the Graduate Program in Visual and Cultural Studies at the University of Rochester. Lisa Cartwright, my dissertation adviser, offered the perfect balance of criticism and encouragement. Kamran Ali, Douglas Crimp, David Rodowick, and Sharon Willis shared with me the critical tools to conceptualize and carry out the first iteration of this project. I also learned a great deal from Robert Foster, Eva Geulen, and Rosemary Kegl. I am particularly grateful to Douglas Crimp for providing a model of political engagement and intellectual production that takes into consideration not only the work itself but also the reason for doing it. So much of what I encountered in Rochester has stayed with me through the years and has informed what I have in turn shared with my students.

My friends and colleagues in the Visual and Cultural Studies Program provided good food, drink, and conversation through the long, cold winters (and brief, glorious springs). I am especially grateful to the members of the reading group for their enthusiastic support and productive criticism; the cocktails, wine, and meals were excellent as well. These gatherings with Mario Caro, Bridget Cooks, Lisa Finn, Eloy J. Hernández, and Tina Takemoto are among my warmest memories of Rochester. It has been a pleasure carrying on the spirit of the reading group with Tina Takemoto in our post-Rochester long-distance writing camp endeavors. Her rigorous interrogations of my writing have been instrumental to the expression of my argument, and her moral support and shared appreciation for the punch-me-harder film have helped me weather the inevitable vicissitudes of work and life. Although we only overlapped briefly in Rochester, in recent years I have had the honor of becoming one of Karen Kosasa's friends. Her commitment to ethical scholarship and pedagogy inspires me to try to do more.

During my year in Atlanta, Cindy Patton and Robert A. Paul graciously welcomed me to the Graduate Institute of Liberal Arts at Emory University as a visiting research associate. At Oberlin College it was my great fortune to be awarded both predoctoral and postdoctoral fellowships from the Consortium for a Strong Minority Presence at Liberal Arts Colleges. There I met many extraordinary colleagues and students who at critical moments in my professional development shaped my thinking about my work as a scholar and a teacher. Dean Clayton Koppes, the Department of Theater and Dance, and Professor Daniel Goulding brought me to Oberlin and provided me with an institutional home. David Kamitsuka offered wise and strategic counsel that taught me a great deal about the workings of academic institutions and my place within them. My intellectual and social life in rural Ohio was greatly enlivened by Antoinette Charfauros McDaniel, Meredith Raimondo, and Moon-Ho Jung. Our conversations about our research and our pedagogical experiences expanded my vision of interdisciplinarity, and our social interactions offered energizing distractions. I think back to the passion and political commitment of the students of Oberlin's Asian American Alliance with a sense of awe and respect. However my presence contributed to their intellectual and political development exemplifies the best of what I have to offer as a teacher.

At George Mason University, Peter Brunette and Cynthia Fuchs invited me to join them in the Film and Media Studies Program and then generously supported my teaching and scholarship. I am especially grateful for Cindy's willingness to read my work in the midst of zillions of looming deadlines; many of the chapters benefited from her sharp editor's eyes. In the English Department, Zofia Burr, John Burt Foster Jr., Devon Hodges, Deborah Kaplan, and Alok Yadav offered support, advice, and encouragement. Their steadfast belief in the value of my work has been heartening. For the many shared meals and movies, as well as amusing and insightful discussions of the critical as well as the superficial issues of the day, I thank Jessica Scarlata and Scott Trafton.

One of the greatest pleasures of researching this book was meeting some of the knowledgeable and generous people who staff libraries and archives. A Mathy Junior Faculty Fellowship from George Mason University enabled me to spend a semester conducting research at the Library of

Congress, where, while viewing films from the turn-of-the-century Paper Print Collection, I first began seriously rethinking this book's historical focus. Zoran Sinobad in the Library of Congress's Motion Picture Reading Room provided invaluable assistance in locating films, film catalogs, Japanese TV documentaries about early U.S. films, and other critical information. Over the years, I've made several visits to the Margaret Herrick Library of the Academy of Motion Picture Arts and Sciences, and the staff there have been unfailingly efficient, resourceful, and genuinely devoted to facilitating the study of the history of U.S. cinema. Janet Lorenz provided cordial and able assistance in locating and reproducing several of the images in this volume. At the University of Southern California's Cinematic Arts Library, Edward Comstock led me to fascinating material about the production history of the film *The Good Earth.*

While I was still in the early stages of researching this work, I received an e-mail from Michael Ward, who had seen a reference to a conference paper I had given about E. Burton Holmes. Michael put me in contact with Genoa Caldwell, whose 1977 book, *The Man Who Photographed the World,* had introduced me to Holmes's extensive travels. This early electronic correspondence initiated a conversation among the three of us that has spanned nearly a decade. Genoa and Michael have worked tirelessly to promote recognition of Holmes's achievements, including sharing a great deal of information with me, and I am delighted to be able to add to the growing body of literature about this extraordinary traveler. Although each of the three of us undoubtedly has personal reasons for being interested in Holmes's travelogues, I believe we share a common conviction in the richness and historical significance of his oeuvre.

At the University of Michigan Press, Alison MacKeen's enthusiasm for this work was revitalizing. Her efforts, with the assistance of Christy Byks, to shepherd the manuscript through the complex process of review and approval are much appreciated. Upon her departure, Thomas Dwyer and Alexa Ducsay took up the final stages of preparing the manuscript for publication with expertise, patience, and good humor. The two anonymous readers were enormously helpful in pointing out the strengths and, even more important, the weaknesses of my work. I am humbled by the time and attention they devoted to reading and commenting on the manuscript, and I know that the book is better for their criticisms.

I have had the extraordinary good luck of serving as the 2008–9 Visiting Scholar at the Center for the Humanities at Grinnell College. It has been a pleasure working with the center's director, Daniel Reynolds, as well as all of the faculty, staff, and students with whom I have come into contact. I especially acknowledge Judy Hunter, the director of the Writing Lab and next-door-neighbor extraordinaire. She not only generously agreed to read the entire manuscript but also accomplished this task over the so-called winter vacation. I am grateful for her comments and am certain that my readers will benefit from the greater clarity her suggestions have facilitated.

I dedicate this book to my parents, who have provided me with every opportunity they could imagine and encouraged every endeavor on which I have set out. Their unconditional support has sustained me in ways I cannot begin to express. My sister, Florence, the double doctor (MD, Ph.D.), has always been willing to share her logical and scientific perspective on the world while listening to my humanist's views without judgment. I relish all of our conversations about matters personal, political, medical, scientific, and cinematic. It is a remarkable thing to go through life with such a family, with so little drama and so much care. Finally, it is difficult to know where to begin to thank Maxwell Leung and impossible to exhaust the myriad ways in which his presence in my life has made it better. A partial, idiosyncratic list might include always asking the "So what?" question, making dinner while I was in writing camp, moving across the country, coaxing me outside for a walk on a sunny Sunday afternoon, and explaining to me the intricacies of the world of *Battlestar Galactica*. I could not have finished this work without his love and support.

Contents

Introduction

On Location and the Production of Place

The Good Earth (Sidney Franklin, 1937) opens with an onscreen preface that frames the film as representing the essence of China: "The soul of a great nation is expressed in the life of its humblest people. In this simple story of a Chinese farmer may be found something of the soul of China—its humility, its courage, its deep heritage from the past and its vast promise for the future." This representation was reinforced by texts such as *A Guide to the Discussion of the Screen Version of Pearl Buck's Prize-Winning Novel* The Good Earth, whose foreword promises that the film offers not just entertainment but knowledge of the country: "The production of a photoplay based on Pearl Buck's famous novel, *The Good Earth,* offers more than mere enjoyment of a splendid photoplay. The enjoyment is present, to an unusual degree, but *The Good Earth* enables one, in addition, to know China, that vast and great country." The writer continues by comparing traveling in China to watching the film: "Possibly one could travel in China for a year and not learn more of its problems and significance than one obtains from the selected details of the photoplay, conscientiously based on extended researches in China as well as on Mrs. Buck's novel."[1] The claim that viewing *The Good Earth* could enable audiences to "know China" to a degree equivalent to a year's worth of travel in China is truly remarkable. Today, it may be difficult to fathom how viewers could ever have seen the film as an authoritative representation. However, this historical embrace of the film as a text that "enables one . . . to know China" makes *The Good Earth* a revealing example of how a fictional film could produce "China" as an object of knowledge almost independently of the "truth" of its content through the operations of the cinematic apparatus and the deployment of particular discourses of travel, presence, and authenticity.

Both Pearl Buck's longtime residence in China and her reputation as an expert on the country informed the reception of the cinematic adaptation of her best-known novel. To add to this impression of authority, the studio publicized the process of making the film in a way that insisted on the film's authenticity, even as studio officials defined and then redefined "authenticity" to fit the changing circumstances of the film's production over its three-year-long history. Shooting on location was essential to the studio's promotion of *The Good Earth* as a realistic representation of the Chinese and to the understanding that the film, as a substitute for travel, could educate audiences about the country and its people.[2] Significantly, the link the studio made between film and travel as it marketed *The Good Earth* echoed the celebrations by early filmmakers of the virtual mobility and visual pedagogy offered by film. As Jeffrey Ruoff writes of the history of the technology of film, "The cinema is a machine for constructing relations of space and time; the exploration of the world through images and sounds of travel has always been one of its principal features."[3] In this book, I argue that U.S. films shot on location in Asia function as a form of virtual travel through cinema's technological ability to bring the distant near. These films produce an entertaining image of "Asia" that configures it in relation to U.S. interests. Yet these films are also simultaneously received as authentic visions of the "Far East."[4] *Envisioning Asia* thus addresses the ways in which cinema functions as a mechanism of global positioning, a means of pinpointing the place of the Far East to situate the United States in the world. The subject of *Envisioning Asia* is therefore both the method of film production known as shooting on location and the literal and figurative practice of locating—that is, of imagining, establishing, and anchoring national identity within an international framework.

Imaginative Geographies

The overwhelmingly positive reception *The Good Earth* received in 1937 not only resulted from the film's aesthetic achievements and its value as entertainment but also served as an index of the increasing importance of China to the U.S. worldview of the time. The publication of Buck's novel in 1931 coincided with the Japanese invasion of Manchuria. By the time of the film's release, the conflict between the Japanese and the Chinese had grown into a war, and the United States viewed the Chinese with sympathy and the Japanese with suspicion and hostility, feelings that would intensify and then solidify into political alliances during the Second World War. This heightened awareness of China and the belief that it had an important role to play in international politics made understanding the country important to Americans who wanted to be well informed about global affairs and the proper U.S. place within them.

The film's preface identifies its subject as the "soul of China," suggesting a quasi-ethnographic focus on a timeless vision of the Chinese that precludes the explicit representation of Western influence within the world of the film. Yet the fact that the film was an expensive prestige picture produced by a major Hollywood studio and the enthusiasm with which U.S. audiences received it indicate that *The Good Earth* emerged from and successfully engaged with long-standing American preoccupations with East Asia in general and China in particular. The film's representation of China was very much shaped by the history and possible futures of American economic, religious, and political investments in the country and its people, from the missionary enterprise that laid the foundations for Buck's relationship with the Chinese to dreams of the fabled China market and debates about how U.S. foreign policy might foster the development of a more democratic and progressive Chinese nation.

By considering the connections between cinematic representations of Asia and the sociopolitical contours of U.S.-Asian relations, this book examines in particular the ways in which U.S. films shot on location in Asia produce knowledge of "Asia" that furthers the objectives of U.S. orientalism. My analysis is therefore clearly indebted to Edward Said's influential *Orientalism*, which examines how Western Europeans and Americans have come to terms with "the Orient" through marking a distinction between Orient and Occident. This distinction discursively constructs ontological and epistemological definitions of Self and Other, Occident and Orient, in ways that enable Western dominance and authority. Orientalism is thus "an *elaboration* not only of a basic geographical distinction (the world is made up of two unequal halves, Orient and Occident) but also of a whole series of 'interests' which . . . it not only creates but also maintains."[5] Particularly germane to my study is Said's notion of imaginative geography, a conception of space and place that "help[s] the mind to intensify its own sense of itself by dramatizing the distance and difference between what is close to it and what is far away."[6] Within this production of ideas about identity and difference founded on a geographical division of the world, *Envisioning Asia* looks at cinematic projections of "Asia" on U.S. screens not so much for what they tell us about the ostensibly distant, faraway countries of Asia as for what they reveal of how American representations of Asia and its differences from the United States define and maintain the "proper" places of and the balance of power between "Asia" and "America."[7]

Since *Orientalism*'s publication, scholars have critiqued, debated, revised, and extended the ideas presented in Said's book. Here I will not rehearse the long history of critical responses to *Orientalism,* but I will specify how my use of the term differs from Said's, especially in my appending of *U.S.* to *orientalism.* While Said names the United States as an imperial nation alongside Britain and France, noting that it has become the dominant power in "the Orient" since the Second World War, he states from the outset that "the Orient" is a very different thing for Americans than for Europeans. In particular, Americans primarily associate "the Orient" with the "Far East," especially China and Japan, and the idea is of more recent vintage.[8] Indeed, the history of U.S. political, military, and economic engagements in East Asia differs greatly from the history of European interventions in the Middle East and India. One challenge to using the idea of orientalism in the U.S. context is the question of how appropriate this theory is for understanding U.S. overseas imperialism and expansionism in Asia, which occurred under different circumstances and more recently than European colonialism. On this issue, Lisa Lowe offers a useful differentiation:

> U.S. orientalism of the twentieth century—the institutional, scholarly, and ideological representations of "Asia" and of "Asians in the United States"— may be rhetorically continuous but is materially discontinuous with an earlier European orientalism, which relied on representations of non-Western otherness as barbaric and incomprehensible, as well as [on] narrative teleologies of universal development.[9]

In fact, a number of works in Asian American and American studies productively use the term *orientalism* to refer not only to U.S. representations of Asians and Asia but also to the racialization of Asians in the United States.[10] As do these earlier studies, *Envisioning Asia* uses the concept of orientalism as a point of departure while recognizing the need for historical and geographical specificity and taking into account the theoretical particularities of analyzing cinematic images rather than literary texts. Furthermore, in *Envisioning Asia,* as in much Asian Americanist scholarship, the issue is not only how "the West" defines and dominates "the East," but also how the United States has struggled to define itself in relation to the Asians within its borders.[11] In Lowe's formulation,

> In the last century and a half, the American *citizen* has been defined over against the Asian *immigrant*, legally, economically, and culturally. These definitions have cast Asian immigrants both as persons and populations to be integrated into the national political sphere and as the contradictory, confusing, unintelligible elements to be marginalized and returned to their alien origins.[12]

This long-standing association of *American* with *citizen* and *Asian* with *immigrant* not only creates an opposition between American and Asian that makes the Asian American subject difficult to imagine but also disavows the history of Asians in the United States to uphold the abstract ideal of U.S. citizenship. This contradiction between the material history of Asians in the United States and the ideals of democratic citizenship highlights the instabilities of national identity and the differences within the nation's borders.

To understand the history of U.S.-Asian relations, we must view the discursive construction of U.S. identity vis-à-vis Asia not as singular and univocal but as conflicted and ambivalent. Scholars writing after *Orientalism* have insisted on the heterogeneity of various discourses of orientalism and have challenged the monolithic constructions of Occident/Orient and Self/Other.[13] In the U.S. case, it is impossible to view Asia as merely Other given how central the Far East has become to American identity. In Homi K. Bhabha's words, "The problem is not simply the 'selfhood' of the nation as opposed to the otherness of other nations. We are confronted with the nation split within itself, articulating the heterogeneity of its population."[14] Bhabha theorizes the representation of national identity as a temporal process in which a tension exists between the pedagogical and the performative—that is, between "the people" as an "a priori historical presence, a pedagogical object" and "the people" as "that sign of the present through which national life is redeemed and iterated as a reproductive process."[15] By recognizing the challenges of representing "the nation" in light of the large-scale movements of immigrants, exiles, and refugees, Bhabha offers a model for my thinking about U.S.-Asian relations and the function of U.S. cinematic images of Asia that goes beyond merely positing the domination of the East by the West. Instead, this framework addresses some of the ways in which the boundary between the two has been and continues to be both erected and breached. Lowe's analysis of the contradictory desire to both integrate Asian immigrants and return them to "their alien origins" in Asia is therefore analogous to Bhabha's notion of the nation "split within itself," in which "the people" become "a contested conceptual territory."[16] Both scholars make evident the fact that the contestation over who belongs where is ongoing and that these determinations have everything to do with understandings of space, the place of "the people," and the identity of the nation.

This struggle over definitions of "the people" and "the nation" is evident every time an Asian in the United States is asked "Where are you from?" This query is founded on the belief that the space of the United States offers no place for a racialized Asian subject; therefore, that subject must be from elsewhere and could not possibly be at home. This presumption of a unity between race and nation condenses the complex history of imagining Asia as other to the United States despite the formative roles and historical presences of Asians in the United States. In Lowe's words, "The project of imagining the nation as homogeneous requires the orientalist construction of cultures and geographies from which Asian immigrants come as fundamentally 'foreign' origins antipathetic to the modern American society that 'discovers,' 'welcomes,' and 'domesticates' them."[17] In short, the conception of a singular, unified U.S. nation requires the repeated distancing of Asians as foreigners; even as the "model minority," Asians remain different, and this difference is located in their purported cultures of origin. U.S. orientalism, as a mode of thought and a strategy of representation, therefore insists on the geographical imagination of Asia and America as separate and distinct entities despite the realities of the history of Asians in the United States and the United States in Asia. Throughout *Envisioning Asia,* I argue that U.S. films shot on location in Asia perform this distancing particularly convincingly, responding to the ambivalence about the proper place of Asians by reinforcing the orientalist imagination of Asia's distance, both geographic and cultural, from the United States.

The representation of Asia as the proper place for Asians exists side by side with the racist stereotypes of Asians as "perpetual foreigners" in the United States. While Chinatown is not the same as China, similar tropes of exoticism, mystery, and danger permeate popular representations of both as worlds apart from dominant U.S. culture. These patterns of representation have helped shape the image of Asians in the U.S. imaginary as racialized others. They have also limited possibilities for Asian American actors. "Opportunity," a segment from *BLT: Genesis* (2003), Evan J. Leong's documentary about the making of *Better Luck Tomorrow* (Justin Lin, 2002), begins with a scene from *Breakfast at Tiffany's* (Blake Edwards, 1961) featuring Mr. Yunioshi, the infamous caricature of a Japanese man played by Mickey Rooney.[18] A procession of familiar Asian stereotypes from television and film follows, as actors Roger Fan, Parry Shen, Jason Tobin, Sung Kang, and Karin Anna Cheung voice their frustrations with the limited kinds of mainstream media roles typically offered to actors of Asian descent.

The challenges these young actors face in finding fulfilling work suggest that the institutionalized racism that Eugene Franklin Wong described in his 1975 study *On Visual Media Racism: Asians in the American Motion Pictures* persists into the twenty-first century. As Wong documents, racist stereotypes of Asians in U.S. films have a long history. He cites such films as *The Chinese Rubbernecks* (1903), *Heathen Chinese and the Sunday School Teachers* (1904), and *The Yellow Peril* (1908) that feature stereotypical representations of Chinese men, noting, "By the middle to late Teens, the racially antagonistic depiction of Asians had, to all intents and purposes, become an institutional reality."[19] Equally importantly, Wong describes practices of role segregation—that is, limiting Asians to "Asian" roles while allowing white actors the freedom to play any and all roles—and major/minor role stratification, where major roles are reserved for white actors regardless of the character's racial or ethnic identity. Such discriminatory casting decisions, along with techniques such as the racist cosmetology known as "yellowface" that allows non-Asian actors to play Asian roles by simulating racialized facial physiognomies, have severely constrained representations of Asians in the U.S. media. Little wonder, then, that Lin's 2002 film, with its representations of a variety of young Asian Americans in Southern California who are by turns endearing, frustrating, frightening, and funny, generated such enthusiasm and support among Asian American communities.[20]

Today, an impressive body of scholarship as well as a number of documentary films critique popular stereotypes of Asians as "Orientals," examining discourses of race, gender, and sexuality in film and television.[21] These works have collectively challenged racist images, narratives, and practices in mass media, identifying recurring patterns of representation and highlighting unconscious assumptions that might otherwise go un-noticed. *Envisioning Asia* contributes to this ongoing interrogation of representations of Asians but adds a different emphasis. Rather than fo-cusing primarily on individual stereotypes and specific narratives, many of which other scholars have examined in considerable detail, I demon-strate how the very nature of the cinematic apparatus (by which I mean the technologies of making and viewing films as well as their effects on spectators) is suited to a production of place that accords with the imag-inary geography of U.S. orientalism. This perspective will broaden the conversation about images of Asians to include the analysis not only of the texts themselves but also of the technologies used to produce them.

Said reminds us that orientalism is more about the West than the East: "That Orientalism makes sense at all depends more on the West than on the Orient, and this sense is directly indebted to various Western techniques of representation that make the Orient visible, clear, 'there' in discourse about it."[22] Although I do not believe that film should be char-acterized as an essentially Western technology, I argue that the verisimil-itude of the cinematic medium itself, in addition to any particular tech-nique of film style, makes it a uniquely powerful means of representing the Far East as distant, and distinct, from the United States in every way. At the same time, the effort to draw an absolute boundary between the West and the East, to imagine a United States separate from Asia or "the American people" without Asians, is ultimately futile. According to Kandice Chuh and Karen Shimakawa, "That Asia consistently has been a significant determinant in the formation of U.S. national identity since this nation's inception has been well-established, if not yet popular-ized."[23] The history of Asians in the United States is not the primary sub-ject of *Envisioning Asia*, given its focus on the travels of Americans to Asia, yet knowledge of this history motivates this book's critical aims. The traffic between the United States and Asia has always been in both directions. My use of the term *orientalism* therefore refers to the con-struction of the foreignness of Asians and Asia but also challenges the ef-fort to locate Asians solely in Asia by recalling the history of Asian pres-ences in the United States that contradict this imaginary binary of U.S. identity and Asian difference. Thus, this work demonstrates how visions of Asia on U.S. screens are complicit in obscuring what should otherwise be common knowledge: historically, Asians and Asia, both within and outside the borders of the U.S. nation-state, have helped constitute American national identity.

Locating Films

Travel is an extraordinarily complex term, affiliated with as well as distinct from a range of different kinds of movements across space. James Clifford suggests, "Everyone's on the move, and has been for centuries," yet he is also careful to recognize that travel overlaps with but is not equivalent to experiences such as diaspora, immigration, tourism, and exile.[24] Clifford's *Routes* examines movements "across borders and between cultures" that have been shaped by three global forces: "the continuing legacies of empire, the effects of unprecedented world wars, and the global consequences of industrial capitalism's disruptive, restructuring activity."[25] Any consideration of modern travel must account for these forces, and they are critical to *Envisioning Asia*. At the same time, since an examination of travel in relation to these social relations is such a vast undertaking, any study within this field would do well to clarify its scope. In *Envisioning Asia*, the movements with which I am especially concerned are the travels undertaken by Americans to Asia in the context of imperial and colonial endeavors. From this point of departure, I examine how U.S. cinematic images of Asia, constructed by a technology that has the ability to conquer space, produces knowledge of Asia that furthers such imperial enterprises. This emphasis leads me to focus on two primary groups of travelers: U.S. businessmen, missionaries, and soldiers in Asia, and filmmakers (including directors, actors, producers, and cinematographers) who go to Asia to produce images of Asia for U.S. audiences. Figures such as the tourist, for example, made famous in Dean MacCannell's classic work, are not central to my study, even though questions of tourism do intersect with my concerns.[26] Similarly, although the history of Asian immigration to the United States helped motivate the writing of *Envisioning Asia*, this work does not offer a detailed examination of Asian immigration, transnationalism, or diaspora.

The places I consider at the historical moments on which I focus were neither completely unfamiliar to U.S. audiences, as they might have been in the case of exploration, nor established stops on packaged itineraries, as they would be in tourism. In China in the 1930s, for example, Americans had a lengthy history of economic, political, and religious interests, but it was not a popular destination for leisure travel, and relatively few people had direct personal experience there. From the vantage point of the United States, therefore, my analysis concerns somewhat familiar and increasingly significant places in the world. Some examples of the

specific places and times I consider are Hawai'i in 1898, the year of its annexation by the United States; the Philippines in 1899, at the beginning of
the Philippine-American War; China in 1901, following the Boxer Uprising, and in the 1930s; and Japan in the two decades following the Second
World War. At such moments, when the U.S. interest in these countries
was most intense, films provided American audiences an opportunity to
better understand the world and their relationship to it by articulating
the distance, and the difference, between the United States and Asia as
well as between the United States and Hawai'i.[27]

The status of the destinations as neither fully assimilated into leisure
and tourism nor entirely unfamiliar distinguishes the virtual cinematic
voyages I examine from a broader consideration of travel cinema. Jennifer Peterson's description of early travelogue films as a genre "obsessed
with *difference*" is certainly accurate, yet when she catalogs the yearnings
to which the travelogue speaks as "a desire to experience someplace (any-
place) different, a desire to leave one's current conditions, a desire for
new experience," her insight does not fully address the historical and political contexts of the films that I examine.[28] However, her observation of
how travelogues create imaginary worlds—"Travel films create places
that are entirely new, geographies that only exist on the screen"—is remarkably congruent with Said's notion of "imaginative geography." At
issue in both ideas is the way in which people imaginatively construct the
world in terms of here and there, home and abroad, Self and Other.
Given orientalism's origin in a geographical division of the world, the interrogation of travel as an actual and an imaginative way of bridging
racial and cultural distance becomes central to the critique of orientalist
discourses. It is not surprising that the analysis of literary travel narratives is an important element of Said's work as well as of many of the
studies that have followed.[29] Furthermore, if travel is central to orientalist discourse, then film is a particularly apt medium for producing
knowledge of the Far East.

As a modern technology, cinema, like the telegraph, railroads, and
steamships, changed conceptions of time and space.[30] To attract audiences, early film producers actively publicized cinema's potential to present scenes from around the world by adopting mottoes such as the Star
Film Company's "The whole world within reach" or the Urban Trading
Company's "We put the world before you." Cinema made the world a
smaller place, making it possible to journey to faraway places in the blink
of an eye; film's function as a form of virtual travel helped constitute it as

a medium. As Alison Landsberg writes, "From its inception, the cinema sought to make visible what, for economic or social reasons, remained beyond an individual person's reach. In part its project was revelation, in both senses of the word, but it was also transportation, the capacity to carry viewers to faraway places and alternative temporalities."[31] In offering views of distant places, early film was but one manifestation of armchair travel.

A number of scholars have written about how cinema relates to nineteenth-century entertainments such as panoramas, dioramas, and international expositions that presented scenes of distant places and cultures to audiences. In these contexts, attendees learned about the pleasures of virtual travel and experienced new modes of spectatorship and ways of consuming racial and cultural difference. These ways of seeing were then put into practice when they encountered the novel technology of cinema.[32] Here, Anne Friedberg's theory of the "mobilized 'virtual' gaze" of the cinematic apparatus is especially useful: "The *mobilized gaze* has a history, which begins well before the cinema and is rooted in other cultural activities that involve walking and travel. The virtual gaze has a history rooted in all forms of visual representation (back to cave painting), but produced most dramatically by photography. The cinema developed as an apparatus that combined the 'mobile' with the 'virtual.'"[33] This mobilized virtual gaze of cinema was put to especially productive use at the historic moments that I consider. As a form of both education and entertainment for U.S. audiences, cinema, as a "machine for travel,"[34] offered not only virtual voyages to faraway places and fascinating escapes into exotic worlds of difference but also, and even more importantly, lessons about Asia's significance to the place of the U.S. in the world.

On what basis does the medium of cinema have the power to produce knowledge of place? The credibility granted to films is founded on the indexical nature of photography, the belief that the image is a direct physical trace of the object pictured. A brief discussion of photography and travel illuminates what makes films shot on location so convincing as substitutes for travel. The ability to mechanically reproduce reality had enormous repercussions for the representation of distant places. Looking back to the 1850s, the era that Susan Sontag has described as "the great age of photographic Orientalism,"[35] we see that English photographer Francis Frith explicitly conceived of his two-volume *Egypt and Palestine Photographed and Described* (1858–59) as a form of virtual travel: "There is no effectual substitute for actual travel, but it is my ambition to provide for those to whom circumstances forbid that luxury, faithful representations of the scenes I have witnessed, and I shall endeavour to make the simple truthfulness of the Camera a guide for my Pen."[36] Such ambitions to provide an accurate representation of the experience of travel are a commonplace in travel narratives. What distinguishes Frith's claims, as Carol Armstrong demonstrates, is his use of the photographic image and the positivistic authority he granted to it.

In the text of his album, Frith critiques the reiterative nature of most travel writing, which in his opinion consists of nothing more than preconceptions accompanied by drawings that illustrate unsupported ideas. The camera, however, offers the foundation of "simple truthfulness." The photographic images, combined with Frith's presence as a witness to the scene, become the basis of the text. Frith seems to have recognized the difficulty of confirming the reality of written travel narratives—the "ready equation of traveller with liar," as Steve Clark has put it—and saw photography as the solution to the problem of verification.[37] Armstrong summarizes Frith's understanding of the role of photography:

> First, the photograph, as a stand-in for and trace of actual experience, has the power to demonstrate or refute imaginative and textual hypotheses; and second, the photographically illustrated book stands in marked contrast to other books. Put one on the table side by side with the other, read and look at each of them, and the reader will discover that the ideas promulgated in the one are proved or disproved by the images in the other.[38]

Frith's faith in the truth of the photographic image was by no means idiosyncratic. The authority, then, of the photographic image as evidence, the indexical nature of the pictures produced by the "simple truthfulness" of the camera, grounds the cinema as a form of virtual travel.[39]

Film has long been associated with verisimilitude, attributed with the ability to capture and reproduce life itself. Accordingly, since the beginnings of film, theorists have pondered the relationship between cinematic representation and reality, with some celebrating film's ability to mechanically reproduce reality and others seeing this association as that which must be overcome for film to become art.[40] In the history of cinema as a commercial enterprise, studios have repeatedly used discourses of realism and verisimilitude to market each new technological development.[41] Thus, the relationship between cinematic representation and reality is complex. Here I simply point to the discursive construction of cinema as a realist medium and suggest that the medium of film works well with the project of orientalism. Film, in its technological capacity to reproduce reality, offers the illusion of simply capturing the profilmic Orient before the camera. Cinema, much like orientalism itself, makes the Orient "visible, clear, 'there' in discourse about it."[42]

Films shot on location most fully exploit cinema's ability to bring the Far East to U.S. audiences. But what exactly distinguishes films shot on location from other films in this nexus of virtual travel, verisimilitude, and cinema? In film production, shooting on location refers to filming at an already existing locale rather than shooting at a studio, whether on a soundstage or a studio back lot. Filmmakers usually decide whether to shoot a scene on location or at a studio based on convenience and economics, but location shooting can also constitute an important aesthetic element of the film. For example, Ruth Vasey, in her work on Hollywood's efforts to negotiate the demands of the global market in the interwar period, shows how the desire to set narratives in foreign locations often reflected merely a search for the picturesque. In these instances, films were usually shot on studio back lots with little regard for realism or authenticity.[43] However, as nations that took offense at Hollywood's portrayal of them threatened rebukes and as such international incidents began to cost money, moviemakers employed new strategies in representing foreign locales. These included setting the story in a "mythical kingdom" or otherwise making it difficult to locate the precise setting of the story.[44] Rather than attempting to produce more acceptable representations, the studios sought instead to protect themselves from charges of misrepresentation by distancing their cinematic worlds from the world itself. In contrast, for the production of the film *The Eternal City* (Madison Productions/First National, 1923), Will Hays, the president of the Motion Picture Producers and Distributors of America, invited the Italian ambassador to become involved because "we wanted to make this picture correctly."[45] As part of this concern with "correctness," a representative of the Italian government was assigned to work closely with the film's producer, writer, and director. *The Eternal City* was also shot on location in Rome, suggesting that while exoticism and a picturesque quality could be manufactured easily enough on a studio set, a more "correct" representation of place required shooting the film on location in the actual place where its narrative unfolded.

In general terms, the location at which a film is shot may have one of several different relationships with the place in which its narrative occurs. First, the film's shooting location might correspond with the setting of the film's action, especially, though not only, when the narrative occurs in a contemporary context, such as when a story that takes place in present-day Los Angeles is also shot in Los Angeles. Particularly when the film includes views of well-known landmarks or landscapes or the story takes place in a distinctive and especially recognizable place, shooting at the actual location where the story unfolds can help the film achieve greater authenticity. In other instances, a film may use topographically and geographically similar landscapes or cityscapes to substitute for more expensive or otherwise less accessible locations.[46] In some cases, a film whose narrative occurs in a fantasy setting or a historically distant time period—that is, in spaces that do not or no longer exist—may be shot on location to offer an approximation of the narrative setting. Finally, a film might give few specifications as to the exact setting of its narrative other than vague signifiers of a generic type of place, in which case the relationship between the place of the narrative and the place of shooting can only be ambiguous.

Thus, the relationship between the physical site of filming and the diegetic setting of a film can be described as correspondence, substitution, or approximation. In instances of correspondence, when a film is shot on location in the place in which its narrative is set, the imaginative geography of the film adheres most insistently to the actual physical site signified in the film and representation comes closest to reality. The discourse of photographic realism manufactures a sense of presence, of having been there, that guarantees authenticity, supplementing other techniques of realist narrative. Even when the narrative of the film is fictional, the profilmic reality of the place before the camera anchors the make-believe characters and story in the real world. Films shot on location in places corresponding to their narrative settings therefore offer a special access to the "reality" of that place at the same time as they shape that "reality" by enveloping it within the conventions of cinema. Such films have the power to create a more engaging and immersive "Asia" than almost any other kind of representation.

Films are, of course, viewed in specific places as well, and the particularity of place locates the viewer within a neighborhood, a city, a region, and a nation. Since I am primarily concerned with questions of the nation and national identity, I will focus on the United States as the place in which the films are seen, as the physical location of the viewers and the point of departure for their cinematic voyages. The virtual travels to Asia that the films offer to U.S. audiences allow Americans to learn about Asia but also ask them to consider the meaning of America. In this way, considering the similarities and differences between home and abroad can deepen viewers' sense of their own identity. However, the shape and contour of this place, the identity of the United States of America, must also be understood as constantly under construction and in flux, as a site of contestation, struggle, and resistance.

Finally, the production of a film on location involves distinctive kinds of labor. James Duncan and Derek Gregory remind us of the need to consider the actual travels necessary for travel writing: "It may seem strange to emphasize the spatiality of travel, but we fear that some critical readings fail to register the production of travel writings by corporeal subjects moving through material landscapes."[47] This cautionary observation brings into relief the entire network of transportation technologies as well as the innumerable individual and collective negotiations that are required to produce representations of distant places. Access to particular locations, for example, is politically and historically conditioned. The U.S. occupation of Peking (Beijing) in the aftermath of the Boxer Uprising gave American travelers and filmmakers unprecedented entrée into the Forbidden City, the spectacular compound of palaces and temples that housed the emperor of China. As its name indicates, the Forbidden City was typically off-limits to foreigners as well as to most Chinese. For audiences of Burton Holmes's illustrated travel lectures during the 1901–2 season, seeing the Forbidden City was literally unprecedented and resulted entirely from the circumstances of the time. In contrast, the very different outcome of the American war in Vietnam and the subsequent lack of diplomatic relations between the two countries made it extremely difficult for U.S. filmmakers to shoot in Vietnam until relatively recently.[48]

The travel that shooting on location necessitates is thus often shaped by national and international policies and may be undertaken by considerable numbers of people, all of whom must contend with the challenges entailed by being on location, away from home. My analysis of the production histories of the films I discuss makes visible the physical displacements and complex compromises required to produce these representations. These travels are the very condition of possibility of films shot on location. Thus, the examination of what Duncan and Gregory call "the material production of imaginative geographies" anchors the more familiar textual explications of a film in the realities of what was required to produce them.[49] Attention to both the material and textual aspects of U.S. films shot on location allows me to examine how cinema, as a manifestation of U.S. orientalism, acts in conjunction with the particularities of the Asian/American dynamic of a given era.[50] This methodology combines the theoretical question of how films function as virtual voyages and as orientalist forms of knowledge with the political and historical specificities of physical movements across international borders.

In practical terms, this commitment to examining "the material production of imaginative geographies" means that my study emphasizes the context of a film, sometimes over the film itself, in a manner that follows from Janet Staiger's historical materialist approach to reception. Staiger argues that no immanent textual meaning exists and that contextual factors are more responsible than textual ones for spectators' experiences at the cinema as well as what they do with these experiences after leaving. This does not mean, as Staiger makes clear, that the text does not exist; rather, it means that the text, a "physical object with sense data," does not signify, in and of itself, apart from larger cultural contexts.[51] Barbara Klinger further elaborates on Staiger's methodology:

> The contextual factors that accompany the presentation of a film, including such materials as film reviews and industry promotions as well as specific historical conditions, serve as signs of the vital semiotic and cultural space that superintend the viewing experience. Further, these factors are not just "out there," external to the text and viewer; they actively intersect the text/viewer relation, producing interpretive frames that influence the public consumption of cultural artifacts.[52]

Only a broad, contextual perspective, such as the one that Staiger and Klinger propose, that moves beyond a text-centered analysis to examine "events of interpretation"[53] can account for the 1930s reception of *The Good Earth* as a reliable source of knowledge of China, a view that would be virtually impossible for a contemporary critic to imagine based merely on the evidence of the film itself.

Within this approach to the interpretation of films, I emphasize the production history of a film, the way in which the narrative of the making of a film is publicized, and how this information circulates within existing discourses of travel and in relation to the international relations between the United States and Asia of the period. I rely primarily on promotional materials, newspaper coverage, and film reviews to establish the historical context of a film's reception. However, I do not pretend to describe how actual audiences saw particular films. As Klinger plainly states, film reviews cannot substitute for audience response; however, "the surviving documents from various contexts provide a glimpse into social constructions of meaning that circulated at the time of reception, shedding light on broader patterns affecting reception than those afforded by the film's formal system itself."[54] Although in some instances, particularly in relation to films from the turn of the century, relatively little information is available about the production, publicity, exhibition, and reception of a film, the later works that I consider in the second half of this study come with a wealth of material traces of these contextual factors. This particular approach to interpretation therefore faces some limitations imposed by the existing archive but also offers the most productive way of accounting for both the actual travels required to make films shot on location and the virtual travels these films make available to audiences.

Travel is inherently disorienting because it forces the traveler to contend with the sights, smells, sounds, customs, and laws of a place that is not home. However, in a completed cinematic text, the experience of travel necessary to shoot on location is mediated through techniques of film form and style. These techniques include strategies as simple as framing and camera angle in early films and as complex as the conventions of classical Hollywood narratives in later ones. The resulting texts, structured according to established stylistic conventions and social expectations, reorient viewers to the place in question by managing the potentially unruly, discomforting, or incomprehensible experience of travel, creating more familiar, recognizable, and entertaining versions of place. Understanding the images and narratives that result from these processes of disorientation and reorientation has an important political stake: how such films, in producing an ostensibly authentic Asia, further U.S. dominance by presenting Asian and American identities and U.S.-Asian relations in a way that sanctions both the expansion of U.S. power in Asia and the continuing disavowal of the place of Asians in the United States.

Beginnings

The technology of cinema and its representation as a form of virtual
travel emerged in the era of high imperialism, at a time when some nations, including the United States, were literally remapping space
through geopolitical expansion. One of the most often cited passages
from Jean-Louis Comolli's "Machines of the Visible" addresses the social
circumstances of cinema's beginnings:

> The second half of the nineteenth century lives in a sort of frenzy of the
> visible. It is, of course, the effect of the social multiplication of images:
> ever wider distribution of illustrated papers, waves of prints, caricatures,
> etc. The effect also, however, of something of a geographical extension of
> the field of the visible and the representable: by journeys, explorations,
> colonisations, the whole world becomes visible at the same time that it be-
> comes appropriatable.[55]

Comolli argues that we must understand cinema not just as a technology
but in terms of social ideology: "The cinema is born immediately as a social machine, and thus not from the sole invention of its equipment but
rather from the experimental supposition and verification, from the an-
ticipation and confirmation of its *social profitability;* economic, ideological and symbolic."[56] While the passage about the "frenzy of the visible" has become very familiar, we have not yet fully integrated the
sociohistorical "appropriations" of the world occurring around cinema's
beginnings into our understandings of cinema's emergence.[57] Observers
from the early years of film's history, however, saw clear connections between "journeys, explorations and colonisations" and the novel technology of moving pictures. For example, French critic and novelist Rémy de
Gourmont notes the productive power of film as a means of knowing
the world in his 1907 article on the cinématographe, the combination
camera, printer, and projector invented by the Lumière brothers. De
Gourmont's early-twentieth-century text suggests that a central feature
of film's early identity as a technology and entertainment lay in the cinematic apparatus's ability to produce knowledge about faraway lands.
Furthermore, he implies that audiences should see these cinematic images of the world as valuable and authoritative in an imperial context.

    De Gourmont finds that cinema is superior to the theater for the pre-
sentation of visual spectacles, especially views of distant places. He de-

picts cinema's ability to allow travel without physical displacement as a harmless amusement, proclaiming, "I love the cinema. It satisfies my curiosity. It allows me to tour the world and stop, to my liking, in Tokyo and Singapore. I follow the craziest itineraries."[58] The essay concludes with a look toward the future of cinema, in which he recognizes the current limitations of the technology, although he seems certain that these impediments will eventually be overcome:

> I do not doubt that one day it will offer us landscapes with all of their colors, and their nuances of sky and forest. Then we will really come to know the vast world, including its most inaccessible pockets, and the diverse customs of men will come alive before us like a troop of charming dancers. Let's take advantage of that. . . . The past year, the cinema taught me more about Morocco than did all the confused tales of travellers. I saw the army on the march and the artillery of the sultan; and I understood the stupidity of those politicians who took the power of that puppet so seriously. It was a lesson for the eyes. That is all that counts.[59]

De Gourmont's article conjoins the technological possibilities offered by the cinematic apparatus with an interest in travel, and he views both from an imperial perspective. This essay, written just after the first decade of cinema's existence, brings to light all of the characteristics that make cinema a powerful instrument of orientalism. The technology of cinema produces knowledge about the "vast world," including "its most inaccessible pockets." This knowledge is ethnographic in kind ("the diverse customs of *men*"), and visual in origin ("a lesson for the eyes"). Travel provides a way to learn about distant places and cultures, and cinematic travel views are a more reliable source of information than the (written and verbal?) accounts of travelers to the region. Finally, the certainty of the knowledge gained from the cinematic image can provide the foundation for a confident assessment of the sociopolitical situation. A century after the publication of this article, cinema has indeed fulfilled the prophecy of providing spectacular Technicolor images of people and places from around the world. However, the implications of the production and reception of these images have not yet been fully considered.

Cinema emerged at about the same time as did U.S. overseas imperialism. The first projected motion pictures were seen in 1895. In the spring of 1898, the United States engaged Spain in a war, purportedly to free Cuba from its Spanish oppressors. In the aftermath of the war, the

United States, a country that saw expansion as nothing less than Manifest Destiny, joined European nations such as England and France in developing an overseas empire by annexing Puerto Rico and Guam and purchasing the Philippines from Spain. Cuba became a protectorate, and Hawaiʻi was officially annexed in the summer of that year, though not as a direct result of the war with Spain. These events, along with the Philippine-American War (1899–1902) and the U.S. participation in the multinational force responsible for quelling China's antiforeign, anti-Christian Boxer Uprising in 1900, constitute the U.S. entrance on the world's stage as an imperial power.

Hearing news of Commodore George Dewey's defeat of the Spanish at Manila Bay during the Spanish-American War, President William McKinley is said to have remarked of the Philippines, "I could not have told where those darned islands were within 2,000 miles." He solved the problem by consulting a globe.[60] McKinley's lack of geographical knowledge revealed his need for a more fully elaborated worldview—a need he shared with all Americans. Perhaps in part as a response to such curiosity, cinema found a new function as a "visual newspaper" during the Spanish-American War.[61] Shortly after the Spanish-American War concluded, the Philippine-American War broke out when Filipinos, who had not battled the Spanish merely to be ruled by a different colonizer, challenged the U.S. occupation of the islands. Short military and scenic views of the Philippines produced by the American Mutoscope and Biograph Company provided Americans an education in the location, landscape, and character of the Philippines. These films were part of U.S. audiences' effort to imagine the world and their place within it according to new configurations of power and notions of imperial nationhood.

Envisioning Asia is not intended as a comprehensive history of U.S. films shot on location in Asia. Rather, it focuses on two especially meaningful moments in the twentieth-century trajectory of U.S.-Asian engagements: the turn of the twentieth century and the beginnings of U.S. overseas imperialism, and the middle of the twentieth century during the rise of the United States as a global power. In the early 1900s, U.S. imperialism took the form of overt domination and territorial conquest (though in regard to China the United States positioned itself against European imperialism); in contrast, midcentury discourses emphasized the spread of freedom and democracy as the goal of American enterprises abroad as the United States attempted to, as Christina Klein writes, "define our nation as a nonimperial world power in the age of decolonization."[62] During these two historical periods, cinematic representations of Asia helped U.S. audiences imagine a national identity first as a newly emerging imperial power in the world and then as a global leader and standard-bearer for liberal humanist ideals of freedom and democracy at the height of the American Century.[63]

The first half of *Envisioning Asia* is devoted to nonfiction films dating from the late nineteenth century to the turn of the twentieth century, while the second half of the volume examines classical Hollywood films from the late 1930s to the early 1960s. The turn of the twentieth century and the mid–twentieth century represent two distinct moments in U.S. film history, each with its own modes of production, distribution, and reception. But examining early films, when cinema was a relative novelty, alongside classical Hollywood films, in which the conventions of form and style had been established according to the dictates of linear narrative, provides an overview of how cinema as a technology of representation allows viewers to know Asia in unique ways. My analysis of cinema as a manifestation of U.S. orientalism highlights both the continuities in the capabilities of the cinematic apparatus and the significance of the differences between early cinema and classical Hollywood films. I consider how fictional narrative films shot on location combine the documentary capacity of cinema and the power of narrative to produce entertaining stories of Asia that are still received as forms of virtual travel and authoritative sources of knowledge despite their avowedly constructed nature. Early film examples that awkwardly (to twenty-first-century viewers) integrate actualities and fictional staged scenes thus provide insight into the classical Hollywood films that smoothly fold "authentic" travel views into the story of the film. It is one thing to suggest that nonfiction films produce a convincing "Asia" for U.S. audiences and quite another to make the same claim for fictional narratives, yet I argue that location shooting and the savvy marketing of it make possible both claims. Moreover, in these later films, the operations of classical narrative further amplify the function of film as a form of virtual travel by offering identifications with both the apparatus and the diegesis, structuring the scenic views of distant lands through the literal and ideological points of view of the characters within the film. Fictional narrative films shot on location thus fully utilize cinema's abilities to bring Asia to U.S. audiences and to make sense of this Asia and what it means to America.

The first two chapters of *Envisioning Asia* examine the ways in which cinema played a role in the culture that gave rise to and supported U.S. overseas imperialism, tracing how film as a form of virtual travel represented, enabled, and was enabled by the commercial, military, and ideological trans-Pacific crossings of the turn of the twentieth century. Chapter 1 analyzes the pleasures and pedagogies of the illustrated travel lectures of E. Burton Holmes. Illustrated travel lectures were often performed at prestigious venues that offered early travel films a respectable context for their projection. Holmes, one of the most popular American practitioners of the genre, was one of the first to incorporate cinema into his work, beginning in 1897. In a departure from the style of his well-known predecessor, John L. Stoddard, who merely showed his audiences images of the subject of the lecture, Holmes organized his images and words to replicate his experience of travel, taking his audiences on the journey with him. Holmes therefore designed his lectures explicitly as virtual voyages. A textual analysis of his lectures, based on the versions published in a multivolume set, demonstrates how the conventions of the illustrated travel lecture anticipated some of the conventions not only of travel films but of narrative films in general.

In each of the chapters of *Envisioning Asia,* the figure of the emblematic American in Asia acts as a model for U.S.-Asian relations on the international level, though the character traits of this American shift with changing historical and political circumstances. In his performances, Holmes comes across as an exemplary American in Asia and Hawai'i who presents U.S. overseas imperialism with an enthusiasm characteristic of the proexpansionist politicians of the time. He did more than "show Americans what the world, outside of America, looked like," as he put it; he embodied a particular kind of American identity as an intrepid traveler, always on the scene of the latest U.S. imperial adventure.[64] This perspective is most apparent in the three lectures this first chapter examines, based on Holmes's travels to Hawai'i in 1898, the Philippines in 1899, and China in 1901. To gauge the reception of his lectures—in particular, how audiences of the time might have seen his representations of the changing U.S. identity in the world—my textual analysis of the lectures is supplemented by an examination of some of the substantial press coverage of Holmes's work, including reviews of the lectures and news items concerning his travels. Holmes's early use of cinema and his personal and professional interest in Asia distinguish his work from that of earlier practitioners such as Stoddard and suggest his prescience in recognizing the importance of both cinema and Asia to the formation of U.S. national identity.

Holmes's work drew on a long-established tradition of travel lectures, with cinema as an added draw, and he both educated and entertained his elite audiences. In contrast, the films of the dominant filmmakers of the period, such as those produced by the Edison Film Company and the American Mutoscope and Biograph Company, were often shown as part of a variety format in venues such as vaudeville theaters, and their meanings varied according to the practices of individual exhibitors. Chapter 2 considers the productions of the nascent U.S. film industry, beginning with the films of the Occidental and Oriental Series, sponsored by the steamship company of the same name and produced by Edison filmmakers in the spring of 1898. Even though they were most certainly shaped by the racial beliefs of the era, these representations offer an unexpected and surprising contrast to the existing images of Asians and Asia in U.S. popular culture of the period. Among other things, they express the distinction between "Occident" and "Orient" primarily through the conventions of early cinema's street scenes and travel views, celebrating Western modernity at the expense of less "developed" non-Western cultures. Yet these films also offer the possibility of less dichotomous views of cultural difference, as seen in the occasionally unruly reality that the films recorded. The films of the Occidental and Oriental Series thus reveal the technological specificity of early cinema actualities, or films of actual events, as representations of racial and cultural difference.

The second half of the chapter examines how the events of the Spanish-American War, the Philippine-American War, and the Boxer Uprising changed existing cinematic representations and conventions. Compared to the films of the Occidental and Oriental Series, in which the emblematic American was a businessman with private interests in Asia, the figure of identification in the films made during and after these military endeavors was a U.S. soldier. The new national imperative to understand Asia and America in terms that justified U.S. overseas military intervention challenged filmmakers to create new kinds of images and narratives. Rather than adhering solely to the principles of the "cinema of attractions," in which films were seen "less as a way of telling stories than as a way of presenting a series of views to an audience," filmmakers began to explore precisely how to tell stories about U.S. national identity.[65] This shift to story films was occurring on an industry-wide level as early cinema transitioned to an era when the classical narrative dominated. Chapter 2 therefore concludes with a brief overview of the role of location shooting within this transitional era in U.S. film history as a foundation for analyzing classical Hollywood films in the second half of the study.

Chapter 3 continues the analysis of *The Good Earth* that opens this introduction. Pearl Buck's 1931 novel, her best-known work, was almost unanimously received as an "accurate" representation of China. By examining the history of Metro-Goldwyn-Mayer's cinematic adaptation of this novel, this chapter takes up the issue of how classical Hollywood cinema could best produce a text that audiences would view as a credible source of knowledge of a faraway place. Since this chapter seeks not to evaluate the realism of the film's representation of China but rather to examine why the film was seen as a way to know China, the critical focus is not on the text of the film but on how the promotion and reception of the film articulated popular discourses of accuracy and authenticity. The point of departure for this discussion will be debates about accuracy—or, more specifically, the lack of it in prior Hollywood representations of China and the abundance of it in Buck's work. The studio faced the challenge of making a film that retained the celebrated authority of Buck's novel, since the studio saw this quality as critical to the success of its production. Correspondence among Buck, studio executives and staff, and George Hill, the film's first director, indicates initial plans to film on location in China using Chinese actors and subtitled Mandarin Chinese dialogue. The film did not realize these preliminary aspirations; most of it was shot in Chatsworth, California, with Paul Muni and Luise Rainer in the lead roles, speaking English-language dialogue. Yet the film was still promoted as a way to see and know China. MGM's efforts to produce and market the film and the results of those efforts reveal a great deal about what constituted an "authentic" representation of China in a Hollywood film of the 1930s. In this juxtaposition between the desire for authenticity and the laborious efforts necessary to define, produce, and promote it, *The Good Earth* serves as a remarkable example of the potentially convincing nature of films shot on location, even though the film departed considerably from contemporary notions of what an "authentic" portrayal of the country and its people should be.

Both Buck's novel and MGM's cinematic adaptation of it were noted for their sympathetic portrayals of the Chinese, in contrast to existing images and narratives of the Chinese in the United States that showed them as exotic, threatening, and essentially foreign. Karen Leong has characterized this shift in representations of the Chinese as "the China mystique," a particular expression of U.S. orientalism that began in the 1930s and emphasized a "new China" that above all highlighted China's potential role in developing the identity of the United States as an international leader with the power to transform the world by spreading freedom and democracy.[66] Although these U.S. hopes for China would be dashed by the rise to power of the Chinese communists, the desire to promote U.S. political ideals in Asia would continue in a form Klein has called "Cold War orientalism," an expansion of many of the principles that defined the China mystique—in particular, the promise that American-style democracy would better the world.

Chapter 4 commences just after the end of the Second World War, during the U.S. occupation of Japan, and traces the changing U.S. perspectives on Japan from the mid-1940s to the early 1960s. Given the lengthy time period addressed in this chapter and my desire to demonstrate shifts in U.S. attitudes toward Japan during this era, the chapter is structured as a series of case studies presented in chronological order. In each of these films, the figure of the emblematic American in Asia is apparent in both the production histories and the diegetic narratives. These figures demonstrate how Americans are primarily a force for the worldwide spread of democracy and how Japan is not America's wartime enemy but its strongest Asian ally against the threat of communism.

Chapter 4 begins with *Tokyo File 212* (Dorrell McGowan and Stuart McGowan, 1951), the first American feature film shot on location in Japan. The film offers intriguing images of a reconstructed postwar Japan yet struggles to reconcile these scenic views with its narrative. Both the lighthearted representation of the U.S. occupation of Okinawa in *The Teahouse of the August Moon* (Daniel Mann, 1956) and the "enlightened" attitude toward interracial relations of *Sayonara* (Joshua Logan, 1957) presented narratives of anti-conquest, in Mary Louise Pratt's term, in rationalizing the U.S. presence in Japan.[67] These diegetic narratives were further reinforced in the publicity surrounding the experiences of filming in Japan, which were uniformly represented as exemplars of international cooperation and understanding. The chapter concludes with the nostalgic search for the spirit of traditional Japan in *My Geisha* (Jack Cardiff, 1962), in which the narrative of the film's production parallels the narrative of the film itself and the privilege of being an American abroad is taken to its furthest extreme as the pleasures and pedagogy of the film's travels to Japan are underwritten by Euro-American expertise in Japanese culture and customs.

The four chapters of *Envisioning Asia* thus trace a historical path through the development of U.S. national identity from emerging imperial power to global superpower. At the height of the American Century, Hollywood produced Technicolor fantasies of Japan that imagined a new era of U.S.-Asian integration. The coming years would seriously challenge such views of U.S. involvement in Asia, yet even in the waning years of the twentieth century, cinematic fantasies of the Orient persisted. *Envisioning Asia*'s conclusion considers the reception of the film *M. Butterfly* (David Cronenberg, 1993), based on the play by the well-known Chinese American playwright David Henry Hwang, as symptomatic of contemporary attitudes toward cinematic virtual voyages to Asia on U.S. screens. Shot in part on location in China, including one significant scene staged at the Great Wall, *M. Butterfly* defies audience expectations derived from the earlier visions of films shot in exotic locales. However, Cronenberg's film was not popular with audiences or critics and was especially disparaged for its lack of realism and believability. As this case suggests, the appeal of a particular kind of cinematic travel to Asia over a more critical approach to shooting on location in an exotic setting apparently continues to the present day.

CHAPTER ONE

"*To travel is to possess the world*"

The Illustrated Travel Lectures of E. Burton Holmes

"The World 100 Years Ago"

The illustrated travel lecturer Elias Burton Holmes began his 1953 autobiography *The World Is Mine* with his motto, "To travel is to possess the world." He intended the phrase metaphorically: "I know that through travel I have possessed the world more completely, more satisfyingly than if I had acquired the whole earth by purchase or conquest." Yet despite his care in setting apart travel, which "takes naught from any man," from the brute economic, political, and military realities of purchase and conquest, Holmes's remarkable career as a professional traveler was made possible in many ways by precisely these practices.[1] At the turn of the twentieth century, the entertaining narratives and picturesque images of the Burton Holmes Lectures represented the world to Americans at the dawn of the American Century. Holmes claimed, not without reason, that "many lands became, through my efforts, visibly familiar to my increasing audiences."[2] In keeping with Edward Said's imperative to "look carefully and integrally at the culture that nurtured the sentiment, rationale, and above all the imagination of empire," we must analyze such representations as more than merely entertainment.[3] Viewed in the context of the imperial contests of the turn of the century, these representations constituted an important element of a national culture struggling with questions of economic expansion, racial and cultural difference, and colonial conquest.

As a young boy, historian Arthur M. Schlesinger Jr. attended the Burton Holmes Lectures at Boston's Symphony Hall in the 1920s with his mother. Many decades later, he wrote the introduction to *The World 100 Years Ago*, a 1998 publication that reprinted abbreviated versions of some of Holmes's lectures. The essay begins:

> Burton Holmes!—forgotten today, but such a familiar name in America in
> the first half of the 20th century, a name then almost synonymous with
> dreams of foreign travel.... He taught generations of Americans about the
> great world beyond the seas. His books are still readable today and show
> new generations how their grandparents learned about a world that has
> since passed away but remains a fragrant memory.[4]

Holmes's photographs, films, and lectures are indeed valuable documents of the "World 100 Years Ago" and as such also provide important
evidence of United States overseas expansionism at the turn of the twentieth century. Holmes had extraordinary timing: he was on the scene in
Hawai'i as the Senate was voting to annex it, in Manila near the beginning of the Philippine-American War, and inside the Forbidden City in
Beijing, formerly Peking, soon after the conclusion of the Boxer Uprising. He characterized the first fourteen years of the century as "those
happy years" when "I was almost alone in the then peculiar field of showing Americans what the world, outside of America, looked like."[5] Holmes
was not, of course, the first or the only person to bring images of foreign
countries to U.S. audiences. But at the very moment that Holmes was
"showing Americans what the world, outside America, looked like," a
dramatic redefinition was occurring not only in technologies of showing
but also in the concept of America as a nation and its relationship to the
world outside. Holmes enthusiastically embraced each of these changes;
his sense of the historic, along with the size and demographic of his public following, makes him an especially important purveyor of travel images in this period. He was also one of the first, if not the first, illustrated
travel lecturer to incorporate moving pictures into his presentations.
This fact makes his work particularly relevant to this book's examination
of U.S. films shot on location in Asia. In sum, Holmes combined the visual and dramatic possibilities offered by cinema with the well-worn
conventions of the travel lecture. Thus, his lectures offer an early vision
of the power of film as both a form of virtual travel and a form of knowledge of faraway places.

Holmes's lectures, initially accompanied only by hand-painted photographic slides, are part of the history of what Charles Musser calls
"screen practice," which situates cinema within a historical model that
addresses a range of related technologies, representational strategies, and
social and cultural functions.[6] This model therefore allows film historians to consider texts, such as Holmes's early lectures, that do not con-

form to what we would today recognize as "cinema." Yet his lectures utilized structures and stylistic strategies that would later become familiar in narrative cinema. Thus, as we examine the discourse of travel that undergirds shooting on location, Holmes provides a link to the past as he exemplifies the conventions of illustrated travel lectures; he also provides a connection to the future development not only of travel cinema but also more generally of fictional narratives in moving pictures. As Rick Altman argues, "In terms of the history of cinema, the editing strategies evident in Holmes's lectures are precisely those that cinema needed in order to develop beyond its early photographic, documentary, mimetic approach."[7] Examining Holmes's lectures therefore allows us to compare still photographs to moving images and nonnarrative cinematic travel views to more familiar story films. However, my analysis in this chapter not only sheds light on the history of cinema but also answers the question of how these modes of representation shaped the imaginative geography of Japan, China, the Philippines, and Hawai'i for turn-of-the-century Americans.

Holmes lectured about these faraway lands and distant cultures at a time when Americans were beginning to see Asia and the Pacific from the perspective of owners of newly acquired territories and occupiers of defeated nations. How might Holmes's travels, as represented in words, still images, and moving images, help Americans to reimagine their place in the world and their new identity as an overseas imperial power? As Said has said of Joseph Conrad's *Heart of Darkness*, the novel was "part of the European effort to hold on to, think about, plan for Africa." In effect, "To represent Africa is to enter the battle over Africa."[8] Similarly, Holmes represented parts of Asia and the Pacific to Americans at a time when their relationship to these places was changing. As he encountered these redefinitions of national identity in an international context, he maintained a spirit of optimism, curiosity, and national pride. In projecting this attitude, he clearly exemplifies the figure of the emblematic American of the period, enthusiastic about the new responsibilities of the nation and confident about its abilities to fulfill them.

Since Holmes was the sole author of his lectures and almost always the speaker at the podium, he was the primary figure of identification for his audiences.[9] Therefore, I begin by recounting some details of his life to illuminate the subjective positioning he offered in relation to the people and places he encountered in his travels. Holmes was not always a travel lecturer, and the circumstances that led to his decision to become one

demonstrate how his lectures were a part of a larger national effort to
understand the world and the place of the United States within it. I then
compare his work to that of John L. Stoddard, his famous predecessor, to
examine the innovations in technique and technology Holmes brought
to the genteel illustrated travel lecture, not least by introducing films to
the format. In the second half of the chapter, I examine three Holmes
lectures—on Hawaiʻi, Manila, and the Forbidden City—that depict the
U.S. expansion into Asia and the Pacific. Although Holmes's professional
life as an illustrated travel lecturer began in 1893 and continued for several years after World War II, in this chapter I focus only on these early
lectures. My analysis is based on the versions of Holmes's lectures published in a multivolume book collection that purports to reproduce the
spoken text in full but includes only a selection of the accompanying
slides and films. Since the lectures are available in book form, they are accessible primary texts. However, the book versions are not the same
thing as the performed lectures, so in addition to analyzing the texts of
the published lectures, I consult reviews of his performances for details
of how they were promoted to and received by audiences.

Orientations

Both of Holmes's parents were descended from English settlers who arrived in New England in the seventeenth century. Holmes was born and
raised in Chicago, in a socially prominent family. He received relatively
little formal education, choosing to leave Chicago's Harvard School for
Boys at the age of sixteen, though most of his friends continued on and
many eventually attended Yale University. According to his autobiography, he first traveled abroad to Europe with his mother and grandmother in 1886, shortly after leaving school. In 1890, he again accompanied his grandmother to Europe, and a year later, the pair toured Mexico
by train. In 1892, Holmes's boyhood friend, Albert W. Goodrich, invited
him on a trip to Japan. Holmes felt an immediate affinity for the country: though he arrived on a stormy day, "From the first moment, despite
the gloomy aspect of everything that morning, Japan fascinated me."
Years later, he reflected, "I doubt if I have ever been happier than during
the four months I spent in the as yet unspoiled *Japanese* Japan of 1892."[10]
Holmes wholeheartedly embraced Japanese culture, boasting of how he

could use chopsticks by his second Japanese meal. Despite his numerous visits to the capitals of Europe, which clearly thrilled and delighted him, and his brief excursion into Mexico, something in Japan enthralled Holmes as no other place did. The beginnings of Holmes's lifelong passion for travel and vocation as a travel lecturer thus lie in this fascination with the difference of Japan.[11] Judging from the content of his lectures and autobiography, however, Holmes was enchanted not with the history and politics of the country but with what might be understood as lifestyle—that is, "customs, dress, food, [and] manner of life."[12]

In the fall of 1893, shortly after his return from Japan, the twenty-three-year-old Holmes attended the World's Columbian Exposition in his hometown. He was one of more than twenty-seven million adults and children to see the exposition over its six-month duration. He described the experience with great enthusiasm, recalling, "I found in that great exposition an epitome and a foretaste of the great world that I longed to see. I travelled around the world within the gates of the Chicago Fair." Furthermore, "the Fair had so intensified my love for things foreign, exotic, far-away and unfamiliar that I resolved, before going back to work, to try to find a way to keep on going places, seeing things, indulging my *wanderlust*."[13] He soon abandoned his job as a photo supply clerk for a career in travel:

> The photo supply house offered me fifteen dollars a week to return. But I didn't want to work. The trip to Japan, the Oriental exhibits of the Exposition, were still on my mind. I thought of Stoddard. I thought of the slides I'd had hand-colored in Tokyo. That was it, and it wasn't work. So I hired a hall and became a travel lecturer.[14]

Holmes explicitly conceived of his lectures as an extension of or even a substitute for the immensely popular exposition: "When the Columbian Exposition closed its gates in November, 1893, I felt that the world needed something important to fill the void! I decided to present 'The E. Burton Holmes Lectures' to the local public of my native city and then— who knows?"[15] Film scholars have frequently noted how world's fairs and international expositions at the turn of the century influenced early cinema.[16] Writing specifically of the Chicago Columbian Exposition, Lauren Rabinovitz argues, "Fairgoers learned about a new modernist, cinematically situated spectatorship because it was part of the overall

discursive formation of visual culture and social practices acting upon
the observer's construction of knowledge."[17] Therefore, the Columbian
Exposition influenced Holmes's decision to become a travel lecturer not
only by reinforcing his interest in "things foreign, exotic, far-away and
unfamiliar" but also by providing a model of a spectacular form of entertainment that offered up the world for visual consumption. Just as
Holmes traveled and learned about the world by visiting the exhibits of
the exposition, so too would his audiences see the world by attending his
lectures and viewing the slides and films of the places he had seen, learning about the world and their place in it in a pleasurable but also educational manner.

Although Holmes, as a member of the Chicago Camera Club, had
presented an earlier illustrated travel lecture based on his tour of Europe,
he debuted as a professional lecturer on November 15, 1893, at the Recital
Hall of Chicago's Auditorium Building.[18] He presented "Japan—The
Country" in front of "a fairly large, fashionable and feminine audience."[19] (The audience members, each of whom paid $1.00 for a single
lecture or $1.50 to attend the two-lecture course, had been culled from
Holmes's mother's visiting book and *The Blue Book*.) One week later, he
presented "Japan—The Cities" to an even larger audience of well-heeled
Chicagoans. This first professional venture, which included one matinee
and one evening performance of each of his two lectures, yielded seven
hundred dollars in ticket sales. These lectures also marked the beginning
of Holmes's long association with Oscar Depue, who was hired to project the lantern slides at this performance and later became Holmes's
motion picture cameraman. Although an appearance in Milwaukee one
month later cost Holmes the profits of his debut engagement, he persisted, and in 1897, Stoddard, the preeminent travel lecturer of the time,
retired and anointed Holmes as his successor, greatly enhancing
Holmes's growing professional reputation. An article announcing
Holmes's upcoming January 1899 lectures in Washington, D.C., assured
readers that he was "fully worthy of the recommendations and sponsor-
ship extended to him by his illustrious predecessor," naming Stoddard as
"one of Mr. Holmes' greatest friends and admirers." The article reprinted
the text of a December 16, 1897, letter in which Stoddard congratulated
Holmes on securing an engagement at Daly's Theater in New York City
as Stoddard's replacement.[20] Perhaps not coincidentally, 1897 was also
the year Holmes began using motion pictures.

Tradition and Innovation

The addition of moving pictures was only one indication of how Holmes differed from his predecessor in the way he conceived of travel and the techniques and technologies of illustrated travel lectures. When Stoddard crossed paths with Holmes on the way to Vancouver, where they would both board the steamship *Empress of Japan* for Yokohama, he was embarking on his first and only trip around the world. Stoddard held a nostalgic view of travel and lamented the advent of modern technologies of communication and transport, accusing them of robbing the earth of its romance. His wistful longing for a vanishing era of travel is apparent in the opening sentences of his lecture on Japan:

> It is now nearly four hundred years since the brave discoverer, Magellan, first sailed around the world. Yet, till comparatively recent times, three years were necessary to complete the circuit. To-day, some Phineas [*sic*] Fogg can put a girdle round the earth in less than eighty days, and messages are flashed to us from China and Ceylon in less than eighty seconds. The old-time spirit of adventure amid unknown scenes, which thrilled the traveler of former years, has, therefore, well-nigh disappeared.[21]

Stoddard notes disapprovingly that a man who had journeyed around the world two centuries earlier would have been heralded as a hero, whereas "to-day the name he earns is merely—'Globe-trotter.'"[22] In contrast, Holmes often used the term *globetrotter* as a descriptive rather than pejorative expression. Stoddard and Holmes also differed in their means of presenting their lectures.[23] While the illustrations for Stoddard's lectures included lantern slides of landscapes and of staged studio scenes along with drawings and engravings, Holmes used only hand-colored lantern slides and films. From the outset, Holmes dispensed with traditional ways of signaling the changes of image in a travel lecture—flashes of light, bells, clickers; he preferred instead to create the illusion of travel. In his foreword to the book version of the Burton Holmes Lectures, he emphasized the importance of this illusion. Even as he celebrated the wider audience the volumes would bring, he pointed out that the public performance of an illustrated lecture differed fundamentally from the lecture as it appears on the printed page: "In an illustrated lecture the impression upon eye and ear should be simultaneous, that the suggestion of travel may be successfully produced."[24] He then asked his readers to "listen with the mental ear to catch the shade of meaning that should be conveyed by every phrase" and to "project the illustrations, through the lenses of imagination" to participate fully in the illusion.[25] According to film historian Rick Altman, Stoddard's lectures were designed not to recount the narrative of his travels but to impart knowledge and information about the country in question. In contrast, Holmes turned his audience into members of his traveling party; the basic stylistic strategies he used to accomplish this feat are evident as early as his first public presentation.[26] Thus, Holmes's illustrated travel lectures are important to the history of film not only for his early incorporation of cinema but also for this conception of his lectures as virtual voyages for his audiences.

A scene from Holmes's lecture on Peking shows how the mere idea of cinema, even without actual moving images, could change the audience's experience of an illustrated travel lecture. In describing the discomforts of a Peking cart, Holmes included an image of the backside of a mule with a person by its side along with the written description of the cart and the physical effects of traveling by such means. Architectural details of the city are visible in the background of the photograph, which is labeled "The Passenger's Point of View" (fig. 1.1). The accompanying text reports, "The passing panorama, framed by the awning and the mule, gave me much the same impression as a very jerky motion-picture projected by a shaky cinematograph—this effect is due to the cruelly continued jolting of the cart."[27] The metaphor of a flickering film would not have been available to Stoddard in 1892, of course, but the differences between the two lecturers go beyond the choice of descriptive language. Holmes's privileging of the passenger's perspective places audience members in the seat of the cart, transporting them to Peking and recreating for them his experience of Chinese transportation in a manner Stoddard never imagined. Given a similar experience of a mode of local transport, traveling in a kago in Japan, Stoddard offered a much more artificial, staged, and stationary image (fig. 1.2). Where Stoddard's lecture merely recounted his experience of traveling in a kago, Holmes invited his audience to feel the "cruelly continued jolting of the cart" for themselves through what would be known today as a perceptual point-of-view shot (a shot that shows what a character within a film is seeing from his or her perspective). In this case, the origin of this perception is Holmes himself.

When members of Holmes's audience imagined themselves riding in

FIGURE 1.1 "The Passenger's Point of View," from Burton Holmes, *Burton Holmes Travelogues* (New York: McClure, 1910), 9:159.

a Peking cart, they became not only subjects who see the street scene and feel movement but also Westerners, like Holmes, trying out an amusing form of local transport though they were accustomed to more modern kinds of mobility. As in the lectures on Hawai'i, Manila, and the Forbidden City discussed later in this chapter, Holmes serves as a figure of identification for his audience, rarely as literally as in this example but rather as a character on the scene and the narrator of the drama, shaping listeners' views of the places to which he traveled. These lectures engaged the audience in visions of the world, as structured by Holmes, that not only assumed an interest in "things foreign, exotic, far-away and unfamiliar" but also told a reassuring, entertaining, and very particular story of the United States as an emerging political force in Asia and the Pacific.

Holmes's lectures often referred to current world events but were not generally designed to report on them in a journalistic manner. Holmes typically traveled during the summer months and then lectured during the fall and spring. This schedule allowed him to spend weeks or even longer in a single country and therefore to present a relatively in-depth view of the world. In these turn-of-the-century lectures, he offered his audiences a leisurely reflection on the rationale for imperial expansion, the benefits of territorial possession, and the pleasures of colonial power; the "ever-shifting boundaries" between the foreign and the domestic that Amy Kaplan has examined can be viewed as they begin to take shape and solidify in the negotiations that Holmes undertakes in his travels as an American abroad as well as in his representations of his travels for his

FIGURE 1.2   "A Kago," from John L. Stoddard, *John L. Stoddard's Lectures*
(Boston: Balch, 1898), 3:133.

audiences at home.[28] As a result, these lectures may be seen as one effort,
among others, to negotiate a new understanding of America's place in
the world via Holmes's experience of it.

In addition to showing how these lectures represented "home" and
"abroad"—that is, the United States of America as compared to Hawai'i,
the Philippines, and China—I draw attention to how they used protocinematic stylistic strategies and incorporated actual films. For
Holmes, cinema offered the ideal means of recording life. In his biography, Holmes describes his desire for an as yet unavailable technology to
record movement during an imperial garden party he attended in Japan:

> Bustles are funny. As worn in Japan in 1892, they were a scream. The dainty
> Japanese ladies, who would have looked so charming in kimono, had

adopted western fashions but not western manners. When they bowed, they bent forward at the waist, again and again, jack-knife fashion. As their heads went down, up came the bustles. Oh, that the movies had been invented then![29]

In Holmes's view, the Japanese women's attempt to assimilate Western fashion while retaining traditional forms of greeting symbolizes the difference between East and West. He also believed that neither still images nor words could capture this difference as effectively as could moving pictures. Similarly, in the lecture "Seoul, the Capital of Korea," Holmes bemoans his inability to provide the readers of the book with a film that would capture the sensation of rushing about Seoul in a trolley car, telling them that "animated photography" could reveal "the very *life* of foreign lands."[30] Holmes's faith in the representational capabilities of cinema mirror discourses of photographic truth except that in his view, the ability to show movement elevates films above still photography. Holmes designed his lectures to function as a form of virtual travel, and cinematic views added immeasurably to his representations of foreign lands and peoples; such views could show not only what people looked like but also how they lived.

At a very early date, Holmes and Depue, recognizing the significance of moving pictures, set about finding ways to produce and use them in the lectures. According to Depue, "In 1896 we realized that we had a growing rival—the motion picture. As a result, in 1897, at the end of the 1896 season, Mr. Holmes sailed for Sicily and Italy and I sailed for London, the Mecca for motion pictures at that time. My intention was to search out and buy a motion picture camera."[31] Having little success in London, Depue traveled to Paris, where he purchased a 60mm camera from Leon Gaumont, before continuing on to meet Holmes in Rome. Depue's first film was of the plaza of St. Peter's Cathedral. Holmes and Depue initially showed films at the conclusion of the lectures as what Depue called "a fifteen- or twenty-minute added attraction" to the lecture. The introduction of moving pictures to the lectures was very well received: "With the spontaneous outburst of applause that followed the first roll, we had the great satisfaction of feeling that it was a real success, which, indeed, it proved to be during the rest of the season."[32] Holmes soon incorporated films into the lecture itself.

The program for Holmes's 1899–1900 season explained that films were "to be projected during the lecture at moments when movement is essential to complete and vivify the impressions produced by the spoken words and colored illustrations."[33] The program also claimed that the use of moving pictures "marks the beginning of a new epoch in the treatment of the illustrated lecture."[34] Film therefore functioned in part as a novelty with which to attract audiences; however, its selective use "at moments when movement is essential" also demonstrates how the technology of film could supplement existing forms of representation. Virtually all of the reviews of Holmes's lectures from around the turn of the century mention the projection of motion pictures, and in some instances, the reviews even list films by title.

Holmes gave his first lectures in Washington, D.C., during the 1898–99 season. These performances in the U.S. capital highlight the overlap and intersection of political and cultural discourses about American identity at this historic moment. Holmes initially appeared at an "invitation lecture" on Yellowstone National Park on December 28, 1898, at the Columbia Theater.[35] An early review praised the hand-colored photographic views as well as a series of motion pictures that "add reality to his entertainment." The writer saw the experience of the lecture as a substitute for actual travel, since "those who heard his description of the National Park and enjoyed the pictures accompanying it, gleaned as much of the beauty of this 'Wonderland' as the tourists generally do in their five days' exploration, without any of the discomforts attending travel and mountain climbing, to say nothing of the expense."[36] Such references to the lecture as a form of virtual travel and to the quality of his photographic slides and the realism of his motion pictures typified reviews of Holmes's lectures.

In attendance at this invitation lecture was "a representative gathering of Washington people," including "Secretary Long, Secretary Gage, Senator Mason and party, and J. Dumont and party."[37] If the audience at this lecture was any indication of the people who would attend Holmes's lectures in the future, then some of the nation's most prominent politicians would see and hear of Holmes's travels. "Secretary Long" was John Davis Long, a former governor of Massachusetts who was appointed secretary of the navy by President William McKinley in 1897. "Secretary Gage" referred to U.S. treasury secretary Lyman Gage, and "Senator Mason" was Senator William E. Mason of Illinois. The patrons at Holmes's lectures were usually a relatively elite audience in search of both entertainment and education. The distinctiveness of the Washington, D.C., audience lies in the political power held by some of the audience members, who would make decisions about the issues of national identity and overseas imperialism that Holmes's lectures implicitly raised.

During this first season in Washington, D.C., Holmes's lectures were presented on Wednesday afternoons at 4:15 P.M. at the Columbia Theater, beginning with "The Hawaiian Islands" on January 18, 1899, then "Into Morocco" on January 25, "Fez, the Metropolis of the Moors" on February 1, "Grecian Journeys" on February 8, and finally "The Grand Canyon of Arizona" on February 15. Tickets to a single lecture were available at $.25, $.50, $.75, or $1.00, depending on seating, or audience members could purchase tickets for the entire course of lectures for $2.00, $2.50, or $3.00. A few days before the first lecture, readers of the *Washington Post* were reminded of how well received the invitation lecture was: "The press of this city, with one accord, pronounced Mr. Holmes and his lecture to be both charming and highly entertaining and instructive." The article reported that the subjects of the upcoming lectures "are new and interesting. Two of them in particular should prove so, as they both pertain to our own country, and one of our recently acquired possessions."[38] Although it is impossible to say exactly how Holmes's lectures shaped his audience's views on U.S. overseas imperialism, the lecture on Hawai'i occurred just as the Senate was debating annexation of the Philippines. During these debates, Mason presented a resolution to the Senate on January 7, 1899, arguing against annexation of the Philippines: "Whereas, all just powers of government are derived from the consent of the governed: Therefore, be it Resolved by the Senate of the United States, That the Government of the United States of America will not attempt to govern the people of any other country in the world without the consent of the people themselves, or subject them by force to our dominion against their will."[39] A week and a half later, Holmes spoke to his Washington, D.C., audience about the Hawaiian Islands, but he did not engage with the anticolonial perspective expressed in Mason's resolution despite the timeliness and relevance of the debate to his lecture topic.

Imperial Travels

"The Hawaiian Islands"

On June 15, 1898, the U.S. House of Representatives voted 209–91 in favor of a joint resolution calling for the annexation of Hawai'i. According to

Holmes, the steamer on which he was traveling to Hawai'i, the *Moana*, brought the islands their first news of the annexation, since no telegraph cable to Honolulu yet existed. Holmes's lecture begins with an evocation of the "two thousand miles of peaceful ocean . . . between our coast and the palm-fringed shores of the Republic of Hawaii." But, he notes, by the end of his trip, the ocean will have been transformed into an "American channel," and "the trans-Pacific steamers will have become boats that convey the traffic of mere 'ferries,' running from San Francisco, Cal. to Honolulu, United States of America."[40] Of course, the distance between San Francisco and Honolulu would not have changed; rather, what the distance signified was rearticulated as the borders of the United States were extended out into the Pacific. This geographic reimagining of the Pacific Ocean as an "American channel" is a striking example of what John Eperjesi refers to as "a moment in which a particular representation, or misrepresentation, of geographical space supports the expansion of the nation's political and economic borders."[41] Similarly, reinventing transoceanic steamships as local ferries posits a sense of proximity between the United States and Hawai'i that the lecture repeatedly reinforces. In this historical context, by bringing U.S. audiences with him to Hawai'i (and bringing Hawai'i to the United States through words and images), Holmes's lecture bridges the distance between the two places and thus transforms the Pacific Ocean into an American channel on an imaginative and cultural level, mirroring the political transformation soon to occur. At the moment of Holmes's visit, however, the U.S. Senate was still debating Hawai'i's status in relation to the United States, and the lecture reveals both the habit of seeing Hawai'i as a foreign site and the imagination of it as a territory of the United States.

"The Hawaiian Islands" opens with Holmes describing the vessel's departure from San Francisco in June 1898, giving a brief account of the week at sea, and then announcing the early morning arrival in Honolulu Harbor. The published text includes one or two images per page of text. In this version of the lecture, typographic strategies further the illusion of travel by integrating the images with the words.[42] The first image is "The summer sea," a rectangular photograph divided horizontally between ocean and sky, followed by a view of "Honolulu Harbor" from a distance. This series of images concludes with a view looking down on the crowd on the dock as the ship comes ashore. This beginning transports audiences with Holmes to Hawai'i; he creates the illusion of travel by showing visual images seen from the perspective of a passenger on the steamship, while his text narrates the passing scenery and views. Thus, he organizes the opening according to the logic of departure, approach, and arrival. However, Holmes deliberately withholds his first impressions of Hawai'i because "I trust that all of you are some day going to the islands, and believe no one has a right to rob you of your first impressions."[43] Later in the lecture, he makes apparent the fact that many other travelers have been to Hawai'i before him, including Mark Twain: Holmes scans the "tourist-register" at the Volcano House in Kilauea and shares some of the thoughts left by travelers as early as 1863.[44] This history, along with Holmes's stated belief that many of his listeners and readers would eventually visit Hawai'i, reveals the status of Hawai'i as an established travel destination for Americans.

Holmes sought to avoid the subject of politics in his lectures, noting, "When you discuss politics, you are sure to offend."[45] Many commentators on his work repeat this assertion. Irving Wallace wrote in 1947 that "the emphasis is on description, information and oddity. Two potential ingredients are studiously omitted. One is adventure, the other politics."[46] More recently, Arthur M. Schlesinger Jr. describes Holmes as "uninterested in politics and poverty and the darker side of life, in love with beautiful scenery, historic monuments, picturesque customs, and challenging trips."[47] Fred Israel portrays Holmes as "a conservative man" who "avoided political upheavals, economic exploitation, and social conflicts in his travelogues."[48] These writers followed Holmes in casting his lectures first and foremost as entertainment rather than as sociological or anthropological treatises or platforms for partisan views. However, traveling as an American in Hawai'i in 1898 (or in the Philippines in 1899 or China in 1901) inevitably situated Holmes within a politicized context. Despite his efforts to avoid controversial topics, Holmes's lectures of this period clearly engaged with and took positions on challenging questions of racial difference, national sovereignty, and the place of the United States in the world. For example, throughout "The Hawaiian Islands," he considers the identity of Hawai'i in relation to the United States. This focus results partly from acknowledging the role that American settlers had played in Hawai'i as well as from considering the question of how annexation will redefine both the United States and Hawai'i in the future. Opinions about the annexation of Hawai'i were by no means unanimous. However, Holmes's lecture not only presumed that annexation was a positive development but also helped his audiences to understand the pleasures that Hawai'i could offer and to imagine for themselves the advantages of "possessing" such a tropical paradise.

As a white American of considerable social standing, Holmes enjoyed the hospitality of his compatriots, and he presented the islands to his audiences from the perspective of the wealthy American settlers in Hawai'i. Nevertheless, Holmes initially experienced Hawai'i with ambivalence, since he traveled looking for difference, and the effects of the long presence of the Americans in Hawai'i sometimes made the exotic islands seem a little too familiar. Arriving in Honolulu and traveling to his hotel, Holmes remarks,

> Surely this is no foreign country; this street is like a dozen streets that we could name in the minor cities of America. . . . The traveler from the United States instantly feels at home. This is delightful in one sense, in another it is a less welcome sensation. The traveler who seeks novelty and strangeness may be at first rebellious when confronted by a typical American thoroughfare, in which there is not one beautiful or exotic note.[49]

Soon enough, Holmes finds evidence of local color in the form of indigenous flora and fauna, though he still takes note of what he considers the banality of parts of Honolulu: "When on King Street the traveler can easily imagine himself in the business district of a small American town; he sees familiar articles exposed for sale, reads signs that he has read before, meets people like the people whom he knows at home."[50] Throughout the lecture, Holmes makes evident the influence of the American settlers in Hawai'i, from the early missionaries to the prosperous owners of the sugar plantations. By reacting negatively to the unexpected familiarity of Hawai'i, Holmes emphasizes the expectation of difference and distance between the United States and Hawai'i and thereby underlines Hawai'i's uncertain status. Is Hawai'i a distant, independent kingdom (though at the time of Holmes's visit it was known to Americans as a republic), or a part of the United States just across the "American channel" from San Francisco? However, even if Holmes objected to how typically American certain aspects of Hawai'i seemed, he was unequivocal about how the American settlers, whom he describes as "men and women of our race" and "fellow-citizens of our race," had improved the place.[51] In his opinion, "Christianization, civilization, and [the] present prosperity of Hawaii are the fruits of the efforts of English-speaking men and women."[52]

References to the imminent annexation are scattered throughout the text, beginning with the news of the House vote and including Holmes's meeting with Dr. John Strayer McGrew, known as the Father of Annexation for his ardent advocacy. However, when Holmes recounts the history of U.S.-Hawaiian relations, he concocts a euphemistic tale that skirts the issue of exactly why Honolulu's streets, signs, and people are so familiar. In this tale, Holmes describes the diverse populations of Hawai'i, including native Hawaiians, Portuguese, Japanese, and Chinese, as clay in the hands of American potters, molded through Christianity, broken through revolution, and finally reshaped into a republic to be given over to the protection of "a certain Uncle Sam." This Uncle Sam, "who had recently developed a passion for 'insular ceramics' . . . enthusiastic collector that he is now become, has placed this beautiful Pacific specimen securely on the shelves of his National Museum, to rest in definite security forever side by side with other lovely tropic curios recently acquired in the Caribbean and the China Seas."[53] Holmes's story represents imperial expansion in reassuringly benign terms. "Insular ceramics" is an obvious reference to "insular imperialism," with "curios" standing in for tropical island nations. Holmes stresses the novelty of American overseas imperial ambitions by translating it into a "recently developed passion," while he insists on the success of recent excursions by gesturing toward the "other lovely tropic curios" in the collection. He even broaches the idea of national identity by positing the image of an architectural unity that houses the individual objects. This remarkably elaborate metaphor for U.S. expansion insists on an entirely passive Hawaiian populace that is literally objectified in this narrative and goes to extraordinary lengths to find neutral equivalents for overtly political terms. By abstracting a political history into a story of collecting curios, Holmes legitimates the American claim on Hawai'i and clears the way for his focus on scenery and attractions.

Holmes also references the future of Hawai'i as a U.S. military base, although its significance is muted since it is placed within Holmes's description of one of the highlights of his visit, a shark hunt at Pearl Harbor. The description of Pearl Harbor as both an ideal site for a naval station and a place of exotic adventure combines Holmes's interest in the picturesque aspects of Hawai'i with an awareness of how its geography gives it potential military uses:

> As the haunt of man-eating sharks and as the scene of many an exciting chase, Pearl Harbor is famous in Hawaii; but it has, as we know, a wider

fame, as the only available site for a naval station in all that vast watery
desert between California and Asia, between Alaska and the Antarctic seas.
It is not only the sole safe harbor of Hawaii, it is as perfectly adapted to the
needs of a modern naval power as if it had been planned and dredged and
blasted out by naval engineers.[54]

Holmes mentions the value of Pearl Harbor to "a modern naval power"
only as an aside, as an incidental observation woven into a lengthy and
detailed narrative of the shark hunting expedition, accompanied by
serene images of the harbor, group portraits of the shark hunters, a
photo of the unfortunate goat that will be used for bait, and two views of
the equally ill-fated shark. Nestled among the illustrations of the hunt is
an unremarkable image of four people dressed in suits and dresses,
standing with their backs to the camera, looking out over a watery landscape. The image is captioned "Our Future Naval Harbor" (fig. 1.3).[55] The
assured tone of both the image and its caption conveys a certainty about
what is to come that is in fact realized. The visual representations of the
tranquil harbor and quaint dock are lovely and inviting and are typical
of the images of Holmes's lectures. Slightly more unexpected is the information about the strategic configuration of the harbor, which acknowledges U.S. national interests in the area and foresees a time when
the harbor will be known for its naval base rather than as "the haunt of
man-eating sharks." However, Holmes's attention to military concerns
becomes more understandable when we recall that the Spanish-American War was under way at the time of Holmes's visit.

While Holmes was in Honolulu, a steamer full of U.S. soldiers on the
way to Manila stopped over, and Holmes devotes ten full pages of the
written version of the lecture to the enthusiastic reception they received.
The effect on the locals was, in his estimation, significant: "Cheered by
the populace, followed by children of every age and color, stared at by
Chinamen and Japanese and natives, who thus receive an object-lesson
in the strength of the United States, our boys march on at a swinging
pace."[56] Such a description makes evident that U.S. military might was
instrumental in underwriting Uncle Sam's collecting mania. The images
provide ample visual support of this point. The still photographs associated with this part of the lecture begin with "Transports for Manila,"
showing a large number of soldiers sitting and standing on the decks of
a ship. "Marching to Waikiki," on the next page, depicts another large
group of soldiers from the back, marching diagonally into the back-

FIGURE 1.3   "Our Future Naval Harbor," from Burton Holmes,
Burton Holmes Travelogues (New York: McClure, 1910), 5:68.

ground. A similar image of marching soldiers follows, this time shown
from the front. A large, full-page photograph of Holmes and another
man in the foreground comes next, showing them standing next to a
motion picture camera on the beach pointed toward soldiers enjoying
the water in the middle ground, with an American flag at the end of the
pier in the background. This image is labeled "Volunteers at Waikiki."

In viewing Holmes's lectures in light of the development of screen
practices, what is most striking about the still images preceding "Volunteers at Waikiki" is just how much they read like a film meant to emphasize U.S. military power, even though the narrative progression is toward
a moment of leisure. As Kaplan writes about early films of the Spanish-
American War,

> The appeal of these war films lay less in their exhibition of exotic foreign
> lands and people, who were rarely visible, or in the battle scenes than in
> the spectacle of American mobility itself—in the movement of men,
> horses, vehicles, and ships abroad and in their return home. The films cel-
> ebrate the capacity of military power and the camera to encompass the
> globe.[57]

In the series of still images of soldiers in Honolulu, the camera is turned on "our boys" while "the populace" is relegated to the background. In other words, Holmes's interest in bringing foreign lands to life is temporarily dominated by his desire to show the spectacle of U.S. military maneuvers. The inviting beach at Waikiki merely provides a setting for a lesson in U.S. power for the local populations and for a proud and reassuring show of strength for audiences at home.

A brief review of Holmes's January 1899 lecture on "The Hawaiian Islands" notes that the lecture concluded with five films: "Travel in Hawaii," "The Hawaiian Militia," "United States Volunteers in Honolulu," "The Honolulu Fire Department," and "Surf-Riding in Native Canoes."[58] Judging from the titles, these films were typical of the time period in that they emphasize movement and topics of local interest, though if the review accurately represented their placement at the conclusion of the lecture, then they had yet to be integrated into the lecture itself. Significantly, in Depue's recollections of his work with Holmes, including their visit to Hawai'i, he mentions only, "We then went on to Honolulu for a tour of the Hawaiian Islands. The American troops were passing through Honolulu on their way to Manila, for the Philippines had come into our possession through Dewey's victory at Manila Bay."[59] In an essay that traces Depue's developing grasp of the uses of cinema in the early years of his association with Holmes, that he mentions only the marching troops suggests just how compelling these soldiers were as cinematic subjects.

Near the end of Holmes's visit, a passing stranger relayed the news of the Senate vote favoring annexation, and Holmes concludes his lecture on Hawai'i by describing the effect of this announcement on him and his two hosts, both of whom were entrepreneurial American coffee planters: "At his next words, 'Annexation is an accomplished fact,' we fix our feet more firmly on this lava shore, for we, who a moment since were as strangers in a strange land are now at home—Hawaii has become part of the United States."[60] The dramatic impact of this final sentence of the lecture derives from the way Holmes erases the distinction between "home" and "abroad," thereby defining the American presence in Hawai'i as permanent and proprietary. Holmes's audiences in the United States shared this sense of possession since they were invited to view his illustrated travel lecture as their first (virtual) visit to their new Pacific territory. According to one review of the lecture, "Mr. Holmes spoke of the native life on the islands, the hospitality of the Hawaiians, and their food and habits, sketching in brief many of the important historical incidents of the country. He dwelt also on Pearl Harbor, our future naval station, and outlined its possibilities and value to the United States, concluding with an enthusiastic prophecy of the future of Hawaii."[61] The review's attention to native Hawaiian life and customs, on the one hand, and the "possibilities and value" of Hawai'i to the United States on the other, neatly reflects the double vision of Hawai'i in the lecture itself: it is both distinct from but also a future part of the United States. In Holmes's telling, the annexation took on a sense of accomplishment and celebration. From the perspective of native Hawaiians, however, the change in ownership can only be understood as a forced expropriation.[62]

"Manila"

Historians have long speculated about President McKinley's opinions regarding the drama of overseas expansion. Julius Pratt, for example, argues that McKinley did not foresee the eventual consequences of war with Spain, while well-known expansionists Henry Cabot Lodge, Theodore Roosevelt, and Albert Beveridge did.[63] (Beveridge, a senator from Indiana considered to have presidential potential, was a close personal friend of Holmes's.) Regardless of McKinley's personal views, his legendary lack of knowledge regarding the location of the Philippines suggests that American attitudes toward expansion rested on a certain level of ignorance about the world. The geographic and cultural distance between the Philippines and the United States was undoubtedly great, and, prior to Commodore George Dewey's defeat of the Spanish at Manila Bay, many people likely lacked the most basic information regarding the archipelago. But some entrepreneurs, politicians, and missionaries were quite familiar with the geography of Asia and the Pacific, including the strategic placement of Hawai'i and the Philippines for military purposes and for the advancement of trade with China. At the conclusion of the Spanish-American War, curiosity about the region was heightened, not least because of the impassioned debate concerning America's proper role in the Philippines. In this case, as in others described in this volume, the desire for information arose from imperial foundations, and cinema was seen as a suitable medium for the production of knowledge about distant countries.

Proponents of annexation used arguments ranging from economic necessity (domestic overproduction created a need for overseas markets) to religious rhetoric (America's divine destiny required expansion). Anti-imperialists warned of the dire consequences of allowing more "Asiatics" into the country, conjuring nightmares of miscegenation. Many also questioned the constitutionality of the endeavor. In the end, the United States and Spain negotiated a settlement that allowed the United States to purchase the Philippines from Spain for twenty million dollars. Although the Senate ratified the treaty, the decision to annex the Philippines remained controversial. Even *Leslie's Official History of the Spanish-American War,* which bore the imprimatur of the federal government, betrayed some doubts about the decision, offering, "While the wisdom of Philippine annexation is a disputed question, there can be no difference of opinion regarding the courage, discipline and efficiency of American troops."[64] When hostilities broke out in February 1899 between U.S. and Filipino forces, questions about the wisdom of annexation appeared to be well founded. Despite periodic and very public assurances of the imminent subjugation of the "insurrectionists," the war continued for three years.[65]

Holmes visited the Philippines at a relatively early stage of the war. At this point in his career, he was well known enough—and perhaps the trip was newsworthy enough—that his departure from Vancouver for China, Japan, and Manila warranted mention in the "Theatrical Gossip" section of the *New York Times:*

> Burton Holmes, the lecturer, who recently filled an engagement at Daly's Theatre, will sail May 8 on the steamship Empress of China from Vancouver, B.C., for China, Japan, and Manila for the purpose of procuring material for his lecture tour next year. Mr. Holmes is supplied with letters of introduction from Federal officials to the commanders of the army and navy at Manila, asking them to extend all the facilities at their command to Mr. Holmes so he may be enabled to obtain pictures to illustrate his lectures.[66]

Similarly, several newspapers, including the *Times,* noted Holmes's return from the Philippines at the end of the summer: "Burton Holmes, lecturer, is expected to land in Vancouver on Aug. 30, on his return from the Philippines, the cities of the Chinese coast, and the mountains of Japan, where he has spent the last four months obtaining material for lectures in this city during the coming season."[67] The *Chicago Tribune* told its readers, "Among the passengers arriving [in Vancouver] by the

Oriental steamer yesterday were several direct from the Philippines, among them being E. Burton Holmes, the Chicago lecturer."[68] As these news items indicated, during the following lecture season, Holmes would be presenting his experiences with regard to the newest U.S. colonial possession. In Washington, D.C., Holmes again spoke at the Columbia Theater, opening the series, featuring "illustrations in color and appropriate Motion Pictures," with "Manila" on December 26, 1899, and continuing with "Japan Revisited" on January 2, 1900, "Round about Paris" on January 9, "Grand Canyon" on January 16, and "Mokiland" on January 23.[69]

In the opening of his lecture on Manila, Holmes summarizes the situation at the time of his visit:

> In 1899 America was looking with anxious interest toward the Philippines. Admiral Dewey, his work accomplished, had left Manila; General Otis, as military governor, was in command; the Filipinos under Aguinaldo were successfully defending themselves, and all the American forces were confined to the immediate surroundings of Manila.[70]

Holmes's arrival in Manila Bay was not auspicious. As in his earlier lectures, he begins with the departure of his steamship—from Hong Kong this time—before recounting the conditions of the sea voyage and depicting the approach to Manila. Once the vessel arrived, however, passengers were not allowed to disembark; the steamship was quarantined for three days. During this time, Holmes and his fellow passengers witnessed American warships shooting at "insurgents" on shore and heard reports that land forces were also involved in the fighting. The passengers noted launches patrolling the bay and cheered the arrival of the Oregon volunteers. They reacted to news of the fighting not with alarm but mostly with surprise and a hint of recognition that the war was not going exactly as planned: "We are astounded to find the fighting line so near the city; for men are killing one another there, not eight miles from the gates of Old Manila, and this after a six-months' pursuit of an enemy whom we, contemptuous white men, have pretended to despise."[71] Despite the challenges of being in the Philippines during the fighting, Holmes told his readers, "Manila itself was accessible, and the situation, political and military, presented picturesque aspects that appealed even to the globe-trotter intent only upon what is called in the East a 'Look See.'"[72]

Given Americans' relatively recent arrival in the Philippines, Holmes, like many of his countrymen, may well have been curious to learn more about Manila, "our new Oriental city" in the "Far Eastern archipelago that fate had assigned to Uncle Sam."[73] The construction of this sentence, in which fate is the party responsible for the current state of affairs, is characteristic of Holmes's efforts to refuse to take a position on the larger political implications of colonization. While the political status of the Philippines appears clearer than that of Hawai'i in some respects, since Holmes deems the U.S. possession of the Philippines an already established fact, the relationship between the United States and the Philippines is more tenuous in light of the relatively recent U.S. arrival there and the ongoing military conflict over the terms of the U.S. presence. Holmes does find some encouraging signs of change on the Escolta, which he had earlier characterized as "the busiest, most interesting street in all Manila":

> The Escolta is rapidly assuming an American complexion. If you believe in *signs,* you may, without the least difficulty, imagine that you are in one of our cities. The tide of street life runs much higher than in the days before the war; new currents are flowing through the narrow thoroughfares; even the natives seem to have caught the restless spirit of the conquerors, for they step out more briskly than they did.[74]

An accompanying photograph of "The Main Thoroughfare"—presumably the Escolta—shows a street lined with shops, many of which have English-language names and signage in their windows. Rather than expressing disappointment in the loss of the indigenous exotic, as he did in Honolulu, Holmes views this example of Americanization optimistically, as an indication of the improvements that will result from American colonization. His reference to "conquerors" is a far more straightforward and explicit acknowledgment of the circumstances that brought American troops to the Philippines than his strange fable of American potters and tropical curios regarding Hawai'i. Perhaps he could not have done otherwise given the obvious presence of American military forces in Manila. The lecture includes numerous images of American soldiers, and accounts of men fighting and dying testify to the ongoing conflict. Holmes took the disruptions of the war in stride, but the lecture reveals a palpable contrast between his lighthearted and bemused tone and the realities of the ongoing military maneuvers.

A Chicago review of Holmes's lecture on Manila emphasized the martial context of his visit to the Philippines yet also noted his reluctance to express a clear political position on this controversial subject:

> In all the long list of views, colored and motion pictures alike, there were none which showed the brutality of war and few that showed its suffering, yet there were not many which did not owe their effectiveness to military significance. The uniform of a soldier would thrust its way into the most peaceful scenes, and the ruins, which were picturesque, were of modern making. The comments and explanations of the lecturer himself seemed framed to avoid any direct reference to the war and its progress without ever letting the fact of hostilities be forgotten. It was evident, also, that he desired covertly to convey the impression that he would have liked to tell more did he not think the frankness might be an injury to him as an entertainer.[75]

Holmes apparently received full cooperation from the military throughout his visit and thus may well have been constrained, whether contractually or merely out of a sense of obligation, gentlemanly reserve, or patriotism, in his ability to fully represent his experience of the Philippines. Regardless of Holmes's personal opinion of the U.S. colonization of the Philippines and of whether he felt the need to exercise restraint in expressing his views, it was very clear that he sought to represent the Philippines from the point of view of a traveler rather than of a politician or soldier, for example. The author of the *Chicago Tribune* review was aware that Holmes did not wish audiences to see his lecture as a political statement, conceding, "Perhaps he would be better pleased if more attention were paid to the excellence of his views and the raciness of his descriptive utterances, but, inasmuch as he has insisted upon dragging matters of news into a place of amusement he must bear the penalty."[76]

In Chicago, however, more than in the other cities in which he lectured, Holmes's views on the Philippine-American War were solicited and publicly disseminated. After he returned from the Philippines, the *Chicago Daily Tribune* reported that Holmes had stayed with General Elwell Stephen Otis, the commanding general and military governor of the islands, and had found him to be in poor health in part because of "the difficulties and anxieties of the campaign and outspoken criticism indulged by the home newspapers, which for the present his physicians have advised him not to read."[77] "Holmes' View of Manila," another article published well in advance of the opening of his lecture series, offered his surprisingly candid and critical opinions of what he saw of the military conflict. Since Holmes was a member of a prominent local family, perhaps his personal perspectives on the war found a more receptive public in Chicago than would have been the case elsewhere. Most reviews of the lecture from other cities provided relatively neutral descriptions of the event and its reception; these reactions were more in keeping with Holmes's insistence that his observations were those of a traveler, not a report on the military conflict. As the program for a supplementary series of lectures given by Louis Francis Brown (Holmes's manager) said of the "Manila" lecture, "The public has already listened to the story of the correspondent and the returned soldier, but the story of the traveler has not been told."[78]

The lecture's popularity—the audience reportedly burst into applause and cheered—clearly resulted from the current events cachet of the topic. The *Washington Post* observed, for example, that "from the spontaneous applause that frequently interrupted Mr. Holmes, it was evident the audience took a keen interest in his remarks." The review traces the itinerary of the lecture by reporting on the itinerary of Holmes's trip itself, and it singles out a number of films as "among the best moving pictures shown": "The Olympia, from a moving launch; gun drill on the Baltimore; Ninth Infantry crossing the bridge of Spain; a caravan of Caraboa [*sic*] carts; and a military train."[79] The motion picture component of the lectures clearly emphasized U.S. military might. Even the film of the caravan of carabao (a type of water buffalo), though partly a scene of local life, is also an element of the military effort. Scenes of local life dominated in the earlier lecture on Hawai'i, even though the appearance of the U.S. troops on the way to Manila garnered a disproportionate amount of attention. In the lecture on Manila, the opposite is true, as the *Washington Post*'s list of film subjects suggests.

In the opening of his lecture, Holmes describes himself as a "globetrotter" in search of the picturesque elements of the Philippine political and military situation. But the contrast between what a traveler might wish to see in Manila and what a U.S. citizen might want to know about the war gave this particular lecture a divided focus. For example, Holmes's discussion of carabao juxtaposes the picturesque with life and death in war—what Holmes saw as a traveler and what Holmes saw as an American. He begins by describing their use as beasts of burden in the Philippines and then notes their present function of pulling carts full of supplies to soldiers at the front during the day and returning in the evening with the dead and wounded. Holmes tells his readers that the road the water buffalo travel leads directly to the front, less than a dozen miles away. But then he veers off into an exasperated declamation about the idiosyncrasies of the carabao—in particular, their slow pace.[80] Holmes concludes the passage by stating, "But you, whose daily downtown perplexities are occasioned by swift trolley-cars may look with interest on the slow caravans of carabaos."[81] This "Oriental" means of conveyance exemplifies the exoticism of "native" life for U.S. audiences who commute by trolley rather than water buffalo, but the example also offers a glimpse of the ongoing war. However, rather than commenting on the use of water buffalo in the war effort, he moves on to describe them as aspects of local culture.

Another example of how Holmes alternates between the point of view of a traveler and that of an American interested in the wisdom of the annexation of the Philippines involves his description of the institution of the curfew in Manila. Before the law was strictly enforced, according to Holmes, "a section of the city was set on fire every night by lawless Filipinos, but now that every man must stay in his own house, the malcontents have lost their eagerness to play with fire."[82] Despite such restrictions, Holmes and his friends still attended dances and receptions using passes that granted them permission to travel past the hour of the curfew. Holmes emphasizes the excitement of the process, describing the need to produce the passes every time they encountered a sentry as "the most picturesque, exciting party-going that you can imagine. At every gate or at street intersections we hear the cry '*halt!*' and the click of a Krag-Jorgensen."[83] In these two examples, as in the lecture as a whole, Holmes produces an intense awareness of the military realities that permeated life in Manila during the war but also reveals his determination to treat these realities as minor inconveniences. The description of the curfew as designed to curtail the "eagerness to play with fire" of "lawless Filipinos" makes it seem as if the Filipino resistance to U.S. occupation was nothing more than mischief undertaken by childlike "malcontents." The juxtaposition of "party-going" with the name of the principal weapon used by U.S. forces in the Philippine-American War is at the very least unsettling. In the context of Holmes's lecture, the anecdote demonstrates how he and his friends attempted to carry on with some semblance of their normal life despite the ongoing conflict. Yet turning a military curfew into an aspect of picturesque partygoing retains some unseemly elements. Overall, Holmes conveys that he felt neither threat-

ened by the Krag-Jorgensen nor likely to find himself in need of one.
This relative remove from the famous firearm allowed Holmes to see it as
just another interesting feature of life in Manila in 1899.

In the lecture, Holmes resists addressing why the Filipinos were fighting U.S. forces and what the long-term American plans in the distant
country might be; thus, he effectively ignores the controversy of the decision to annex the Philippines. Since Holmes's visit occurred before the
U.S. occupation of the Philippines had been firmly established, he found
it necessary to include scenes that show the ongoing conflict even while
he emphasized the picturesque and exotic aspects of the city. The strange
combinations apparent in the lecture—the contrasting perspective of a
Western traveler and an American colonist in Holmes's attitude toward
water buffalo, and the description of traversing the streets during the im-
position of a curfew as "picturesque" and exciting—indicate the challenges of the political circumstances of the Philippine-American War for
a man such as Holmes. Holmes journeyed to Manila in search of the picturesque, but the war did not allow him to be merely a traveler. However,
the lecture generally gives the impression that an American victory is inevitable and justified and assumes that the Philippines will be an American colony. Yet the difficulties of governing such a distant land are already apparent to Holmes: he writes that the Luneta, a park facing
Manila Bay, "is a place to inspire loneliness and homesickness; it brings
to us that sense of exile, which will be the bane of future colonists."[84]
From Holmes's lecture, it is difficult to imagine that Manila will ever become as familiar to American travelers as Honolulu. In Hawai'i, Holmes
was received and entertained by the islands' white American elite, and he
identified with the settler colonialists even if he felt a slight sense of dis-
satisfaction about how much they had remade Honolulu into an American city. In the Philippines, he arrived as a globetrotter, but his travels
were clearly made possible by the American military, and he saw the
country as a member of the occupying forces, albeit an unofficial one.

In much of his lecture on Manila, Holmes focuses on U.S. soldiers
and their efforts to pacify the "insurrectionists." At one point during his
visit, Holmes left Manila and accompanied the Twelfth Infantry to the
front. From the town of Malolos, he traveled with the daily supply train
to Baliuag, which he described as "the most isolated outpost now held by
the American forces."[85] The images of Baliuag focus on American troops,
including two images of soldiers garrisoned at the local church, another
unsettling combination of the local picturesque and the realities of war.

Holmes gives the impression that the insurgents might attack Baliuag at any moment. Although hostilities do not break out during his visit, the Third Infantry obligingly stages a battle for Holmes to demonstrate what would happen in the event of an attack, and Holmes filmed this drama. "The day was dark and wet," Holmes wrote, "but the motion picture successfully reproduces the dramatic sequence of incidents as they occur."[86] The battle as described in the published lecture begins with an alarm, the exchange of gunfire, and the call for reinforcements, who arrive from the town and join in the battle. As the imaginary enemy begins to fall back, the soldiers are ordered to charge. They pursue the phantom enemy across the fields and attend to the "dead" and "wounded."

Holmes singles out the death of a soldier as the most convincing aspect of the film—"So realistic is the feigned death of one soldier that spectators will not believe that the picture represents only a sham battle"—a curious emphasis given that the book version of Holmes's lecture pictures no real war dead anywhere, even though he frequently refers to men fighting and dying.[87] It is as if images of actual war dead or wounded would ruin the tone of the lecture, whereas Holmes can accommodate the exciting battle reenactment as a "picturesque" event. Like the Edison and Biograph military actualities discussed in chapter 2, this film demonstrates the U.S. military's capabilities. What was unique about Holmes's film was his ability to situate these scenes within the narrative of his visit to the front lines, as a battle reenactment staged specifically for him and his future audiences to demonstrate how the U.S. Army would defeat the insurrectionists. Unlike the famous Edison battle reenactments set in the Philippines but filmed in New Jersey, the fact that Holmes was there, on location in the Philippines and on the front lines, made his film an especially convincing and effective document and a precursor to later fictional films shot on location to give them authenticity and credibility.

The Hawai'i lecture from the previous season reportedly concluded with a handful of films, but the lecture on Manila appears to incorporate films into the lecture itself, including scenes from the voyage across the ocean and subjects that were apparently not shown in still images, such as the carabao. An announcement of the lecture in the *Chicago Tribune* provided an extensive list of the films to be shown:

> Crew and stewards at fire quarters on the Empress of China. Coaling the Empress of China in Nagasaki harbor. The Olympia in Hongkong harbor,

from a moving launch. Gun drill on the Baltimore. Panorama of the Pasig River, Manila. Street crossings and canals, Manila. Ninth United States Infantry crossing the Bridge of Spain. The Carabao. Caravan of Carabao carts. The Manila fire department. A cockfight. A military train and defending an earthwork.[88]

The interest in movement, local manners, customs, and modes of transportation and the spectacle of American military power in these films is consistent with both Holmes's earlier use of cinema and other films of the time period. The number of films shown in this lecture—more than double the number of the previous year's lecture on "The Hawaiian Islands"—demonstrates the increasing importance of cinema. The titles also suggest that the films supported the program's promise to project films "at moments when movement is essential to complete and vivify the impressions produced by the spoken words and colored illustrations," with an emphasis on the voyage across the ocean, military maneuvers, and scenic views.[89] These details suggest that Holmes and his audiences increasingly saw the value of cinema as an aid to creating the illusion of virtual travel, particularly when it was used to punctuate selected scenes with the novelty of moving photographic images.

Although Holmes's lectures varied somewhat in style according to when they were written and their topic, they shared certain features. For example, Holmes never mentions the costs of a particular journey, although they at times must have been considerable. He usually does not represent unpleasant experiences unless they illustrate a comic custom, and his disinterest in politics favored the picturesque. In the Philippines, even though he depended on the American military for his safety and mobility, he maintained the stance of a detached observer, frequently praising the comportment of the American troops but rarely personally participating in the drama of the war. However, an incident in Baliuag revealingly undoes his ability to work and travel with American military cooperation while standing apart from such operations. Holmes's account of this adventure describes a completely unprecedented film that is not reproduced in the book. One morning, the garrison discovers that a telegraph wire has been cut in an apparent act of sabotage. The colonel in charge orders a native house to be burned as a warning to the villagers. But despite efforts to uncover the identity of the culprit, the Americans can find no evidence of guilt. Nevertheless, as Holmes relates, "the wire was cut and a house must be burned."[90] In the absence of evidence of guilt, the captain charged with carrying out the order must choose which house to burn, a problem he solves by asking Holmes to "pick out the house that will make the most effective motion picture as it goes up in smoke."[91] "Fortunately," Holmes relates, "the one lending itself best to artistic necessities was an abandoned nipa dwelling—a pretty little affair with a neat little garden around it."[92]

In looking over the location, Holmes believes that the mise-en-scène can be improved, and in response to Holmes's request, the captain orders a group of Filipinos to cut down a hedge that is partially obscuring the house and to remove several branches from a tree that would interfere with the view of the smoke. Once the scene is set, Holmes writes, "several soldiers enter the house, pour kerosene on the walls and floors of thatch and bamboo, and set fire to the flimsy structure. When we rode on nothing but ashes marked the site."[93] It is surely disturbing that a cut telegraph wire should naturally require the burning of a house as both reprisal and deterrent. But even more remarkable is the way in which Holmes, as a filmmaker, was interpellated as a colonizer by being asked to direct and record a brazen act of destruction. As a film, the scene qualifies as an actuality since it is a film of an actual event; however, the scene is more than a mere record of reality since it was staged and filmed to communicate U.S. military power in the Philippines.

In at least one instance, a description of the film served as a preview of coming attractions. An article published before Holmes's lecture on Manila at Boston's Music Hall recounted the incident that led to the creation of the film and then concluded,

> With the assistance of his associates Mr. Holmes secured a capital motion picture showing the house to be burned, before the torch was applied, as well as after its conflagration had begun, the latter part of the picture showing the particularly lively exit of the guard to whom its destruction was given, and this picture will be one of those shown in the lecture upon Manila in the course announced at Music Hall.[94]

The article, which narrates in detail the circumstances leading to the making of this film, assumed that audiences would be motivated not only by seeing the film but also by learning what it says about the U.S. efforts to combat the Filipino insurgents. Although the burning of the house may have been intended as a lesson for Filipinos, the film of the event was made for U.S. audiences. The anecdote about the cutting of the telegraph wire and the punishment that must follow, the film that results, and the way that it is used to promote the lecture on Manila combine to make this an extreme example of cinema's complicit relationship with the practice of colonial conquest.

Holmes's role in this interaction at Baliuag obviously diverges from the distanced positioning he preferred. The lecture offers little clarification of what the captain intended by the phrase "most effective motion picture," but given the context of the situation, it seems reasonable to assume that he wished to maximize the show of American military capabilities and resolve. By requisitioning, in effect, Holmes and his camera, the captain makes Holmes a member of his army and his camera a military instrument. Holmes was apparently more than willing to oblige, to take advantage of the opportunity to repay the military forces for the support that had been so critical to his work, bringing their mutually beneficial relationship to the fore. In the film itself, the potentially destructive force of the camera's gaze is literalized in a spectacular manner. At another stage of the war, such as during the congressional hearings on reported atrocities in the Philippines, such a film could have been considered not a testimony to the military's effectiveness but instead damaging evidence of its brutality. Despite Holmes's light tone, the image of soldiers pouring kerosene on a house and setting fire to it foreshadows the kind of highly criticized U.S. Army tactics practiced in the Philippines that led historians to look back and compare this war to the U.S. intervention in Vietnam.

Holmes's "Manila" lecture comes closer than any of his other early lectures to standard reportage because it does not emphasize Filipino culture and customs but rather the conditions of life of Americans in the Philippines at a time when the military conflict was getting under way. He suggests as much in the final series of events he recounts. From Baliuag, Holmes proceeded to San Fernando, "the extreme front of our line on the north."[95] On his first night there, the Americans come under attack, and Holmes makes his way to a balcony, where a friend asks, "Have you got your revolver and cartridges?" Holmes replies that he does not, but he does have a camera and extra film. Holmes "wanted to be prepared in case the fighting lasted until sunrise."[96] Unfortunately for Holmes, the fighting ended before sunrise, depriving him of the opportunity to show his audiences the confrontation. His presence at the scene of a battle is, however, an effective and logical way to end the lecture after all the times it mentions men fighting and dying.

"Manila" is one of the shortest of Holmes's lectures, and on the last page, he vows to return after the war is over to explore the rest of Luzon as well as the archipelago's other islands.[97] As he observes, "It is something to have been witnesses of the transformation of Manila, to have seen the sleepy haunt of Spanish inactivity suddenly become the busy center of American enterprise in the Far East."[98] His lecture does indeed bear witness to the transformation of Manila, and Holmes's sense of watching history unfold gives the narrative and images a more ambivalent and contradictory cast than those of the lecture on Hawai'i, which unequivocally celebrated U.S. annexation. Holmes's negotiation of his positioning as both an American tourist and colonialist in Manila is symptomatic of how U.S. national identity was being redefined at this historic moment, as Americans contemplated what it might mean to govern a distant Asian nation whose inhabitants seemed determined to fight U.S. rule.

"The Forbidden City"

Holmes's visit to the Forbidden City in 1901, which came about under still different circumstances than those that brought him to Manila or to Hawai'i, offers yet another version of Holmes as an American in Asia and the Pacific. He arrived in China at a favorable moment in history for someone like himself—the summer after an international force crushed the Boxer Uprising: "Peking is daunted, the Boxers are forgotten, and, for the present, to be a white man or woman is to command respect, and to inspire fear—in fact, to be almost a god in the eyes of the disgruntled natives, who have had at last a lesson that has made an indelible impression."[99] There is little ambiguity in what Holmes represents to "the natives" as he visits Peking—he is a citizen of one of the allied nations that had recently defeated the Boxers and were currently occupying the city. One of the most tangible benefits for Holmes was that he was afforded access to the once highly restricted Forbidden City. Holmes separated the material from this visit to Peking into two separate sections, one on Peking and another on the Forbidden City, which also included a visit to the Summer Palace. As he writes near the beginning of the lecture on the Forbidden City, "We have already seen the Peking of the miserable many, formerly the only Peking known to the alien intruder. We are now to see the once invisible Peking of the 'Son of Heaven,' the Peking of the Celestial princes, and imperial ministers—the Peking of the privileged and semi-sacred few."[100] The *we* of whom Holmes writes refers not only to his traveling party but also to his audience members, who would finally have an opportunity to view this mysterious space.

In the 1900–1901 season, Holmes had lectured on China, taking advantage of the interest in the country following the siege of the foreign legations in Peking the preceding summer, but he used material he had gathered during his 1899 trip to China, Japan, and the Philippines. The lecture on Peking and the Forbidden City given during the 1901–2 season was based on his summer 1901 visit to China, following his travels across Russia on the Trans-Siberian Railway. Throughout the lecture on Peking, Holmes refers to the Boxer Uprising. In "The Forbidden City, " he shows an acute, almost obsessive, awareness of the political circumstances that enabled entry into the Forbidden City. As Holmes stands at the Altar of Heaven, he remarks, "Formerly as inaccessible to the ordinary mortals as the north pole itself, this unique spot now feels the daily touch of foreign heels and the soft tread of barefoot Chinese coolies, who attend the desecrating visitors."[101] In the course of requesting a permit to visit the Forbidden City from Major Robertson, an officer of the Ninth U.S. Infantry who had set up a temporary residence in the Temple of Agriculture, Holmes observes, "What we have already done and are about to do in Peking, are things which a year before no foreigner would have dared to dream of doing. The traveler who reached Peking in the first year of the twentieth century was fortunate indeed. Doors that had been closed for hundreds of years, stood open."[102] Finally, just before he presents his permit at the gate, Holmes once again ponders the historical significance of what he is about to do: "Who would have dreamed, a few years ago, that permits to visit the Forbidden City of Peking, then never violated by foreign intrusion, could be had in 1901 on application to an officer of the Ninth U.S. Infantry?"[103] These and similar statements emphasize again and again that Americans did not, in fact, belong in the Forbidden City. Yet a traveler such as Holmes must have welcomed the once-in-a-lifetime chance to visit these palaces and temples.

Holmes was not exaggerating the significance of the mass dissemination of images of the previously unseen Forbidden City to his U.S. audiences. The popular press reviews of the lecture confirm that the promise of viewing sights never before and perhaps never again seen influenced its reception. The *Washington Post* attributed the sizable audience present to the rarity of the views: "The fact that many of the sights disclosed are again hidden from the eyes of civilization was probably responsible for the large attendance."[104] In Chicago, one reviewer remarked that the lecture "contained some descriptions and views which may never be seen again by the world at large, except through the medium of Mr. Holmes' photographic plates and motion picture films. For the Forbidden City through which he roamed at will last summer has now reverted to its imperial owners and once more is closed to all foreigners."[105] In contrast to Hawai'i, which Holmes felt his audiences would see for themselves one day, the lecture on the Forbidden City was promoted as an unique opportunity to visit what would not be accessible to American travelers in the future.[106]

Although reviews offered enthusiastic plaudits for the motion pictures shown during the lecture on "Peking and the Forbidden City," the descriptions of the films suggest that they were probably of Peking only. Nevertheless, the still photographic images included with the published version of "The Forbidden City" are remarkable. Holmes was impressed by what he saw, and many of his photographs communicate his sense of awe and wonder. Several images emphasize the grandeur of the architecture in sweeping panoramas that spread across two full pages, a format rarely used elsewhere in the lectures, while other full-page images are oriented so that the book must be rotated ninety degrees to view the image properly. Rather atypically for the lectures, many pages feature only images, with no accompanying text. But all of these photographs seem slightly eerie. The photographs reveal virtually no signs of life aside from a few U.S. soldiers and a handful of Chinese attendants. One possible explanation for the lack of moving images in this lecture is that Holmes could not film any movement because the area had already been captured and the enemy had been vanquished. The work of the U.S. military forces was already completed by the time Holmes arrived, and the soldiers had little to engage them except for light guard duty—and issuing of passes granting entry. The absence of the imperial family and its entourage also meant that most of the palaces and temples stood devoid of human presence and therefore of movement. The one exception is the inexorable advance of Holmes and his friends on the Dragon Throne.

Perhaps because of the architecture of the Forbidden City, Holmes's lecture proceeds as a classic penetration into the unknown interior. The emperor's throne is described as "the central object of the Celestial Capital—the Imperial Chair of the Manchu majesty. . . . Until the foreign invaders, in 1901, broke down the barriers of tradition and penetrated to the very heart of this unseen abode of the Invisible, it was one of the

world's mysteries, guarded by the world's most wonderful walls."[107] The
bulk of the lecture on the Forbidden City traces a movement from the
exterior of the city through its interior and finally into its center. Despite
the absence of moving images, this narrative and its visual representation in the book have a cinematic quality; the sequence could be easily
translated into a scene within a classical narrative film.

The visit to the Forbidden City proceeds as a series of passages
through gates, portals, courtyards, and doors. As Holmes describes moving through these spaces, with appropriate illustrations, the audience
passes through the spaces with him. While the palaces, temples, and gates
lend themselves best to majestic still images, Holmes's account of his
voyage into the inner sanctum of the Forbidden City unravels as if long
tracking shots were following the progress of Holmes and his party, with
subjective point-of-view shots showing the audience what Holmes sees.
The first images of this section are panoramas of the Forbidden City,
with text that describes the compound's overall design. The movement
into the Forbidden City begins with two images of the approach to the
city from a distance that would be termed an extreme long shot in cinematic terms, emphasizing the organization of the space and features of
the landscape rather than the human figures within it. As the journey toward the interior continues, the lecture gives the details of the design of
the gates and the color of the walls and pillars. Accompanying images
show these gates from a straight-on angle. At the Gate to the Invisible,
just before the entrance into the first court of the Forbidden City,
Holmes and his party confront a sentry, whom he describes with ironic
amusement as "a smiling, tired looking, khaki-clad Hoosier boy, who
hails from some unknown little town on the banks of the Wabash, very
far away."[108] By pointing out the distance between the soldier's home in
Indiana and his present location, Holmes emphasizes the incongruity of
a young American stationed at the entry to the Forbidden City in China.

At the inner gate of the court, Holmes and his friends confront and
are reluctantly admitted by the Forbidden City's Chinese caretakers. In
the book version of the lecture, a spectacular panorama of the first
court is paired with the advance into the court. Spread horizontally
across two pages, this photograph gives a sense of the vastness of the
grounds, showing a wall in the left foreground, a series of bridges across
what appears to be a river or canal stretching from the right foreground
to the left middle ground, and a large palace filling the right background
and connecting to a number of smaller buildings to the left. Next, "Re-

freshments at the Gate," an image of Holmes standing with a small group of Chinese men, confirms Holmes's presence at the Forbidden City and reestablishes his function as the guiding subjectivity of this experience (fig. 1.4). Finally, accompanied by eunuchs and imperial officials, Holmes and his party travel through more courtyards until they arrive at the Dragon Throne, where "despite the impatience of the attendants we linger to examine things hitherto unseen by foreign eyes."[109] After three stolid, imposing architectural images—of the "Hall of the Throne," "An Audience Hall," and "A Pavilion"—Holmes finally reveals the throne itself. The Dragon Throne is photographed from the right side, emphasizing the steps leading up to the raised platform. Two pages later, a view of the throne from a more frontal orientation more clearly shows the ornate carvings and designs, with Chinese script painted on the adjacent columns. Then, as the written text of the lecture condemns the behavior of the conquering armies, many of whom profited unscrupulously from looting, the travelers press onward into the private dwelling of the emperor to view his sleeping chamber, despite the obvious discomfort of the Chinese attendants. After viewing the quarters of the empress dowager as well, Holmes leaves the way he came, closing this portion of the lecture with an image, "The Gate of Exit from the Forbidden City."[110]

The "suggestion of travel" Holmes hoped to achieve in his lectures comes through intensely, despite the limitations of the book format, because of the sustained sense of a linear progression through space and time and the suspense of moving closer and closer to a previously unseen mystery. The effect of seeing these images of the Forbidden City in 1901 or 1902, hand-colored and projected on a screen, accompanied by Holmes's narration and presence on the stage, must have been profound, enabling Holmes's live audiences to experience with him what it was like to be a white American man strolling unimpeded through the Forbidden City, gazing upon wonders never before seen by foreign eyes. At the conclusion of his lecture, Holmes again considers the immensity of what he and his audience have just witnessed, reminding listeners,

On the 17th of September, 1901, the American detachment retired from the gate and turned over to the Chinese troops the violated sanctum of China, which has again become, though in a sense less absolute, "forbidden" to the foreigner. Never till war shall bring another foreign army to Peking, will foreign eyes look upon its courts and palaces.[111]

FIGURE 1.4 "The Eunuchs Serving Tea to Visitors" and "Refreshments at the Gate," from Burton Holmes, *Burton Holmes Travelogues* (New York: McClure, 1910), 9:283.

In other words, by the time that Holmes was lecturing on the Forbidden City to his U.S. audiences, the Forbidden City had already been returned to China and was no longer open to American travelers. Holmes's presence on the scene is significant in relation to both the past and the future. He not only captured novel images but also presented them knowing that the Forbidden City might never again be accessible to foreigners.

Representing the United States

During his travels in Hawai'i in 1898, the Philippines in 1899, and China in 1901, Holmes enjoyed the hospitality of his fellow Americans and the protection of his national military forces. In both subtle and more obvious ways, his travels represented the power of the United States in the world. Edward Said writes that one of the main methodological devices for studying the authority of orientalist discourse is to identify "strategic location"—that is, to determine "the author's position in a text with regard to the Oriental material he writes about."[112] According to Said,

> Everyone who writes about the Orient must locate himself vis-à-vis the Orient; translated into his text, this location includes the kind of narrative voice he adopts, the type of structure he builds, the kinds of images, themes, motifs that circulate in his text—all of which add up to deliberate ways of addressing the reader, containing the Orient, and finally, representing it or speaking in its behalf.[113]

Holmes certainly utilized in his lectures specific textual strategies to situate himself in relation to Hawai'i, Manila, and Peking. But in these travel lectures, we can also understand the notion of locating oneself vis-à-vis the Orient in a much more literal sense.

Holmes was comfortable and at home among his fellow white Americans in Hawai'i, even though the Senate was still debating the political relationship between Hawai'i and the United States at the time of his visit. Upon arriving in Manila, Holmes had no choice but to recognize the ongoing conflict between U.S. and Filipino forces over the Philippines' identity as either a newly independent nation freed from Spanish colonial rule or a new U.S. colony. As he lodged with, marched with, and photographed and filmed the U.S. Army, his identity as a traveler was often conflated with his presence as an American colonizer despite his best efforts to separate the two. Furthermore, although he was certain that the U.S. forces would prevail, Holmes provided little in the way of a vision of the Philippines' future as a part of the United States, whereas in Hawai'i, he could easily imagine "our future naval harbor" at Pearl Harbor. In Peking, Holmes took advantage of the rare opportunity to see the Forbidden City, but here, he saw the U.S. military presence as only temporary; eventually, the Chinese would return to the Forbidden City, and the U.S. soldiers would go home. Charles Musser writes that audience identification with someone such as Holmes could occur on three levels: as a profilmic figure pictured in the scene, as the cameraperson whose point of view is represented, and as the lecturer at the podium.[114] The published lectures offer plentiful examples of Holmes both as a figure on the scene and as the source of subjective point-of-view shots. But through Holmes, the audience could also, in a lecture such as "The Hawaiian Islands," identify politically and ideologically with the white American settlers in Hawai'i.

Holmes's records of his experiences as an American citizen traveling through these distant places and cultures provide a unique perspective on the changing nature of American identity in relation to Asia and the Pacific. Holmes showed Americans not only what "the world, outside of America" looked like but also what it meant to be an American in this world. Holmes's views of the landscapes and peoples of Hawai'i, the Philippines, and China provided not only picturesque entertainments but also especially effective lessons in U.S. national identity. In part, these lessons resulted from the way he incorporated the technology of film into an established mode of representing the world. Holmes's work thus provides the foundation for the later reception of films shot on location because he used discourses of travel, witnessing, and presence to give his lectures authority, and he used photographs and films as indexical traces of the foreign realities that he had seen. The reception of his lectures confirms the importance of authorship: reviews frequently noted that Holmes photographed the images shown during the lectures, for the lectures were meant to represent Holmes's travels and the images what Holmes saw.

However, in some of his lectures—in particular, the earlier ones—Holmes also utilized photographs credited to others. The lecture on Hawai'i and Holmes's lecture on Greece and the 1896 Olympic Games incorporate a number of images with bylines designating the photographer as someone other than Holmes. Despite the insertion of images taken by others, the lectures create the impression of Holmes's (and the audience's) continuous movement through time and space, testifying to the strength of the expectation of narrative progression.[115] As Rick Altman asks, "What difference does it make ... who took the photograph or when it was taken?" He then explains,

> In order to understand the importance of this question, it is necessary to recognize that two meaning systems here collide, the one becoming visible only because of the temporary failure of the other. We are clearly operating within a traditional photographic system of representation, where images correspond to pro-filmic foreign realities named in captions. Yet each image has become a marker of Holmes's (and our) passage through a foreign space—and thus a sign of the domestication of that space. While the first system is purely documentary or *mimetic* in nature, the second establishes a fiction and its supporting *diegetic* world.[116]

Altman then makes the case that "diegetic coherence has actually taken precedence over mimetic accuracy."[117] Holmes thus marries the power of narrative with the indexical, documentary capacity of the photographic image that travel images are thought to have; in the end, the story of Holmes's travels dictates how his audiences understand the images they see, rather than the images serving as the point of departure for the story.

In the late 1850s, British photographer Francis Frith described his work *Egypt and Palestine Photographed and Described* as a different kind of travel book, one whose text was based on the truthfulness of photographic images. Yet this positivistic view of photography also allowed Frith to illustrate Henry Wadsworth Longfellow's fictional novel *Hyperion: A Romance* (1865). Carol Armstrong explains this seemingly counterintuitive conjunction by saying that Frith "gives us the positivist reason for illustrating [*Hyperion*] with photographs: photographs have the power to confirm the verity of even fictional narratives. Which is to say that so strong is their confirmational capacity that they are even able to turn fiction into fact and verify an author's imagination by tracing the visible world in which it came to light."[118] In this example, the photographic images of the Rhine, Switzerland, and the Tyrol with which Frith illustrates the novel testify to the reality of the world through which Longfellow imagines his fictional character, Paul Flemming, traveling. In contrast, in Altman's reading of Holmes's lecture, the "traditional photographic system of representation, where images correspond to pro-filmic foreign realities named in captions," constitutes only one of the "meaning systems" at work; the power of narrative, rather than the photograph, as in Frith's approach, can "turn fiction into fact" by creating the impression of a coherent world within which Holmes's travels took place. Although these two examples differ in emphasis, with Armstrong highlighting the power of Frith's photographs and Altman underlining the power of Holmes's narrative, both make a productive point about the unstable boundary between fact and fiction in illustrated travel narratives. On a fundamental level, both examples pose the question of how narratives combined with photographic representations function to produce the reality of a place; this dialectical relationship between story and image speaks to the core of the issues surrounding virtual travel, shooting on location, and cinema.

Burton Holmes was in many ways an exemplary man of his time. He embraced emerging technologies of travel and of representation and took advantage of the new possibilities they offered him. His lectures relate not only to the long tradition of written travel narratives but also to other elements of turn-of-the-century visual culture, such as international expositions. Thus, they allow a glimpse of how still and moving photographic images shaped how Americans saw cultural difference and imagined faraway places at a critical moment in U.S. history. Holmes helped his audiences understand distant lands and consider what it would mean to possess them, whether as travelers, soldiers, or colonialists. Holmes's lectures grew out of an established tradition of representation, and his use of cinema gives us many insights into how cinematic travel views could be seen within the context of an illustrated travel lecture. But the emerging filmmaking industry of the time addressed a very different audience, under different kinds of commercial imperatives, and in relation to other kinds of cultural traditions. Chapter 2 considers how early films represented the world to Americans through the developing conventions of cinema itself.

CHAPTER TWO

Asia in Early American Cinema

From Street Scenes to War Stories

110 Years Ago

The title "SHANGHAI STREET SCENE, No. 2" appears first, as white lettering on a black background, along with a name, "Thomas A. Edison," the date of the film, "1898," and a control number, "38218." After a few seconds, we see a black-and-white image of a broad street lined with trees. Our attention is immediately drawn to two rickshaws and a vehicle with small seating areas on either side of a large wheel, fast approaching the camera. The two rickshaws have Asian customers, while the other vehicle, closest to the camera, carries two white men dressed in dark suits and hats. As this vehicle approaches the camera, one of the men looks at the camera and takes off his hat in a gesture of friendly salutation (fig. 2.1). A few seconds later, another such vehicle with similarly attired passengers approaches the camera, and this time, both of the men look to the camera, smile, and tip their hats. (The Chinese drivers barely acknowledge the camera with a glance.) A white man on a bicycle rides by, and then the scene reveals more vehicles of all kinds going in both directions. Pedestrians are visible on the opposite side of the street, and a large, official-looking building can be seen in the far background. Approximately thirty seconds after it begins—less than the time it takes to read this paragraph—the film ends.

Shanghai Street Scene, no. 2 is a typical film of the era in many ways, a record of the lives of people who have long since passed away and a locale that may be barely recognizable after more than a century of change. Yet despite its historical particularity, when we view the film today, it still appears as if the men were gesturing to us, acknowledging all present and future audiences with a hearty hello. Unlike someone viewing photographs or other kinds of visual representations of the period, the

FIGURE 2.1   Frame enlarge-
ment from *Shanghai Street
Scene, no. 2* (Edison, 1898).
Courtesy of the Motion Pic-
ture, Broadcasting, and
Recorded Sound Division of
the Library of Congress,
Washington, D.C.

viewer of the life visible in these passing frames achieves a different kind
of engagement, almost a sense of presence on the scene across space and
time. To see such films is to gain an inimitable glimpse of life at the cusp
of the twentieth century as only motion pictures can provide. But these
brief, sometimes shadowy and indistinct films can frustrate, too, not
only because the images are often not clearly visible, but also because
their meanings are rarely evident to the twenty-first-century viewer.
What is *Shanghai Street Scene, no. 2* about? And what were Edison employees doing making films in Shanghai in 1898?

Early cinema, a period of film history dating to approximately 1907,
has been distinguished from the films that followed in a fairly definitive
fashion. Films of this time do not have many of the characteristics of
narrative films that we have come to take for granted, such as the existence of a story line or continuities of time and space. As Charles Musser
summarizes, "Early cinema was predominantly syncretic, presentational,
and nonlinear, while later classical Hollywood cinema favored consis-
tency, verisimilitude, and a linear narrative structure."[1] Tom Gunning's
influential conception of these films as a "cinema of attractions" describes them as "less a way of telling stories than as a way of presenting a
series of views to an audience, fascinating because of their illusory power
. . . and exoticism." Early cinema is also an "exhibitionist cinema," and "a
cinema that displays its visibility, willing to rupture a self-enclosed
fictional world for a chance to solicit the attention of the spectator."[2] In
this period, actuality films (films of actual events) were far more numerous than staged scenes, and travel views were extremely popular.[3] While
these characteristics make early films more challenging texts for contem-

porary critics to understand, such features are also central to their significance. A film such as *Shanghai Street Scene, no. 2* is intriguing not only for the ways it embodies these traits of early cinema but also for the material circumstances of its production.

Most films from the nascent U.S. film industry were made by film production companies and then sold to independent exhibitors who might use the films in any number of ways and in a variety of programming contexts. These exhibitors generally catered to very different audiences than those who attended travel lectures. According to Musser, "The travel lecture emerged as the antithesis of the dominant film industry. The one appealed to a small elite seeking education and enlightenment, the other to a mass audience seeking amusement. While the mainstream industry rigorously separated film production from exhibition, the lecturer usually took some or all of his films and photographs."[4] For example, while traveling with Burton Holmes, Oscar Depue produced films created specifically for projection during Holmes's illustrated travel lectures. The purpose of the mainstream films is less clear. Within the context of the dominant film industry of the period, one of the questions this chapter will address is why films such as *Shanghai Street Scene, no. 2* even exist. If not for inclusion in travel lectures, why were these films made? Why travel across the Pacific to capture this scene? Chapter 1 examined the illustrated travel lecture as part of a history of screen practice, arguing that Holmes's lectures effectively transported his audiences to faraway lands in Asia and the Pacific in part because he included moving images of life in foreign lands and used modes of presentation that created a sense of narrative progression. The lectures thus functioned as virtual voyages that allowed audiences to experience a new American identity as embodied by Holmes: owners of newly acquired territories and occupiers of defeated nations. This chapter shifts the focus to how the dominant film industry of that time represented Asia and Asians in early American films. Did moving photographic images offer another vision of Asians and Asia in a culture already accustomed to seeing these subjects in drawings, photographs, dime museums, and world's fairs? Instead of considering the ways in which films were incorporated into an existing tradition of representation (the illustrated travel lecture), I focus on the unique characteristics of early cinema and the difference that cinematic modes of vision made.

As in the previous chapter, my concerns lie not only with the history of early films but also with the ways in which this emerging technology engaged with, represented, and enabled contemporaneous practices of U.S. overseas imperialism. "The beginnings of the cinema, as is well known, coincided with the height of imperialism,"[5] writes Ella Shohat, but the coincidence itself has only recently begun to receive the scholarly attention it deserves. I begin this chapter with an examination of the films of Edison's Occidental and Oriental Series, including *Shanghai Street Scene, no. 2*. James White and Frederick Blechynden produced these films in China, Hong Kong, Macao, Japan, and Hawai'i from February to May 1898, on the threshold of a series of dramatic events that would reshape U.S. national identity. The films in this series, like other early films, were designed to emphasize the technological capabilities of cinema, whether through the street scenes that highlighted the ability to capture movement or through the travel views that underlined cinema's capacity to bring scenes of distant lands to its viewers. Because these films adhered to early cinematic conventions and because they were connected to the commercial interests of their sponsor, the Occidental and Oriental Steamship Company, this series offered depictions of Asians that differed noticeably from the vituperative anti-immigrant caricatures of the Chinese found in the popular press of the time or the exaggeratedly exotic Others of world's fairs and dime museums. Although hardly free of the racist assumptions of the period, the films of the Occidental and Oriental Series provided their audiences with scenes of life in Asia that allowed relatively unembellished versions of the profilmic reality before the camera to show through, thereby highlighting the modern technology that made the films possible.

Twelve days after the two Edison filmmakers left San Francisco for Yokohama, the USS *Maine* exploded in Havana Harbor. By the time of their return, the United States and Spain were at war. White and Blechynden remained in San Francisco long enough to film the departure of the first U.S. troops for the Philippines. The second half of this chapter considers how the Spanish-American War, the Philippine-American War, and the Boxer Uprising affected the conventions governing the representation of Asia in films made by U.S. film producers. Prior to 1898, commercial and religious groups pursued their interests in Asia and the Pacific primarily as private individuals and organizations, though often with the support and blessing of the U.S. government. After this series of turn-of-the-century military engagements, U.S. national interests in Asia and the Pacific differed radically from what they had been just a few years earlier. As these political situations increased Americans' interest in

China and the Philippines, a range of different types of early films represented the two countries, from actuality films of street scenes and scenic
views to trick films, staged reenactments, and even protonarrative sequences that combined two or more films to present a story to the audience. Each of these types of films offered different opportunities for
shaping U.S. images of faraway places across the Pacific. Over the course
of a few years, the touristic street scenes and travel views of the Occidental and Oriental Series would be replaced by images of U.S. soldiers in the
Philippines and in China, ostensibly pursuing Filipino "insurrectionists"
and antiforeign Boxers and establishing an occupying force in these
countries. For U.S. audiences, the pleasures of virtual travel in Asia offered by the Occidental and Oriental Series disappeared; in their place
were the responsibilities of imperial domination.

The shift in subject from illustrated travel lectures to the dominant
U.S. film industry necessitates a shift in my methodology as well.
Holmes's lectures are available in book form at many public libraries
across the United States, and these texts provide an extensive and detailed framework of signification within which the films of his lectures
were embedded. His popularity as a lecturer and the high-profile audiences who attended his performances also led to regular coverage of the
lecture series in the popular press; however, the films that the reviewers
praised so highly are no longer available for viewing.[6] Thus, I have found
a great deal of information about the exhibition and critical reception of
Holmes's films but have been unable to examine the primary texts themselves. In contrast, most of the films discussed in this chapter may be
viewed thanks to the preservation efforts of the Library of Congress and
other early film archives.[7] However, much less information is available
about the viewing contexts and reception of these films. Individual exhibitors had a great deal of control over how early films were shown, and
programs could vary considerably. This chapter therefore emphasizes
textual analyses of early films within their general cultural contexts but
can only speculate about how the films were received.

The Edison Manufacturing Company and the Occidental and Oriental Steamship Company

Edison's first images of Asians (as distinct from images of the geographical spaces of Asia) portrayed performances staged at the Black Maria,

the Edison studio in West Orange, New Jersey, with the performers isolated against a black background for dances or against a rudimentary set
for vaudeville routines.[8] Edison's staff recorded these films using a kinetograph (a camera they developed) and the films were viewed using the
kinetoscope (a peephole-viewing device designed for a single person).
The subjects of these films tended toward popular amusements such as
vaudeville shows and circus acts. In 1894, William Heise filmed *Toyou
Kichi,* a performance by a Japanese acrobat by that name, and *Imperial
Japanese Dance,* featuring three Japanese women.[9] That same year, white
performers Robetta and Doretto performed their comedic sketches pur-
porting to portray Chinese men on vaudeville stages in New York City
and then restaged the skits in three Edison films, two set in a Chinese
laundry and one set in an opium den.[10] Spurred by both a new portable
camera available beginning in May 1896 and by awareness of the work of
the Lumières in France, Edison filmmakers traveled further afield from
the studio to shoot films in New York City, Pennsylvania, Ohio, Brook-
lyn, and Coney Island. They began with street scenes of New York City
that were projected before audiences in New York, providing viewers
with what Musser describes as, "local views of locations they encountered in the course of their everyday lives."[11] Actuality films showing Li
Hung Chang, the Chinese statesman who visited New York City in 1896,
were among the few cinematic images of Asians of this period that did
not feature either Asian performers or white actors pretending to be
Asians. When Li Hung Chang met with President Grover Cleveland and
some of the leading businessmen of the day, these events were covered
widely by newspapers and documented by both the Edison and the
American Mutoscope and Biograph Companies.[12]

    James White was hired to head the Kinetograph Department of the
Edison Manufacturing Company in October 1896, when motion picture
profits were coming primarily from films rather than from equipment
such as the kinetograph and the kinetoscope.[13] In July 1897, the twenty-
five-year-old White, accompanied by cameraman Frederick W. Blechyn-
den, embarked on a ten-month trip to the American West, Mexico, and
Asia. The U.S. portion of their adventure included stops in Yellowstone
National Park, Washington, California, Oregon, Colorado, and New
Mexico. In Mexico, they visited Sabinas, Durango, and Mexico City. The
Denver and Rio Grande Railroad, the Atchison, Topeka and Santa Fe
Railroad, and the Mexican International Railroad subsidized their ex-
penses in the interests of promoting tourism. In return, a number of the

films featured the railroads and nearby attractions, exemplifying "mutual promotion" between railroad lines and cinema.[14] These scenic views served as cinematic attractions in their own right—that is, as forms of virtual travel that could replicate the experience of railroad travel and offer the visual charms of the destination stops. However, they were also enticing advertisements aimed at prospective passengers, promising the pleasures to come.

On February 3, 1898, White and Blechynden left San Francisco for Hong Kong on the Occidental and Oriental Steamship Company's SS *Coptic*. After a brief stop in Yokohama, White and Blechynden arrived in Hong Kong on March 6, 1898. They filmed there and in Macao and Canton before leaving for Shanghai. They arrived in Shanghai around April 7, sailed for Nagasaki and Yokohama on the SS *Gaelic* on April 8, and departed from Japan at the end of April on the SS *Doric*. After a little more than a month, White and Blechynden set out on their return to San Francisco, with a one-day stopover in Honolulu before arriving back in the United States on May 16, 1898. This was the first overseas voyage Edison employees took for filmmaking purposes. Their travel across the Pacific took place under similar financial arrangements as their railroad trips: the steamship company provided free travel and possibly some additional financial incentives.[15] This support was duly acknowledged in a manner typical of the time. The films that resulted were organized under the heading of the Occidental and Oriental Series, and Edison film catalogs preface the listing, "The following subjects were taken aboard ship and in the Orient; China, Japan, and Hawaii being the countries in which the scenes were taken. It is entirely due to the obliging courtesy which distinguishes all the high officials of the Occidental and Oriental S.S. Co., of San Francisco, that the efforts of our artists proved so successful."[16]

In the March 1900 issue of the *Edison Films* catalog, a brief paragraph precedes the list of the films produced during White's and Blechynden's ten-month voyage, which included descriptions, lengths, and prices for each of the films. This preface clearly connects the technology of film and its unique ability to bring images of life from around the world to U.S. audiences:

The established popularity of moving pictures led Mr. Edison to believe that a series of views photographed in various parts of the world would prove a most valuable addition to our list of subjects, thus combining instruction with interest. We therefore sent an efficient corps of photographers on an extended tour, and the results are now placed before the public. The pictures cover noted natural scenery and institutions, places of interest in cities, and scenes depicting phases of life, customs, amusements and occupations characteristic to the different localities in which they are taken. The views are actual reproductions, and are in every instance photographed from life. We feel satisfied they are of the highest interest to the public; thereby increasing still more the popularity of moving pictures, especially when presented through the efficient and satisfactory "Edison Stereo-Projecting Kinetoscope." Send for a descriptive pamphlet of the 1899 model.[17]

This introduction reaffirms the educational value of travel views and the fascination of the faraway so important to the appeal of Holmes's illustrated travel lectures. The language also suggests that cinematic views reinforced the interest of already established sights; the films reproduce "noted" scenery and institutions, while the depiction of images of life "characteristic" to specific places establishes the logic for the filmmakers' selection of subjects. In emphasizing notable sights and characteristic views, these cinematic scenes function within a discourse of travel and tourism, while the established cultural value of travel buttressed the growing popularity of the new medium of moving pictures. What is somewhat curious about this preface, however, is the apparent need to inform the exhibitors that the views are "actual reproductions, and are in every instance photographed from life." The reiteration of the reality of these actuality films suggests some lingering anxiety that viewers might not recognize the authenticity of these films as travel views, forcing the producers to insist on this fact at the outset.

The catalog text thus articulates the rationale behind producing travel views and offering them to exhibitors, but other questions remain. Why were China, Japan, and Hawai'i in particular filmed? And why does the Occidental and Oriental Series receive pride of place at the beginning of these various series of films? To address the "material production of imaginative geographies"[18]—that is, the question of how and why Edison filmmakers traveled across the Pacific in 1898 to produce films—I examine the history of the Occidental and Oriental Steamship Company. The company's history is significant within my larger examination of U.S. films shot on location in Asia because it demonstrates how these early cinematic images of Asia were situated within a larger context of U.S. interests and investments in the region. Of particular importance is the fact that the Occidental and Oriental Steamship Company came into being as a cooperative venture of the Union Pacific and the Central Pacific railroads as a result of their desire to gain control of a through route to East Asia.

The first trans-Pacific steamship line was the Pacific Mail Steamship Company, which began service in 1867. After the transcontinental railroad was completed in 1869, the railroads and Pacific Mail initially agreed to coordinate their sea and land transportation services, although Pacific Mail abandoned the arrangement in 1873. In response, the railroad executives drew up initial plans for the Occidental and Oriental Steamship Company in 1874, with service expected to begin in 1875. The threat of competition was enough to bring Pacific Mail to a renewed agreement with the railroad companies, and the Pacific Mail and Occidental and Oriental Steamship companies established a schedule in which each company would sail across the Pacific to Yokohama and then on to Hong Kong once a month, with the Pacific Mail steamers leaving on the first of the month and the Occidental and Oriental steamers departing in the middle of the month. After 1883, service was offered every ten days. The average round-trip voyage required approximately three months. In 1896, the two companies added Kobe, Nagasaki, and Shanghai to their ports of call. After 1898, Honolulu became a regular stop. Manila was added to the itinerary on occasion starting in the summer of 1902 and on a regular basis by the end of 1905.[19]

The competitive business dealings that led to the establishment of the Occidental and Oriental Steamship Company indicate that it was economically desirable to control travel across the Pacific in the last quarter of the nineteenth-century. This inference leads to the question of who and what were being transported on these steamships. According to historian John Kemble, each ship carried between thirty and sixty-eight first-class passengers, including "missionaries, government representatives, naval officers, merchants, and tourists."[20] Asian passengers traveled in the steerage section, and prior to the Chinese Exclusion Act of 1882, ships sometimes carried more than a thousand passengers. After the passage of this legislation, the number of Asian passengers declined, but even in 1895, a steamer arrived in San Francisco with seven hundred Asian immigrants.[21] In terms of freight or cargo, eastbound income (from Asia to the United States) was far greater than westbound (from the United States to Asia). From Asia came "tea, silk, merchandise, rice, gunnies, sugar, and opium." In the other direction, "flour led by a large margin and was followed by treasure in the form of refined silver, Mexican dollars, and jewelry."[22]

Along with the flour, silver, jewelry, and other cargo making its way from San Francisco to Hong Kong came a few of the Edison Manufacturing Company's products. A May 17, 1898, letter from Gorham and Company in Hong Kong to the Edison Laboratory suggests that White's and Blechynden's trip across the Pacific at least partly represented an opportunity to further Edison's global commercial expansion. The letter acknowledges receipt of "the Phonograph, Records, etc." and makes note of arrangements for payment. The writer also expresses interest in the kinetoscope and the purchase of twenty-eight films but regretfully refers to "the Plague" and its effects on the Chinese, implying that the public health environment was not conducive to the kinetoscope business in Hong Kong at the moment. The author also provides the sad news that two Chinese men who were in conversation with the company about purchasing kinetoscopes had died. However, the Hong Kong correspondent viewed favorably the possibility of setting up a showroom of Edison products on the company's premises, requesting samples of the commodities for sale and specifics regarding their "prices, shipment, packing, etc., etc." Finally, the letter reiterates a suggestion given to White about showing lantern slides while films are being changed, and the company offers to provide slides of "Chinese and tropical subjects on very reasonable terms."[23] Although Gorham and Company apparently did not ultimately establish a permanent relationship with Edison, this communication provides one small example of Edison's far-reaching commercial aspirations.[24]

White's and Blechynden's Far Eastern itinerary was determined by the paths already laid down by railroads and steamships, and these routes were initially established to further a variety of interests, including the accumulation of profit and the expansion of U.S. national ambitions. But if the railroad emblematized American westward continental expansion, the vast watery expanse between the United States and Asia required another mode of transport to navigate. As Kristen Whissel points out, overseas empire

> entailed a shift in the technology of American expansionism. In proimperial discourse, the railway lost its status as the primary mechanical icon for expansion, functioning less to expand the nation's continental boundaries than to bind the nation into a coherent commercial whole. . . . [T]he

steamship emerged in the 1890s as the primary technology for imagining and acquiring a new commercial and territorial overseas empire.[25]

The Occidental and Oriental Steamship Company, as its name implies, was particularly invested in establishing new commercial and territorial empires in East Asia, as its ships traversed the distance between "the Occident" and "the Orient." By publicizing the routes of the Occidental and Oriental Steamship Company, the films of the Occidental and Oriental Series helped to promote the movement of capital, goods, and ideology across the Pacific.

As in the films taken during their railway travels in the American West and Mexico, White's and Blechynden's films of their travels on-board the ships of the Occidental and Oriental Steamship Company and in the port cities they visited functioned both as cinematic attractions for U.S. audiences and as promotional tools for the steamship company. These existing routes of exchange allowed Americans to traverse the ocean as first-class passengers, pursuing religious, economic, and political interests, while thousands of Asians endured steerage conditions in search of opportunities in the United States. Seeing the films of the Occidental and Oriental Series within the context of these existing trans-Pacific crossings shows how White and Blechenden were following what was already in some respects a well-traveled path.

If U.S. commercial interests in Asia had previously been established at the time of White's and Blechynden's voyage, the market for representations of Asia in the United States was also a familiar and significant one.[26] An 1898 advertisement for the Edison Projecting Kinetoscope included a "Special Notice" of the images of "the Orient" to come, promising, "Our artists are now working in Japan and the Far East. We shall shortly have ready for the market new and interesting subjects taken in the Orient."[27] This notice, the only mention of specific films in the ad, demonstrates an existing demand for "Oriental" subjects. Indeed, a tradition of representations of the Orient existed in the United States long before the emergence of cinema. As historian John Kuo Wei Tchen observes, various Asian peoples and cultures were displayed as "edifying curiosities" in the West throughout the nineteenth century. These exhibits commodified difference, highlighting the contrast between an exotic otherness and the European American norm, and functioned as a way for people to see the world and understand their place in it:

Much in the way aristocrats and patricians engaged in travel writing, the urban middle classes could now consume a visual array of commercial "edifying curiosities" to discover their own personal relationship to other cultures, peoples, and parts of the world. To survey a panorama of China, a miniature of a primitive village, or a living animal or exoticized human on display or to witness an "oriental conjuror" all evoked a sense of wonderment and situated one's place in the world.[28]

Tchen continues, "Transglobal trade made possible the transglobal process of collecting from 'remote' cultures. Curiosities, then, were often objects or subjects brought back from colonial hinterlands to the metropoles for possession, collection, and display."[29] The travel views of the Occidental and Oriental Series participated in this long-standing tradition of collecting and then displaying Asians and Asia in the United States, though the film series displayed moving photographic images rather than actual people or objects. Similarly, these images were literally made possible by the existence of trade between the United States and Asia. In other words, although the technology of cinema was new, the intercultural exchange it fostered was not: Americans were accustomed to viewing distant cultures at home through metonymic fragments, to the dependence of this exchange on "transglobal trade," and to its function as a way to situate Self and Other in the world.

However, the films in the Occidental and Oriental Series cannot be fully understood within the terms of either the exotic curiosities that Tchen describes or the racist anti-Chinese images that were widely circulated in late-nineteenth-century U.S. culture in support of anti-immigration legislation. This is not because the Edison filmmakers were more enlightened than most or because they were unaware of or unaffected by the virulent anti-Chinese campaigns of the period; rather, the difference results from the specificity of the medium in which they worked as well as the conventions of the genres they employed. In illustrations and editorials published in magazines such as *Puck, The Wasp, Harper's Weekly,* and *Frank Leslie's Illustrated Newspaper,* the Chinese were routinely depicted as patronizing opium dens and gambling houses, menacing white women, and competing unfairly for American jobs.[30] They were drawn with stooped shoulders, exaggerated grins and pigtails, and sometimes with subhuman or animal-like characteristics. In contrast, a film such as *Hong Kong Wharf Scene* from the Occidental and Oriental Series shows Chinese workers on a crowded pier and resembles films shot in the

FIGURE 2.2 Frame enlargement from *Hong Kong Wharf Scene* (Edison, 1898). Courtesy of the Motion Picture, Broadcasting, and Recorded Sound Division of the Library of Congress, Washington, D.C.

United States depicting the loading of cargo or ship launchings (fig. 2.2). The camera is stationed close enough to passersby that viewers can see their faces.[31] The busy workers seem remarkably ordinary, though still racially marked. But the individuality and humanity of their faces is a striking rejoinder to the distorted drawings of the Chinese of the era as well as to many of the other existing representations of Chinese available in the United States around the turn of the century.

The Occidental and Oriental Series

Racial and cultural beliefs of the day undoubtedly shaped the scenes of foreign life in this series of films. But the images of Asians they depict were not fully circumscribed by existing racist and exoticist formulas, partly because they used an indexical medium such as film and partly because they adhered to the formal dictates of early cinema actualities, established to maximize the representation of movement. As actuality films rather than staged scenes and as actualities filmed on location in Asia rather than produced in the United States, these films proved relatively resistant to racist manipulation and staging. All this is not to say that White's and Blechynden's films were neutral, unmediated representations. As always, the filmmakers chose which subjects to film, privileged particular framings, and made the many decisions required to produce a text. In addition, the catalog descriptions of these films reveal stereotypical understandings of Asia, and these descriptions may have accompanied the films during exhibition—for example, by being read by a lecturer. The summaries express an ethnocentric and often racist perspective that situates the films within turn-of-the-century attitudes of racial hierarchy, progress, and civilization. The catalog description of *Hong Kong Wharf Scene*, for example, refers to the workers as "coolies," a term with prejudicial connotations of lower-class, expendable labor. But these descriptions exceed what can be seen in the films themselves. This disjunction suggests that stereotypical cinematic conventions of racialization were not yet fully developed in these early actualities of Asians, especially when compared to existing written or visual portrayals, including caricatures, photographs, and displays in dime museums and at international expositions.

The films of the Occidental and Oriental Series also utilize few recognizable "ethnographic" conventions.[32] In Alison Griffiths's thorough study of images of native peoples in turn-of-the-century U.S. visual culture, she situates cinema in relation to a range of other representations: "In its textual practices, critical discourses, and exhibition contexts, early cinema, like the other new sites of urban spectacle, choreographed the complex juxtapositions of the urban metropole and the exoticized Other."[33] Griffiths suggests that the commercial imperative behind the production of early ethnographic travelogues favored easily recognizable images that conformed to audience expectations: "A film series shot in Japan, for example, would not signify 'Japaneseness' to an American audience unless it featured geisha girls dressed in kimonos."[34] However, although they were frequent subjects of Holmes's illustrated lectures on Japan, geisha girls dressed in kimonos were not foregrounded in any of the films of the Occidental and Oriental Series. *Street Scene in Yokohama, no. 2* is described as showing "a typical group of jap [*sic*] men, women and toddling children [who] are gathered on the roadside, watching the native band," but neither the film nor its catalog description suggests what exactly makes these people "typically" Japanese.[35] Furthermore, the concept of ethnography often evokes the idea of a culture's defining rituals and customs. In contrast, the films of the Occidental and Oriental Series focus on unremarkable scenes of everyday life in the public spaces of the relatively cosmopolitan port cities of Hong Kong, China, and Japan. Representations of an "exotic" culture frequently highlight the distinctiveness of the culture, the differences between lives there and the norms of the intended audience. Yet the films of this series approach their subjects in a relatively matter-of-fact rather than sensationalist manner. As a result, these films show less stereotypical representations of

Asians and Asia than usually appeared in the handful of cinematic performances and staged scenes that preceded them. Not least among the cultural complexities these films display is the degree to which Westerners were already a part of the life of many of the cities the Edison filmmakers visited; the films thus banished fantasies of timeless, essential, and untouched Asian cultures that U.S. popular culture often reiterated.

People in early films frequently acknowledged the camera, whether through a sidelong glance, a conspiratorial wink, or overt staring, challenging the absolute divide between those in front of and those behind the camera. In White's and Blechynden's films, Westerners often acknowledged the camera directly, as in *Shanghai Street Scene, no. 2*. Local inhabitants captured on film tended to respond to the presence of the camera more subtly, perhaps with a quick glance while going about their daily business. Regardless of how U.S. audiences of the time might have seen their racially marked bodies, this awareness of the camera made many of the people in the Occidental and Oriental Series not passive objects of the gaze but participants in a cross-cultural exchange. As Griffiths argues, this kind of active subjectivity on the part of the "native" was precisely what made anthropologists consider cinema, with its potential to unsettle scientific certainty and control, a suspect medium: "Ironically, cinema's ability to represent reality with such compelling verisimilitude may have contributed to anthropologists' ambivalence about the medium, since the sense of agency afforded native peoples for the duration of a performance also threatened to undermine the specular authority of an idealized scientific observer."[36] While the films of the Occidental and Oriental Series were not intended as scientific documents, this potential for individual agency in cinematic representations of the native suggests that early actuality films could offer a vision of the native beyond the familiar stereotypes, even when white Westerners wielded the camera.

One film in the Occidental and Oriental Series, *Theatre Road, Yokohama*, offers a somewhat unusual though highly instructive example of how cinema could capture a reality that exceeded the expectations of both the filmmakers and their audiences. It ostensibly avails the audience of a view of a street in Yokohama lined with theaters, but in the end, the American cameramen elicit most of the attention. According to the catalog description, the film shows "the native quarter of the city. Rickshaws pass in and out among the crowd, which is composed of typical Japs [*sic*]."[37] *The Phonoscope*, a trade periodical, gives a slightly more de tailed summary: "An excellent view of the busy thoroughfare in the native quarter of Yokohama. Most of the Japanese theatres are on this street, and crowds are always to be seen gazing at the old theatre posters. In the immediate foreground is a group of curious Japanese children, attracted by our artists."[38] What is actually visible in the film, based upon a screening of the print housed at the Library of Congress, is the following. As the film begins, crowds of people on a busy street walk past the camera. Many adults glance at the camera as they pass by but keep walking. The less inhibited children, however, stop and stare to see what the visitors are doing, looking around at the camera, what the camera is filming, and ongoing activities in the area. Within seconds, children occupy nearly half of the space of the frame, threatening to block out most of the street scene (fig. 2.3).

Although the children's proximity to the camera obviously allows it to record intimate details of their appearance and behavior, their frank interest in and reactions to the act of filming draw attention to the activity of the men behind the camera. The film does indeed depict an area of Yokohama filled with native inhabitants, as the catalog description promises. These natives are not, however, engaged in their usual activities but are instead gathered around the American cameramen filming in their city. Tom Gunning discusses a similar reversal in the 1903 Edison film *Native Woman Washing a Negro Baby in Nassau, B.I.* He writes that the film begins in a way that is "typical of a large number of travel films in which the inhabitants of other lands, particularly of less industrialized nations, are treated as curious sights not unlike the landscape." Partway through the film, however, the camera pans and shows a group of adults and children who have been observing the filming. They then run away from the camera, out of the frame. Gunning interprets this part of the film as an example of how "the spectacle makers themselves have become a spectacle, the tables turned with the camera's pivot. And finally, a sublime moment as this witnessing audience refuses to become a spectacle in turn and takes off, escaping the frame and the camera, running off into unimaged space."[39] Gunning borrows the term *transito* from film scholar Giuliana Bruno to describe how this film offers a glimpse of the utopian possibilities of early cinema—that is, how it exemplifies what cinematic travel views could show that no other kinds of travel representations could: "The escape of its subject, its pure transito and flight."[40]

In *Theatre Road, Yokohama*, the children remain within the camera's gaze. However, their reactions highlight the presence of the cameramen

FIGURE 2.3   Frame enlargement from *Theatre Road, Yokohama* (Edison, 1898). Courtesy of the Motion Picture, Broadcasting, and Recorded Sound Division of the Library of Congress, Washington, D.C.

and their actions; they call the attention of viewers to the physical presence of White and Blechynden shooting on the scene in Japan. Ironically, a film meant to display a part of the city devoted to the performance of Japanese culture becomes a record of the acts of the American filmmakers. Classical narrative films draw viewers into the scene as invisible voyeurs, encouraging them to look without consequence and to turn a blind eye to the processes responsible for the existence of the images. In contrast, *Theatre Road, Yokohama* makes audiences aware of the circumstances of the film's production. The children's intense curiosity regarding the activity of filming makes us wonder how the two white American men in their suits and ties, with their pale skin and prominent noses, appeared to the Japanese children. Moreover, the children's unabashed gaze straight into the camera's lens makes the audience potential objects of their examination as well. Like the filmmakers, the viewers are also on the other side of the camera, a doubling that normally functions as a pleasurable identification. But this film has the potential to make viewers consider what their status would be as visitors to the town of Yokohama, subject to the curiosity of the natives even though they are supposed to be the attraction of the trip and the film.

Not all the films of the series challenged established views. Holmes's lecture on Hawai'i included a photograph of "Diving for Coins" in the series of images representing the steamship's arrival in Honolulu Harbor. In the lecture, this image of native Hawaiians supposedly diving for coins, as seen from the passenger's perspective on the ship's deck, appears as part of the touristic ritual of arriving in Hawai'i. During White's and Blechynden's brief stopover in Honolulu, they depicted a similar event in *Kanakas Diving for Money, no. 1* and *Kanakas Diving for Money, no. 2.* While these two films and *Theatre Road, Yokohama* all feature explicit interaction between the children being filmed and the filmmakers, the monetary exchange at the center of *Kanakas Diving for Money* radically alters the nature of the engagement and the looking relations of the film. As a result, the two films shot in Hawai'i position the viewers far more explicitly as subjects gazing upon native objects.[41] Both of these films show groups of young boys in the water from the perspective of the dock, with the camera looking out toward the harbor. The boys then cup their hands, turn their heads, and dive into the water after coins tossed by someone outside the frame. The boys in *Kanakas Diving for Money,* unlike the children in Yokohama, who spectacularize the filmmakers even as they themselves are being filmed, never look directly at the camera but rather focus all their attention on the coins. Of all of the films of the Occidental and Oriental Series, these films are the clearest examples of a touristic and ethnographic spectacle being performed for the camera; these scenes also suggest the nature of U.S. imperialism in Hawai'i as compared to U.S.-Japanese relations of the period.

Theatre Road, Yokohama had the potential to make U.S. audiences uncomfortably aware of how the denizens of a Japanese street might perceive and react to Americans' foreignness, thereby instilling some sense of racial and cultural relativism. In contrast, *Kanakas Diving for Money* and Holmes's "Diving for Coins" further reinforced racial and cultural hierarchies, not only in the subject they represented but also in the actual relationship between the subjects of the images and the image makers. These scenes draw paying audiences in as parties to the exploitative exchange that takes place on the screen. Although viewers obviously would not have paid to see the film or the photograph and accompanying lecture until after they were produced, the boys in the film can be seen as diving for the coins of U.S. audiences who were both potential viewers and tourists. *Kanakas Diving for Money* not only offered a quasiethnographic image of a purportedly local custom but also fed the fantasy of a benevolent and paternalistic relationship between Americans, like the "generous" filmmakers, and native Hawaiians, represented by eager young boys competing for tourists' spare change.

The reception of this and other early films is difficult to ascertain given the diversity of the exhibitor-centered practices of the time, the variety show format in which many early films were exhibited, and debates about the demographic composition of early film audiences.[42] Neverthe-less, at least to the contemporary viewer, the images of *Hong Kong Wharf Scene* and *Theatre Road, Yokohama* clearly differ from the racist drawings or exotic displays of the period, even if the historical reception of the films cannot be precisely determined. These Edison films did not merely replicate existing stereotypes and clichés of the Orient, though such stereotypes also were not completely absent. The films' recordings of everyday street life, undertaken in a way typical of early cinema actuali-ties, allowed a less exotic view of Asians to show through, free of the ori-entalist conventions of other forms of representation. The fact that these films were actualities matters: staged films frequently relied heavily on orientalist conventions, an issue to which I return later in this chapter. But these early films, by emphasizing the experience of travel and move-ment, made visible other aspects of the difference between "the Occi-dent" and "the Orient" that were tied to cinema as a novel technology and its relationship to modernity.

Orientalism and the Occidental and Oriental Series

In the films of the series, as in much of early cinema, the filmmakers dis-play a marked interest in moving vehicles. The first films of the trip were taken from the deck of the SS *Coptic* while it was traveling across the Pacific. Like the "phantom ride" films traditionally taken by a camera from a moving train, these scenes offered views from the passenger's per-spective. In two of the films, the camera is near the railing, and as the ship bobs in the water, the image of the sky, ocean, and ship shifts within the frame as well, imitating the visual cues of standing on the deck of a ship at sea. Two other films show scenes taken by a camera stationed far-ther away from the edge of the ship. The catalog descriptions and reviews of these films remark on the exciting action shown in the scenes. A re-viewer in the *New York Clipper* wrote,

> In some miraculous manner with the ship pitching and heaving at a tremendous rate, the operator was able to lash his camera to the deck of the vessel, and to get a thrilling picture of the ocean rising and falling in the great fury of a storm. A portion of the ship is shown very plainly, and the effect of the waves has never been equaled in any film so far produced.[43]

The image of a ship tossing about in a storm might not seem to be a particularly convincing advertisement for traveling on that ship, but part of
the appeal of the phantom rides was the thrill and potential danger of
travel. Exhibitors sometimes built entire attractions around phantom
ride films, as in Hale's Tours, perhaps the most famous and literal use of
the viewer-as-passenger convention.[44] In this fairground attraction, introduced at the 1904 St. Louis Exposition, audiences were seated inside a
railway car to view films projected on a screen. At the 1900 Paris Exposition, amusements such as the Lumière brothers' *maréorama*, which
placed passengers on a simulated ship with projections of films of sea
voyages, and the *cinéorama*, which simulated riding in a hot air balloon,
also offered variations on the phantom train ride.[45]

Other films of the Occidental and Oriental Series taken on the
steamship depicted first-class passengers lounging on deck, swimming,
and taking afternoon tea. (The films show no images of the Chinese
members of the crew or of steerage passengers.) Shown individually,
these views represented the experience of traveling on a steamship, allowing the audience to appreciate the excitement of crossing the Pacific
and to view the leisure activities available on the long journey. As part of
a series of travel views, they could serve as connecting scenes signifying
the traversal of space and function as an authenticating touch for staged
travel views. However, White and Blechynden were not onboard the
steamship merely to document the crossing of the ocean but rather to
get to Hong Kong. These films allowed steamship travel, as a general experience, to be packaged and sold, but the Occidental and Oriental
Steamship Company was in the specific business of transporting goods
and people across the Pacific. For the filmmakers, as for all the passengers, the time spent on the ship was merely a means to an end, so images
of the destinations far outnumbered images of travel on the ship.

In Hong Kong and almost every other city they visited, White and
Blechynden made at least one "street scene" film. The compositions of
these films resemble those taken in the United States, in which horse-
drawn carriages and the occasional early automobile usually approach
the camera at a diagonal, creating a dynamic sense of movement across
planes, from background to foreground and beyond into offscreen
space. These films generally included some view of the buildings lining
the street, pedestrians, and sometimes even bicyclists. In some films,
passing trolleys or streetcars bisect the frame, either vertically or horizontally. Overall, street scene films were set in urban cityscapes, filmed

from a distance, and filled with the movement of people, whether on foot or in some other mode of conveyance. But instead of the carriages, trolleys, and automobiles depicted in American street scenes, White's and Blechynden's street scenes from the Occidental and Oriental Series show rickshaws and other human-powered modes of transport.

In the Occidental and Oriental Series, difference is most clearly expressed not in the exotic appearance of the people but in their quaint means of transit. These human-powered vehicles called immediate attention to the scenes' foreignness, as they did in Holmes's and Stoddard's lectures. The film *Government House at Hong* Kong shows the arrival of distinguished guests at a garden party in honor of Prince Henri of Prussia. The guests arrive "in chairs carried on the shoulders of Chinamen, who make their living at this occupation."[46] However, rather than focusing on the government house or the distinguished guests attending the event, the film emphasizes their means of arrival. The government house and its entrance are at the far right. The center of the frame features the area where partygoers disembark. As a result, the view from this camera positioning shows the arriving chairs and the backs of the passengers. In this example, the filmmakers clearly favored the representation of movement over either the architecture or the guests. Similarly, *Tourists Starting for Canton*, according to the Edison catalog, shows "a party of English people in their chairs. This is the only safe way of getting about in Canton, as the streets are indescribably filthy."[47] However, the tourists of the title are barely visible under the sheltered canopies of their chairs, while the bearers and the chairs are clearly depicted. (The condition of the streets is difficult to determine from the film.)

In *Shanghai Street Scene, no. 2*, "peculiar wheelbarrows prove to be the central attraction. Evidently some tourists are enjoying the novel vehicle, as shown by the hilarity of the party that passes by in front of our artists. A barrow is often loaded with three or four passengers, although but one man propels it."[48] The salutations from the tourists in this film acknowledge both the cameramen and the viewers of the film, all sharing a laugh over the absurdity of their means of transportation. Both *Tourists Starting for Canton* and *Shanghai Street Scene, no. 2* invite the viewer to delight in what the white, Western visitors see as the amusing, exotic modes of conveyance used in China. In Japan, rickshaws merited attention in *Street Scene in Yokohama, no. 1*, while *Japanese Sampans* shows "peculiar crafts" charged with taking passengers from the jetty to the steamships.[49] The film depicts several sampans moving in a diagonal line across the frame, from the far left background toward the right front foreground. Two men propel each boat by maneuvering an oar at the back. Three steamships are visible against the distant horizon, creating a subtle but unmistakable contrast between the two types of vessels. These scenes from the Occidental and Oriental Series not only allowed viewers as virtual tourists to compare the urban scenes of the United States with those of Asia but also permitted technologically advanced Westerners to evaluate these differences. The phantom ride films taken from railroads imparted a sense of the thrill of traveling via modern modes of transport. In comparison, sedan chairs, rickshaws, and sampans could only seem hopelessly outdated. The fact that these images of older, premodern modes of transport were made available through new moving picture technology further emphasized the developmental differences between the United States and Asia.

One film in the series, *Arrival of Tokyo Train,* foregrounds steam power. Both its title and its staging bring to mind one of the most famous early films, the Lumières' *Arrival of a Train at La Ciotat* (1895), suggesting a view of Japan as a more Westernized and modernized country than China. But demonstrating precisely how Japanese trains resemble or differ from American or British ones seems to be one of the main goals of the description of the film:

> Here is a Japanese railway depot, something quite different from the bustle and hustle of our American railroad stations. A train is just arriving at Yokohama. The engine is of a modified American type, while the passenger coaches are similar in construction to the accepted English idea. The first and second-class coaches are quite modern looking and have glass windows, in distinction from the third class.[50]

The comparisons among Japanese, American, and English trains and stations also offer an evaluation of relative levels of modernization. Even if Japan is more modern than China, it is still not quite as advanced as either the United States or Britain.

An even more explicit statement of this principle can be found in a 1908 lecture on "Queer Methods of Transportation" by O. P. Austin at the American Museum of Natural History in New York. An *American Museum Journal* advertisement for the lecture, which was also the occasion for the first screening of films at the museum, heralds, a view, by moving pictures and stereopticon slides, of the curious methods of travel and transportation encountered in a trip around the world; the crude methods of the Tropics and the Orient are contrasted with the modern systems of Europe and America, and some suggestions are presented regarding the possibility of development of the Tropics and the Orient through the introduction of modern methods.[51]

This lecture apparently confirms cinema's suitability to represent travel and transportation and uses these representations to construct a hierarchical division of the world between Europe and America, with their modern systems of transportation, and "the Tropics" and "the Orient," where curious and crude methods of travel remain in use. Although the films of the Occidental and Oriental Series did not make this point as explicitly as Austin apparently did, their fascination with human-powered modes of transport supports the same kind of division of the world, one that resonates strongly with the "basic geographical distinction (the world is made up of two unequal halves, Orient and Occident)" at the heart of Edward Said's theory of orientalism.[52]

The fascination with the rickshaw and other similar vehicles in the Occidental and Oriental Series makes it seem as if the Chinese had not yet entered into the modern world of steam-powered travel. Yet Chinese immigrants were crucial to the completion of the transcontinental railroad in the United States. As David Palumbo-Liu writes, "The very revision of modern American time and space was enabled by Chinese labor on the transcontinental railroad, that concrete, modern technological link that, in a particular enactment of time/space compression, shrank the distance between the Atlantic seaboard and the Pacific coast and allowed America to imagine more precisely its particularly modern dream of an American Pacific 'lake.'"[53] The depictions of China in the Occidental and Oriental Series obscure the history of Chinese immigrants who helped to produce American modernity and the role of the Occidental and Oriental Steamship Company in bringing Asian immigrants to the United States; instead, they present a vision of a world unambiguously divided into Orient and Occident. The representations of transportation offered by this film series, in their emphasis on human-powered modes of mobility, thus reinforce dramatically the racial and cultural divisions apparent in the name of the steamship line.

Cinema itself was a modern technology, like the railroad and the steamship, and it is no accident that films offered phantom rides and scenic views that paralleled the experiences produced by these technologies of travel. Lynne Kirby argues that both railroads and the cinema "revolutionized the ways in which people perceived their world, and each created a new kind of subject."[54] She suggests that the railroad provided perceptual and ideological paradigms for cinema, creating "a new, specifically modern mode of perception" and "a subject invested in the consumption of images and motion—that is, physical displacement— for entertainment."[55] While this "new kind of subject" refers to a general effect of the technologies of cinema and of the railroad, the theoretical framework might not be universally applicable, given the uneven history of the development of railroads around the world. The advertisement for Austin's lecture suggests that the Tropics and the Orient might be "developed" by introducing modern methods of transportation. In fact, the development of railroads in China was part of the imperialist division of the country into spheres of influence over which the British, French, Russians, Japanese, Americans, and Belgians fought.[56] Therefore, if we associate both railroads and the cinema with modern perceptions of space and time, we must also account for how railroads and cinema were instrumental to the practices of imperialism and capitalist expansion that accompanied the modern age.

Imperial Visions

On February 15, 1898, the U.S. battleship *Maine* exploded while anchored in Havana Harbor. Despite the lack of evidence, many Americans were convinced that the Spanish were responsible, and patriots were exhorted to "Remember the Maine!" Two months later, on April 25, the Spanish-American War officially began when President William McKinley and Congress declared war against Spain. White and Blechynden returned to San Francisco on May 16, in time to film troops shipping out from San Francisco to the Philippines. They then made their way back to the East Coast. By mid-August, the Spanish-American War was over, though fighting between U.S. forces and Filipinos over Philippine independence would continue for years. The United States thus became involved in a war of colonial conquest in the Philippines and gained an overseas empire, including the separate though not unrelated annexation of Hawai'i. When the Boxer Uprising broke out in 1900, proponents of American overseas expansion noted the relative ease with which troops could be transferred from the battle in the Philippines to Peking. In mid-August, the United States contributed five thousand soldiers to an international force of sixteen thousand that crushed the antiforeign uprising, drove the imperial family from the Forbidden City, and exacted a heavy indemnity from the Chinese government.

These turn-of-the-century military conflicts created a new national imperative to articulate expansionist ideologies. The films of the Occidental and Oriental Series presented Asia as a destination where visitors could delight in quaint modes of human-powered transport, while the rationale behind the production of the series promoted the economic interests of U.S. companies. In particular, these representations encouraged the traffic of goods and people back and forth across the Pacific, an exchange that benefited the sponsor's bottom line. With the inauguration of U.S. overseas imperialism, viewers saw images of Asia within a new context, in relation to the evolving political interests of the U.S. nation-state. Whereas White and Blechynden traveled to where the Occidental and Oriental Steamship Company took them, other filmmakers would follow in the footsteps of the U.S. Army. The earlier delight in the modern technological possibilities of virtual mobility, such as the ability to see street scenes from halfway across the world, was replaced by a demand for information about the progress of imperial military campaigns also taking place halfway around the world.

In his influential *The Emergence of Cinema: The American Screen to 1907*, Charles Musser explores the Spanish-American War's effects on the fledgling film industry, concluding that cinema was entangled with American imperialism but refraining from specifying cinema's role in overseas expansion:

> Moving pictures projected a sense of national glory and outrage. It would be a gross exaggeration to say that cinema launched a new era of American imperialism. But cinema had found a role beyond narrow amusement, and this sudden prominence coincided with a new era of overseas expansion and military interventions. Who can say what fantasies of power audiences experienced in those darkened halls, and how these emotions continued to resonate outside the theater?[57]

Fantasies of power and emotional affect are impossible to quantify, but they are precisely the kinds of issues that we must consider to understand the relationship between cinema and imperialism as more than mere coincidence. I now turn to an examination of how films produced beginning in the latter half of 1898 make visible some of the fantasies of power and emotions that accompanied U.S. overseas imperialism. As Whissel argues, "Early cinema's developing formal features made it particularly well suited to frame the [Spanish-American] war through spectacles of shock, surprise and trauma recuperated as documents of national unity and imperial resolve." She continues, "While actualities of the war promoted a sense of the inevitability of U.S. overseas expansion, the story film accommodated shifting discourses on race and nation that followed the USA's transformation from nation to empire."[58] The conventions of the Occidental and Oriental Series both reinforced and challenged certain orientalist traditions of representation. How did the formal and stylistic features of early films represent Asia as a space of U.S. imperial domination and colonial conquest? I address how the specificities of four different types of early films—actualities, trick films, reenactments, and story films—shaped the imagination of the United States as an emergent imperial power in Asia.

Documents

The actuality films of the Occidental and Oriental Series are open in their signification, offering viewers many possible interpretations. In distinguishing between *document* and *documentary,* Philip Rosen describes actuality films as "relatively pure instances of documents."[59] In his view, actuality films "provided fewer means for the filmmaker to attribute significance to the real. . . . [S]uch films possessed much less of the textually saturating directionality of meanings based on internal sequenciation and elaboration to which we are so accustomed after seventy-odd years of narrative dominance."[60] While both the Griersonian documentary tradition and classical narrative films prize the stabilization of meaning, Rosen observes that in early actuality films, meaning could be stabilized only at the time of exhibition, perhaps by the accompaniment of a lecturer or by the structuring of the program in which the film appeared.

At a time of war and heightened nationalistic fervor, exhibitors could encourage audiences to take away more specific meanings from such films. One example was the program devoted to the Spanish-American War at Proctor's Theatre in New York City. As described in a *New York*

Journal and Advertiser report, Biograph actuality films and slides were shown, along with live musical accompaniment (a bugler behind the screen played "Taps" during a film of the burial of the victims of the *Maine*) and a live reading of a bulletin about the war's progress. Audience members reportedly reacted enthusiastically to the program, as they apparently felt deeply the tragedy of the dead soldiers from the *Maine*, cheered each image of the U.S. flag, and hissed at the appearances of the Spanish.[61] This account suggests that in the proper context, actuality films could produce specific emotional reactions from audience members. The Eden Musee in New York City also devoted entire programs to the Spanish-American War, as Musser has detailed, serving as "a kind of patriotic news service . . . dedicated to heroicizing the United States' imperial adventures and those who implemented its policy."[62]

At a textual level, the actuality films produced during these turn-of-the-century wars followed established cinematic conventions: they depicted military views, well-known personages, and scenic views. Some films showed U.S. troops performing maneuvers and drills in the United States, shipping out to or returning from Cuba or the Philippines, and marching in parades. Others featured U.S. battleships or famous military personalities such as George Dewey. A handful of films showed views of Cuba, but no actuality films showed the Philippines prior to 1899. The Philippine-American War created a new demand for views of the Philippines, however. The "Military" section of Biograph's November 1902 catalog lists twenty-nine films related to the Philippine-American War, most of them filmed in the Philippines; the "Scenic" section offers eight more Philippine views. These new images did not radically transform existing principles of actuality filmmaking; rather, filmmakers chose subjects and scenes for a U.S. audience that they imagined wanted to learn about the newly acquired territory and their relationship to it. Films of the Spanish-American War and subsequently of the Philippine-American War and the Boxer Uprising were produced according to the formal dictates of the "cinema of attractions" but within the context of the imperial project. According to Whissel, "Such images trade upon both the moving pictures' ability to harness the visually kinetic mobilizations of imperial expansion and, moreover, its ability to redirect inwardly the outward thrust of imperial expansion by circulating images of US soldiers, naval parades, and re-enactments of battles throughout the nation."[63] Films of the Philippines and China brought the spectacle of the U.S. military forces in Asia to U.S. audiences. Whereas earlier representations had shown Hong Kong, China, and Japan as sites of commerce and leisure, the newer films showed these countries as sites of military maneuvers and imperial domination.

Although on a formal level, these later films were not distinctive, the references to the foreign occupation scattered throughout the catalog summaries are striking. Instead of the "tourists" who frequently appeared in the descriptions of the films of the Occidental and Oriental Series, these later entries highlight the presence of the U.S. Army. Biograph's *The Escolta* (sometimes listed as *The Escalta*) has the visual composition of a typical street scene, but its catalog listing also notes the historical context of the film's making: "An interesting view in Manila's busiest street during the early occupation by the American Army. Various types of native life are shown, and a very good idea is given of the general character of the city."[64] *Making Manila Rope,* one of the few films of the Philippines focused on commercial production, illustrates "one of the chief industries of our new possessions, taken during the occupation by the American Army."[65] In these summaries, which exhibitors may have used to accompany the screenings of the films, the scenes of "native life," the city, and its industries offer not just views of Manila and its inhabitants but rather illustrations of Manila and Manilans under U.S. occupation. However, like the earlier examples from the Occidental and Oriental Series, the catalog descriptions often overstated what could be clearly seen in or understood from the films themselves. Once again, the visual conventions of the films were not developed to convey meanings equivalent to those offered by the accompanying written descriptions.

The military films on offer, however, clearly focus on U.S. troops in the Philippines. Many films show U.S. soldiers marching or charging, and the description of *General Bell's Expedition* is typical: "Showing General Bell's famous expedition of picked men, with native scouts and pack train coming down the mountain near Sual in Northern Luzon. This picture gives an excellent view of the character of the country through which the American troops fought in their chase after Aguinaldo."[66] As this description indicates, this actuality was intended not as a scenic view of an exotic land but rather as a record of the resources of the U.S. Army and the terrain it covered in pursuing the leader of the Philippine resistance. Despite mentions of the Filipino "insurgents" throughout the descriptions of the films, no insurgents were shown, perhaps because of the difficulty of "capturing" the insurgents on film, but also because the films emphasized the strength and abilities of the American forces rather than those of their enemies. Whissel argues that in the midst of anxieties about American manhood, cinematic images of U.S. soldiers represented an imperial white masculinity: "War actualities displayed a high-tech, complex, hierarchical formation in which physically developed bodies and powerful machines worked efficiently to extend the nation's political and commercial power around the globe."[67] Like Holmes's lecture on Manila, such films demonstrated U.S. soldiers' fitness for the imperial task ahead rather than the character of the Filipinos on the scene or the Philippine landscape.

Just as the Philippine-American War led to greater curiosity about the Philippines, so the Boxer Uprising piqued further U.S. interest in China, though China and the Chinese were somewhat more familiar to U.S. audiences. "China" warranted a separate listing in the July 1901 Edison film catalog, which began, "The Boxer Massacres in Pekin May, 1900 have turned the eyes of the civilized world toward China. Public interest is now intensely aroused, and people will eagerly appreciate any pictures that relate to the localities in which the war in China was prosecuted."[68] However, the catalog lists only three new films in this section: *Bombardment of Taku Forts by the Allied Fleets* (a battle reenactment) and two street scenes, *Street Scene in Pekin,* and *Scene in Legation Street, Shanghai.* For a "Complete List of Chinese Picture Films," exhibitors are told to refer to the Occidental and Oriental Series.[69] Thus White's and Blechynden's 1898 films are seen in an entirely new frame, no longer in relation to the commercial interests of the Occidental and Oriental Steamship Company but now in relation to the anti-Christian and antiforeign uprising of the Chinese Boxers. In this instance, not only the conventions but also the films themselves literally remained the same. The difference between seeing the Edison films of China before the turn of the century and after was therefore located primarily within viewers and their historical milieu. Whereas the films had previously served as invitations to and virtual experiences of travel that reaffirmed U.S. modernity relative to Asia, the changing international political situation turned them into documents of Chinese life and culture, full of information about the world of the Boxers.

Biograph found "the War in China" worthy of two expeditions. The company's catalog underscored Biograph's reliance on and cooperation with the Allied military forces: "In the case of the China campaign, our operators were recognized and assisted by the American, English and

German War Departments."[70] Biograph's efforts resulted in twenty-eight films in the series the War in China, along with twenty-one scenic views. Most of the military scenes depicted familiar maneuvers, charges, and exercises. The addition of views of German, Japanese, British, and Russian troops called attention to the international coalition of Allied nations, but the Boxers themselves were nowhere to be seen. The scenic views of China resembled those given in earlier films, though the views were mainly of Tien-Tsin, Peking, and Shanghai instead of the cities on the steamship company's itinerary. Many of the descriptions of these new views mentioned the Boxer Uprising and the foreign occupation, just as descriptions of the Biograph views of the Philippines had emphasized the war and the U.S. occupation of Manila. The film *Street Scene*, for example, shows "Street Scene in Tien-Tsin. United States officers in Jinrickishas. Characteristic life during the foreign occupation."[71] Once again, even though many of these films bore a close visual resemblance to earlier scenic views, these descriptions make clear that viewers were to look at them in a new way. While the earlier series had shown friendly Western tourists bemusedly experiencing the native modes of transport, these films showed U.S. officers in rickshaws, presumably going about the business of occupying China. This transfiguration mirrored the historical change in the role of the Americans in China from tourists to soldiers; a similar change was also evident in Holmes's lectures in a more personal sense, as Holmes struggled to reconcile his presence as a traveler in Manila and in the Forbidden City with the military power that made possible these travels.

Among the scenic views, a film of the Forbidden City stands out. It is described as a "Panoramic view in the Forbidden City, or private palaces of the Emperor of China, from the Wu-Men Gate, showing the buildings reserved for the exclusive use of the Emperor, and the court-yard in which millions of dollars of treasure were buried at the time this picture was taken, during the flight of the Chinese court."[72] The existence of this film is remarkable for the same reasons as Holmes's images of the Forbidden City: both were unprecedented. However, this panoramic view of the city as seen from a distance is much less impressive than Holmes's detailed penetration into the interior. Nevertheless, the thrill of seeing the forbidden still remains, albeit on a much smaller scale; perhaps this difference testifies to the privilege Holmes's audiences enjoyed compared to those who watched the films of the dominant film industry of the time. In both Holmes's lectures and these actualities of the Spanish-

American War, the Philippine-American War, and the Boxer Uprising, cinema brought moving photographic images of life in faraway places to viewers at home not just to promote the pleasures of travel but also to help Americans to understand the work of their army abroad. As unique documents—visual recordings of reality—these actuality films responded to the desire for knowledge about distant wars by bringing China and the Philippines to the United States; they showed American audiences what it was like to be a U.S. soldier in Asia, pursuing Filipino insurrectionists and antiforeign Boxers, or establishing a U.S. occupation in Manila and Peking.

Movie Magic

On the other end of the spectrum from actuality films, trick films portrayed blatantly unrealistic staged scenes featuring impossible acts achieved through manipulations of the camera such as stop-motion or multiple exposures. Most famously associated with French filmmaker and former magician George Méliès, the pleasures of these films derived from their entertaining spectacles. As a rule, trick films did not directly address current events, and they explicitly represented few or no incidents from the Spanish-American or Philippine-American Wars.[73] The Boxer Uprising, however, was the subject of *Congress of Nations,* a trick film produced by the Vitagraph Company's J. Stuart Blackton and Albert E. Smith between September and early November 1900 and distributed by Edison in 1901.[74] The film was made just after the conclusion of the Boxer Uprising, and in its topicality, it resembled an actuality film. The catalog description emphasizes this timeliness: "A new and sensational film, which deals in a highly up-to-date manner with the international situation."[75] The *New York Clipper* reviewed the film as "a stirring and sentimental picture, treating upon the complicated Chinese question, ending with a marvelous tableau that will evoke applause from every audience."[76] The catalog references to "the international situation" and the timing of the film's release suggest that this picture, like the actuality films of China and the Philippines, was produced to take advantage of the U.S. audience's heightened interest in these countries in relation to recent political events. However, what trick films conveyed about the Boxer Uprising differed greatly from what was seen in the military and scenic actuality films of China. *Congress of Nations* depicts a magician on a stage, playing to the audience as he conjures up a series of flags and matching soldiers from Germany, Russia, Ireland, England, and China. The film begins with the magician against a painted backdrop with a large white circle in the center. Each individual then magically appears on stage behind his flag and marches to his place. A "Chinese man" appears last, runs around in a circle, and then is set upon by the soldiers on the stage. The "Chinese man"—in reality a Vitagraph clerk, Morris Brenner—is distinguished from the others by his diminutive stature, long queue, and decidedly nonmilitary clothing.[77] The magician finally halts the action by making the characters disappear and unfurling a giant American flag against the back wall. The image of the empty stage with the flag then dissolves into the concluding tableau featuring representatives of the allied nations with Miss Liberty at the apex. Finally, the tableau comes briefly to life, with Miss Liberty throwing flower petals from her basket and representatives of the United States and Britain vigorously shaking hands.

Edison also distributed a similarly themed film titled *A Chinese Mystery* (1902) that was produced by an unidentified filmmaker, possibly George Méliès or Robert Paul.[78] The film is summarized:

> The scene is before the open door of a Chinese pagoda. A Chinese conjurer appears as if coming from the bowels of the earth, and causes a beautiful Chinese maiden to take her place on the stone steps of the pagoda. The maiden is suddenly transformed into the hue head of a Chinese hobgoblin who emits great volumes of smoke from his mouth. An American traveler then appears upon the scene and seizing a huge sword splits open the head of the hobgoblin, and from its center appear three small Chinamen who dance about in a fantastic manner. Then the allied soldiers of England, France, Russia, America and Germany appear and from the place previously occupied by the Chinese hobgoblin there appears a lily, in the center of which grows the figure of a beautiful woman representing the Goddess of Liberty.[79]

Such films obviously would not teach audiences anything of the "reality" of China or the Chinese, although these images might reinforce stereotypical views derived from popular culture. Nor would the films portray a sense of the work of a U.S. soldier during the occupation of Peking. Actuality films could place spectators on the scene, far from their actual physical locations, to see the curious modes of transport in the Orient or to appreciate U.S. military power at work in a distant land, as the case might be. These two trick films, however, like other films of this kind, developed out of a tradition of magic performances; they were produced according to entirely different conventions than those governing actuality films. Many trick films, including *Congress of Nations,* appear as records of stage performances, with sets featuring anything from relatively minimal backdrops to the elaborately detailed worlds for which Méliès was known. As the Chinese pagoda scenario of *A Chinese Mystery* suggests, the Boxer Uprising served primarily as an inspiration for the exotic setting, populated by stereotypical racialized figures, within which an entertaining series of transformations occurred. Freed from the imperative to represent the reality of China and centering on how cinema could perform magical transformations, *Congress of Nations* and *A Chinese Mystery* use allegories of the United States as part of an international coalition of nations allied against the Chinese as the pretext for inventive acts.

Reenacting Reality

Actuality films offered scenes from real life in a declarative mode: a typical street in Tien-Tsin, a company of U.S. soldiers on the march in the Philippines, a view of a U.S. battleship. While some of these scenes may have inspired patriotic sentiment, these short slice-of-life films could communicate specific meanings only when accompanied by additional interpretation, whether from a lecturer or through some other type of contextual situating. In contrast, a trick film such as *Congress of Nations* created metaphorical connotations by engaging audiences with fantastic transformations. *What Our Boys Did at Manila,* which was staged and filmed in a New York studio rather than shot on location in Manila, as its title might suggest, draws from both traditions as well as from a longer history of staged representations. According to the Biograph catalog, which includes *What Our Boys Did at Manila* among the military scenes,

> This picture makes a quick appeal to popular patriotism, and has been a decided "hit" wherever it has been shown. At the opening a Spanish flag is seen floating from the top of the flagstaff; then a United States sailor appears shinning up the staff with a bundle tied to his shoulders. He rips down the Spanish flag, nails Old Glory to the staff, and as the breeze carries it out, waves his cap to the cheers of his comrades below.[80]

In comparison to actuality films or trick films, this film illustrates a different kind of meaning-making process. It represents the events in the Philippines as a straightforward transfer of power from Spain to the United States. This representation could be likened to the allegory of *A Chinese Mystery,* yet it still functions within a relatively realistic diegesis reminiscent of actuality films. The film features a staged performance, but one that proceeds according to the rules of real life; there are no sudden appearances or disappearances, no hobgoblins, and no metaphorical tableaux. Thus, by combining elements of trick films with aspects of actuality films, *What Our Boys Did at Manila* conveys a precise and succinct interpretation of the colonial conquest of the Philippines far more effectively than could scenes actually shot in Manila.

Reenactments were not uncommon in early film, although they generally depicted newsworthy events or battles such as the explosion of the *Maine* rather than the kind of smaller-scale incident represented in *What Our Boys Did at Manila.* Reenactments also served as a way to offer a version of an event of interest to the U.S. public but without transporting the filmmakers to distant locations; famous examples include the Edison company's New Jersey–based reenactments of battles from the Spanish-American War and the Philippine-American War.[81] Such films often signaled their status as reenactments in either their titles or descriptions, and audiences were most likely aware that these films were staged and acted for the camera. Reenactments do, however, pose theoretical questions of the separation between fact and fiction. According to David Levy, generic distinctions between documentary and fiction were not absolute for turn-of-the-century filmmakers:

> The categories Newsreel, Documentary, Drama and Reproduction do not appear to have been very firmly fixed as production models by early film producers. And because the methods employed in one needed to cross no very strong boundaries to be used in another, there was a lot of two-way traffic across a weak ontological frontier.[82]

Levy argues that a staged or reenacted film of a current event that utilized the visual conventions of actuality footage could effectively create the impression that a cameraman was present and filming at an actual event. Reenactments such as *The Early Morning Attack,* which depicts a military encounter between Filipinos and U.S. troops, or *Bombardment of Taku Forts by the Allied Fleets,* a staging of a Boxer Uprising naval battle, were effective not because they resembled the reality of the Philippines or China but because they gave the impression of a subjective presence, a witness at an actual event.

Where Levy sees battle reenactments as persuasive because they create the presence of the cameraman through newsreel-style cinematic staging and technique, Whissel traces their credibility to the live historical reenactments of the late nineteenth century, such as Buffalo Bill's Wild West show, and the ability of the show's staging to produce an ideal spectator position in relation to the scene.[83] Griffiths also looks back in time when she examines the importance of the reenactment in both nineteenth-century panoramas and early cinema:

> Audiences attending the typical nineteenth-century battle panorama would not only have been entertained by the spectacular painting but would have been interpellated into the roles of historical witnesses or war reporters. The ability to re-experience an event of enormous national significance, to step inside history, which was metaphorically enacted via the spectators' physical location and locomotion around the central viewing platform, were doubtless intended to trigger feelings of nationalistic fervour for early nineteenth-century spectators.[84]

Griffiths goes on to suggest that the connections between panoramas and cinema include not only the fascination with current events but also the panorama's construction of an experience in "proto-cinematic ways, foreshadowing the shot structures of typical early travelogues and inviting the spectator to read the painting as a seamless synthesis of a place and its people."[85]

All of these scholars of early cinematic reenactments emphasize how the reenactment produces the sense of presence, or the impression of witnessing. This impression of a presence on the scene reminds us of how the cinematic apparatus could offer images of distant countries to U.S. audiences curious about their new roles as imperialists in Asia and the Pacific. In the staging and filming of *What Our Boys Did at Manila*, which resembles the realistic style of actuality films, the scene is presented as if it were a record of an actual event carried out by U.S. soldiers and recorded by a camera operator on the scene in Manila. If such a spontaneous action as this hoisting of the American flag ever took place, it would have been a remarkable expression of U.S. imperialism by members of the military, combining a celebration of their victory over

Spain with a proclamation of the status of the Philippines as a U.S. territory. Because *What Our Boys Did at Manila* was a staged scene and not an actuality film, it was able to convey an unambiguous political message. Unlike actuality films as documents of reality, in the sense that Rosen defines them, these films move toward a greater specification of signification, coming closer to the "centralization of meaning production" that typifies classical narrative.[86]

Telling Tales

The final type of early film that I examine in this chapter takes up the challenge of meaning production by combining several strategies of early cinema; these films sequence two or more films, sometimes showcasing very different types of cinematic conventions, that are held together by the logic of a story. Biograph's *The American Soldier in Love and War* (1903) combines staged interior and exterior scenes with actuality footage and a battle reenactment to tell the story of a soldier who leaves his sweetheart behind in the United States while he goes to fight in the Philippines. The production is actually a series of three films, each listed separately, though they form a single narrative. The first scene portrays a domestic interior with a woman seated at a table. The soldier enters, the two share multiple embraces, and then he exits the scene. The second film takes place in an outdoor setting represented by a painted backdrop with palm trees, water, and foliage, with a few props in the foreground. The soldier enters the scene and falls to the ground. A dark-skinned man arrives wearing a grass skirt and holding a club; he fights with and defeats the soldier. Just as he is about to strike the final blow, a woman rushes over to defend the fallen soldier. The final scene is set against a different painted exterior backdrop, with a small home on the right side of the stage. The soldier, whose head is bandaged, is seated just outside the house. A woman to his right fans him with a palm leaf, while another leaves the scene briefly and then returns to bring him a beverage. A white woman wearing a white dress then enters the scene, accompanied by a white man. The soldier gestures toward one woman, presumably explaining how she saved his life, and as his sweetheart goes to the woman, the soldier and the father shake hands.

The *Biograph Bulletin* recommended that exhibitors use the "three scenes . . . in conjunction with two war views to make a complete story in one film for projections."[87] Musser identifies the two war views as *Fif-*

teenth Infantry, USA, a view of troops shipping out to war, and *Practice Warfare,* showing a realistically staged battle. The use of these views, says Musser, "provided a credible milieu for the story."[88] For him, the interest of *The American Soldier in Love and War* lies in the way in which continuity in the film depends on narrative and performance within the film's syncretic mise-en-scène. What were previously three distinct kinds of films—actualities, staged scenes, and a reenactment—are linked in the service of a story, with the actuality film and the reenactment providing the backdrop to the narrative.

The incorporation into one film of these different types of scenes, each with its own origin and function, was part of a growing industry-wide emphasis on story films. Edwin S. Porter, for example, made a number of films in 1903–4 for Edison that combined actuality films and fictional, acted scenes, including *Rube and Mandy at Coney Island* (1903) and *European Rest Cure* (1904), which included one of the films from the Occidental and Oriental Series, *S.S. "Coptic" Running Against a Storm* (1898).[89] By incorporating travel scenes into these films, filmmakers looked back to the tradition of exhibitor-centered practices; such arrangements combined and ordered films to suggest larger significances. Such practices of selection and juxtaposition also looked forward to the development of classical narrative films, similarly to Holmes's travel lectures, though from a different point of departure. Yet *The American Soldier in Love and War* not only tells us about the transition to story films but also tells a particular story. Considering the film in relation to U.S. nation-building and imperial policies, Amy Kaplan argues that the film "narrativizes a foreign war in part by negotiating gender and racial anxieties at home. . . . Imperial conquest appears as the restoration of white American domesticity on foreign terrain."[90] This narrative of conquest required "Filipino" characters to be presented in outrageous and grotesque makeup, costumes, and settings designed purely to give them a frightening and "primitive" appearance. Since they function within the film as foils to the American soldier, as representatives of the "savage enemy," these actors, who were dressed, made up, and directed to act their parts, represent the worst American stereotypes of Filipinos. According to Charlie Keil, this exaggerated representation of people of color is a significant feature of the transition from the actuality-film-dominated era of early cinema to the later dominance of fictional narrative films.

Keil asserts, "If the dichotomy of fiction versus fact exists at all in early cinema, it manifests itself most clearly in the representation of people of color, particularly blacks and native Americans, who can be themselves within a documentary format, but are translated into black-faced or war-painted white actors at the point of dramatic representation." Keil continues, "The more independent existence of non-whites within the documentary mode also points to its less controllable aspects (at least on the profilmic level) and indicates the potential for shock that nonfiction film possessed. It is little wonder that as filmmaking moved toward greater emphasis on narrative, attempts were made to exert increasing control over documentary elements."[91] The comparison of films such as *Hong Kong Wharf Scene* and *Theatre Road, Yokohama* to films such as *Congress of Nations, What Our Boys Did in Manila,* and *The American Soldier in Love and War* bears out Keil's argument, demonstrating that Asians in the Occidental and Oriental Series indeed had a "more independent existence" than in the later staged scenes or racist caricatures of the print media or in the staged exoticism of world's fairs of the period. While the Occidental and Oriental Series did not, of course, simply offer unmediated visions of distant lands and peoples, the films captured something of the life of the people they depicted that exceeded existing orientalist significations. In *The American Soldier in Love and War,* as is befitting for a film whose main character is an American soldier, the one scene of "reality" is of soldiers shipping out. Since the Philippines is important only as the background for the story of the film, it is reduced to a few overdetermined signifiers of tropical vegetation and landscape, while the "Filipino" characters must be grotesquely exaggerated to provide an easily apparent contrast to the soldier and his sweetheart and between the Philippines and the United States.

It is perhaps not surprising that actuality films offered expansive possibilities of meaning, while staged scenes presented stereotypes. But what is compelling about later classical narrative films, especially those shot on location, is the way in which the indexicality of cinema, which lends actuality films their sense of independent existence, could naturalize the control of narrative. That is, the films made it seem as if viewers were indeed experiencing a text made within the documentary mode, even when it utilized a script, actors, and classical narrative conventions. In examining the development of what he calls "the narrator system" in the first decade of the twentieth century, Gunning describes the ways in which cinematic verisimilitude lent reality to stories while stories constructed meaning out of reality:

Film's innate tendency toward mimesis becomes a sign of narrative realism, naturalizing the process of storytelling as the inclusion of apparently useless detail does in verbal narrative. Simultaneously the process of narrativization delivers a sense to this realism, through filmic discourse which "picks up" and selects precisely those meanings necessary for the story to be told. In this way the filmic image, without losing (indeed, using) its capacity for showing, defines its unique way of telling.[92]

Precisely this combination of showing and telling, of offering a seemingly unmediated vision of reality while simultaneously framing and interpreting "reality" in a very particular way, makes cinema a uniquely powerful medium.

Transitional Views

At one point in academic film history, scholars referred to the first decade of cinema's existence as the era of "primitive cinema," a nomination that indicated the prevailing view that the films of the period were undeveloped versions of the art's mature form. However, Gunning's influential concept of "the cinema of attractions," along with the work of a number of other historians who have studied early cinema with great care and attention, have amply demonstrated that turn-of-the-century cinema is not merely a prelude to classical narrative but rather a rich and intriguing period deserving of study on its own terms, free of what Gunning calls "the hegemony of narrative films."[93] The first two chapters of this book explore how material circumstances, discursive traditions, and aesthetic conventions shaped early cinematic travel views. The actuality films of Hawai'i, China, Japan, and the Philippines brought the world to U.S. audiences, first within an existing discourse of travel as a means of knowing the world and one's place within it, and then in relation to the ideological demands that emerged with the advent of U.S. overseas imperialism. The latter pages of this chapter touched on the story film and its growing popularity in the first decade of the twentieth century, as filmmakers experimented with new ways of telling stories and creating coherent worlds within which these stories could unfold. The next two chapters, however, fast-forward to the era of classical Hollywood films to consider the functions and effects of filming on location in China and

Japan from the late 1930s to the early 1960s. Such time travel is not undertaken lightly; most books on early film are devoted entirely to early cinema.

By including in my study films ranging from the turn of the century to the 1960s, I do not intend to suggest that films "developed" in a teleological sense. The institution of cinema around the turn of the century was radically different from what it would become by the 1930s. I respect these differences; however, films continued to offer virtual voyages to Asia within an ideology of U.S. orientalism despite the changes that occurred within both film and U.S. orientalism. As the widespread critical embrace of the 1937 silver screen adaptation of Pearl S. Buck's *The Good Earth* demonstrates, the power of cinema to transport audiences across vast geographical distances and to educate them about faraway peoples and cultures remained considerable in the classical era. Yet *The Good Earth* is also a fictional narrative with synchronized sound and a running time of approximately 138 minutes. Metro-Goldwyn-Mayer, a major Hollywood studio, produced the film, and it features two stars in the leading roles. Although both *The Good Earth* and *Shanghai Street Scene, no. 2* have the power to transport their audiences to China, the two films could not differ more in their form and style; in their relations to the structures of cinematic production, exhibition, and reception that they inhabited; and in their representations of China and the Chinese and their significance for the United States. We must examine both their similarities and their differences to consider cinema's power to function as a form of virtual travel to and as a source of knowledge of China.

A detailed account of the history of American cinema from the turn of the century to the 1930s is beyond the scope of this work, but some sense of what occurred in the intervening decades is necessary to understand what shooting on location means and how it functions in relation to classical narratives. The period of film history dating from around 1907 to the early to mid-1910s is known as the transitional era, in reference to the transition from the films of early cinema to narrative feature films. This era is characterized less by specific traits than by the wide-ranging changes that occurred in film form and style, the film industry, and film audiences. According to Eileen Bowser, "Film forms changed as drastically [between 1907 and 1915] as at any point in motion-picture history. At the same time, the film business itself changed from a hand-crafted amusement enterprise and sideshow to a gigantic entertainment industry and the first mass-communication medium."[94] One of the most significant transformations of this era was the emergence of the story film as the dominant product of the film industry.

Story films are distinguished from actualities, which have been the primary subjects of these first two chapters, most significantly by their narrative form. This form, which clearly delineates relationships of cause and effect as well as space and time evolved in tandem with stylistic strategies designed to engage the audience in the good fortunes and dramatic reversals of fictional characters. As is well known, the development of editing and cinematography was important to transitional film form. However, regardless of how the story was told, each story also had to take place some*where*, in some place. The setting of the fictional story, part of the film's mise-en-scène (which traditionally includes setting, lighting, costumes and makeup, and acting), requires the filmmaker to choose between shooting on a stage set or at an actual location.

Edwin S. Porter's *European Rest Cure* follows an accident-prone American tourist on a tour of Europe and Egypt. As in *The American Soldier in Love and War,* the faraway places seen in the film were depicted through less-than-convincing stage sets. In contrast, the use of actuality scenes shot near the shores of the United States emphasized the reality of home.[95] Along with *S.S. "Coptic" Running against the Storm* (1898) from the Occidental and Oriental Series, two other Edison actualities are seen in the first and second parts of the five-part film: *Pilot Leaving "Prinzessen Victoria Luise" at Sandy Hook* (1902), and *Skyscrapers of New York from the North River* (1903). But once the unlucky tourist arrives in Europe, all the scenes take place on stage sets with painted backdrops, which represent Ireland, France, Switzerland, Italy, Egypt, and Germany. Only when he returns to the United States is the action again filmed in an actual location, showing the weary traveler in an exterior scene slowly being helped into a carriage that will presumably deliver him to "home, sweet home."[96] The artificial foreign settings work effectively as the background for the film's illustration of the hazards of travel abroad—What does travel offer but humiliation and danger to the American tourist?— but this type of "syncretic mise-en-scène" (that is, the juxtaposition of actualities and staged scenes in a single film) would be increasingly challenged by the audience's demand for a more coherent and seamless world within which the film's narrative could unfold.

As Gunning observes, "Although its achievement was uneven in 1908, situating stories within a realistic environment became an important element as the narrator system developed. Detailed realistic settings provided a varied spontaneous world beyond the demands of significance and naturalized the narrator's interventions, guaranteeing the diegetic unity of a film."⁹⁷ Held to such standards, the stark stylistic contrasts between actuality films and scenes staged against painted backdrops presented a disjunction that required smoothing over. One strategy to lessen the obvious differences between the world of the film and the "real" world was to quite literally incorporate the real world into the story world of the film. Gunning points to D. W. Griffith's inclusion of scenes of life on the Lower East Side of New York City in the film *The Romance of a Jewess* (1908) as well as shots of Florence Lawrence, the star of *The Christmas Burglars* (1908), among crowds of actual Christmas shoppers on the street as examples of the use of real settings in a fictional narrative. These instances of actuality functioned quite differently from the use of actuality films as merely "touches of realism" in earlier films such as Biograph's *The Skyscrapers of New York* (1906) and *The Tunnel Workers* (1906).⁹⁸ In sum, Gunning tells us, "Staging dramatic action within actual locations exemplifies the homogeneity and continuity the cinema of narrative integration introduced."⁹⁹ In these examples, scenes of real life no longer merely demonstrate the novelty of the technology of cinema, with its ability to capture moving photographic images, but rather situate the fictional story of the film within the familiar, real world.

Griffith and other filmmakers soon discovered the potential of the varied landscapes of Southern California and the year-round shooting the climate allowed. In Keil's account, the growing popularity of location shooting, in California and elsewhere, further heightened the visual differences between exterior and interior scenes. This contrast conjured up the specter of discontinuity between the various worlds of the film, which would have deleterious effects on a realist aesthetic. He describes at length how location shooting challenged the desire for authenticity and realism:

> By 1910, the Eastern-based companies routinely began traveling to distant locales. The landscapes of California, followed by those of the United Kingdom, Canada, and Cuba, among others, functioned as exotica but also as marks of authenticity. Once location shooting emerged as an accepted practice and marketable production value, employing unrealistic sets became even more problematic, especially when meant to represent the outdoors. The principal drawback derived from the discrepancy between the appearance of exteriors and interiors. If a filmmaker chose to use both sets and location shooting in combination, the apparent authenticity of the latter would expose the counterfeit nature of the former. Any open window or

door within a set would necessarily feature a portion of a fabricated landscape, subsequently shown in its actual form via outdoor shots; in these areas, the evident discrepancies would cancel any effect of realism.[100]

This description of the function of distant landscapes—whether located across the country, across the border, or across the ocean—as simultaneously "exotica" and "marks of authenticity" suggests that the fascination of early travel views lingers in location shooting. For Keil, the main issue is the challenge that location shooting represented to the coherence of the world of the film. But the implications of his observations go beyond questions of film style. In this transitional moment in film history, as Keil describes it, location shooting for fictional films had become an accepted and valued practice associated with "authenticity," while sets, especially those representing exterior scenes, were increasingly seen as unrealistic. Keil does not examine the additional question of whether the location is merely *a* location or *the* location where the narrative is set. Nevertheless, his terms—*authentic* as opposed to *counterfeit* or *fabricated*—establish the discursive distinction that defines the value of shooting on location.

Among the earliest films that Edison filmmakers produced with their new portable camera were actualities taken in New York City and the surrounding area, showing audiences "local views of locations they encountered in the course of their everyday lives," in Musser's words.[101] These cinematic views highlighted the amazing capabilities of the new technology of moving pictures, reproducing on the screen places familiar to the audience. In contrast, the need to emphasize to exhibitors perusing the Edison sales catalog that the films of the Occidental and Oriental Series were also "photographed from life"[102] points to how U.S. audiences could not so easily confirm the reality of the largely unfamiliar streets of the Far East. How indeed could exhibitors or audiences be certain that the images of the distant lands on the screen were actually "photographed from life"? And how might such assurances, whether textual or extratextual—that is, within the film itself or through the catalog copy or advertising, for example—be pressed into service to naturalize the fictional story of a film? It is one thing for New York audiences to recognize the world within which they lived their everyday lives as the backdrop for a realistically staged story but quite another for them to believe in the authenticity of faraway places that most would never see or experience for themselves.

CHAPTER THREE

$\mathcal{K}$nowing China

Accuracy, Authenticity, and *The Good Earth*

Knowing China

Pearl Sydenstricker was born in Hillsboro, West Virginia, in 1892 while her American missionary parents were home on leave from China. At the age of three months, she accompanied her parents on their return to China, where she would spend much of the first half of her life. While other Americans read or heard about the violence of the Boxer Uprising, she witnessed the events unfold around her firsthand. She grew up reading and speaking both English and Chinese and was tutored in the Chinese classics. After attending college in the United States, she married missionary John Lossing Buck and returned to China for another decade and a half. Thus, in contrast to the Americans discussed in the first half of this study, Buck was not merely a visitor to China. As the title of her autobiography, *My Several Worlds*, implies, Buck considered both China and the United States home, though whether she was ever truly at home in either nation is another question.[1] However, like Burton Holmes and James White and Frederick Blechynden, she produced representations of China for U.S. audiences.

Buck had minimal involvement in the making of Metro-Goldwyn-Mayer's cinematic adaptation of her novel, *The Good Earth* (Sidney Franklin, 1937), the main subject of this chapter. However, the discourses that surrounded her life and her writings on China were significant factors in the film's initial ambitions, production, and reception. In particular, Buck's work shaped the development of what Karen Leong calls "the China mystique," an expression of American orientalism that presented a "romanticized, progressive, and highly gendered image of China, the 'new China.'"[2] According to Leong, "Beginning in the 1930s Americans began to imagine China differently, no longer as an alien and distant culture and land, but as a demonstration of the promise held by American democracy and culture to transform other nations."[3] The China mystique "bridges the development of American orientalism and its newer, postwar forms to justify American empire as the United States increasingly involved itself throughout Asia."[4] Buck

> internationalized for the American public the concept of cultural plural-
> ism, providing her readers with a cosmopolitan context for the United
> States' increasing role in international affairs. By incorporating China into
> a vision of diverse international cultures sharing in a common democratic
> and liberal ideological vision, Buck contributed to popular understand-
> ings of the United States as a beacon of light and freedom for the world.[5]

Buck's accounts of China and its people, which took the form of novels, short stories, private letters, political commentaries, and invited lectures, encouraged Americans both to see the Chinese with empathy and to recognize the U.S. responsibility to help bring about a better China modeled on American ideals of liberal humanism and democracy.

Within the realm of cinematic images and narratives, perhaps no film embodies the ideology of the China mystique better than *The Good Earth*. As a point of comparison, it is sufficient to mention some of the more well known films and characters from the first few decades of the twentieth century to indicate the cinematic landscape from which *The Good Earth* emerged.[6] Some of the most popular serial films of the teens featured "Oriental" villains, though the two most well known films of the decade with Asian characters are probably *The Cheat* (Cecil B. DeMille, 1915), starring Sessue Hayakawa as a predatory "Burmese" ivory king,[7] and *Broken Blossoms* (D. W. Griffith, 1919), with Richard Barthelmess in yellowface as a homesick, lovesick Chinese man in London's equivalent of Chinatown, the Limehouse district. Although Hayakawa's character was ruthless and threatening while Barthelmess's was timid and gentle, both shared a prohibited desire for white women, and both were portrayed in exotic terms.

The most notorious of the evil Orientals, Dr. Fu Manchu, made his cinematic debut in the English serial film *The Mystery of Dr. Fu Manchu* (A. E. Coleby, 1923). The first of many U.S. productions featuring the fiendish doctor was *The Mysterious Dr. Fu Manchu* (Rowland V. Lee, 1929) starring Warner Oland.[8] The Fu Manchu films continued with *The Return of Dr. Fu Manchu* (Rowland V. Lee, 1930), *Daughter of the Dragon*

(Lloyd Corrigan, 1931), and *The Mask of Fu Manchu* (Charles Brabin, 1932).

In the 1930s, China's political instability provided new kinds of story lines about Chinese warlords, as in *Shanghai Express* (Josef von Sternberg, 1932), *The Bitter Tea of General Yen* (Frank Capra, 1933), and *The General Died at Dawn* (Lewis Milestone, 1936), all of which provoked protests from the Chinese government. However, as Dorothy B. Jones writes, these controversial representations of the political situation in China soon began to give way to a more "realistic" type of representation. This new perspective resulted at least partly from concern over China and the "Manchurian question" (the Japanese invasion of Manchuria in 1931).[9] According to Jones, the number of nonfiction shorts or documentaries made about China increased fourfold between the 1920s and the following decade. She also discerns a new, more sympathetic approach in fiction films, evident in features such as *Oil for the Lamps of China* (Mervyn LeRoy, 1935).[10] *The Good Earth*, however, marks a decisive break with past representations: this film showed the Chinese "not as strange, mysterious, fictional characters of another world, but as human beings whose life story was very much like the life story of people anywhere else in the world."[11] Jones describes *The Good Earth* as a landmark of sorts, a predecessor to a "factual and realistic approach in the feature film on China."[12] However, unlike the films that accompanied Holmes's travel lectures or the actualities produced by the Edison filmmakers, *The Good Earth* is a fictional narrative, and the screen version conforms to all of the conventions of a classical Hollywood film.

Despite *The Good Earth*'s status as an imaginary construction, studio publicists promoted the film as a way to see and learn about China, and newspaper and magazine critics wrote of the film as a source of knowledge of China and the Chinese. Furthermore, the terms of this promotion and reception were remarkably similar to those that framed Holmes's illustrated travel lectures and Edison's films of China "photographed from life." The embrace of *The Good Earth* as a form of virtual travel to China and its reception as a reliable source of information about the country and its people provides a striking example of how a fictional film shot only partially on location in China could produce knowledge of a faraway place and people. Early actuality films had highlighted the technological capabilities of cinema within existing discourses of travel to frame the films as virtual visions of life in distant lands. In contrast, *The Good Earth* was persuasive for reasons far beyond cinema's ability to reproduce moving photographic images. Given the enormous changes in cinema as an institution from its earliest incarnations to the classical Hollywood era, how, and in what form, did cinema continue to operate as a machine of virtual travel, and what role did location shooting play in producing "authentic" imaginary geographies?

This chapter begins with an overview of how Buck's novel was received as an accurate representation of China. I then discuss the meaning of authenticity in mid-twentieth-century Hollywood films. The debates about the accuracy of Buck's works focused on whether they were correct or true representations; Buck, her supporters, and her critics all believed that the stakes of this question were considerable. In contrast, in the case of Hollywood films, authenticity was a far more loosely defined and amorphous term that originated when filmmakers attempted to minimize the economic consequences of negative or offensive racial or national representations. These two related yet distinct modes of evaluation, along with the changing views of how China reflected the promise of the U.S. role in the world, set the terms for how the cinematic adaptation of *The Good Earth* was both produced and received. Within these contexts, my analysis of the production history of *The Good Earth* will examine how the machinery of Hollywood film promotion and marketing in the 1930s used discourses of travel, shooting on location, and cinematic verisimilitude to create a belief that the film's version of China was authentic. Rather than foregrounding the text of the film, this chapter will emphasize the discourses surrounding its production and reception. In particular, drawing on a theory of film reception and intertextuality elaborated by Barbara Klinger, I explain how audiences were encouraged to see a fictional narrative film primarily shot in California as an authentic vision of China. At issue is not whether the film offers a "true" representation of China but rather how the studio attempted to assure audiences of the legitimacy of their production and how this production contributed to a shift in U.S. orientalist visions of China and of the United States in relation to China.

Representing China

Before the academic institutionalization of Asian studies, missionaries were the group of Americans most familiar with Chinese culture and practically the only ones with any knowledge of the Chinese language.[13]

An account of U.S. "sentimental imperialism" in East Asia notes that missionaries were the primary source of firsthand knowledge of China between 1842 and 1942 and thus were a crucial factor in developing U.S. views of and sometimes policies toward the country. Thus,

> Through letters, tracts, books, and speeches, Americans learned more of China from missionaries than from any other single source prior to the coming of sound films and television. Out of such communication grew widely shared national perceptions. Central to them was, inevitably, a hope to help change China—from authoritarian and backward and heathen, to Jeffersonian and progressive and Christian.[14]

Buck's voluminous output of speeches and writings on China educated Americans about the country and its people within this tradition, one that was central to the China mystique. However, her works did not simply extend established missionary positions, for she had a unique perspective, politics, and style; she eventually denounced many aspects of the missionary community and its practices and beliefs. Yet her relationship to China, the expertise and knowledge she gained about the country and its people, and her work representing China to U.S. audiences originated within the world of American missionaries in China. Buck's positioning as a missionary thus framed her writings as authoritative works arising out of a history of Americans who had traveled to China, lived there for significant periods of time, and in some cases even learned the language and customs, all in the hopes of changing the country for the better. It is not surprising, then, that a significant factor in the positive reception of the novel *The Good Earth* was the belief that it offered an accurate portrayal of a country that was believed to have been long misrepresented as exotic and mysterious in the United States.

The John Day Company published Buck's first novel, *East Wind, West Wind* (1930). The manuscript had a divided reception among the staff, but Richard Walsh, the president of the company (and Buck's future second husband), saw promise in her writing and believed her later work would be even better.[15] His instincts proved correct, and her second novel, *The Good Earth* (1931) garnered almost unanimous acclaim from reviewers and critics. The epic story begins with farmer Wang Lung's marriage to O-lan, a "slave girl" at the great House of Hwang, and then follows the birth of their children and their efforts to acquire more land. They refuse to sell their land even in the midst of a severe drought but are eventually forced to migrate south in search of food and livelihood. They eventually return to their homestead, and the family prospers to the point of taking over the former House of Hwang. The children mature, O-lan dies, and Wang Lung enters old age. The novel concludes with a hint of the cyclical nature of history as Wang's sons plot to sell off some of their land.

The Good Earth was a Book-of-the-Month Club main selection and the best-selling book of both 1931 and 1932.[16] It received a Pulitzer Prize and was an important factor in the decision to award Buck the 1938 Nobel Prize in literature; she was the first American woman to receive this honor. In late 1931, Metro-Goldwyn-Mayer paid fifty thousand dollars—at the time the largest sum ever offered by Hollywood for a novel—for the film rights to The Good Earth.[17] The film's production ultimately spanned three years, three different directors, and nearly three million dollars. It won two Academy Awards and reached an estimated twenty-three million American viewers and forty-two million viewers worldwide.[18] In his 1958 study of images of China and India in the United States, Harold Isaacs writes, "No single book about China has had a greater impact than [Buck's] famous novel, The Good Earth."[19] A more recent commentator on Buck's work cites the number of readers of The Good Earth and viewers of the film to conclude that "it is safe to say that no non-Chinese writer in history since Marco Polo (in the thirteenth century) had such an influence on so many millions of people on the subject of China."[20]

In its review of The Good Earth, the New York Times Book Review noted,

> One cannot doubt that Mrs. Buck knows her China. Except for her college years in the United States, she has spent the greater part of her life there. But she portrays a China unfamiliar to the average reader, a China in which, happily, there is no hint of mystery or exoticism. There is very little in her book of the quality which we are accustomed to label "Oriental." Her interpretation of life in the Far East is as far removed from Lafcadio Hearn, on the one hand, as it is from Hollywood on the other.[21]

Most reviews of the novel described The Good Earth as a more accurate and therefore less fantastic representation of "life in the Far East" than those of Hollywood films and nineteenth-century travel writers (though it should be noted that Lafcadio Hearn was known for his works on

Japan, not China). Reviewers often mentioned Buck's long residence in China, which would become an important element of Buck's developing public persona. However, among the mostly adulatory notices of Buck's novel in the United States and worldwide, including China, were two notable dissenting critiques, both from North America: a review penned by Korean American writer Younghill Kang published in the *New Republic* in 1931, and a lengthy critique by Kiang Kang-hu, professor of Chinese studies at McGill University in Montreal, that first appeared in the *Chinese Christian Student* in 1932 and was reprinted, with a reply from Buck, in the *New York Times Book Review* in 1933.[22] These contestations make explicit the terms and stakes of the debate over the representation of China in *The Good Earth* that MGM would inherit. Before turning to the film, I offer a more detailed look at these two significant challenges to Buck's authority as an interpreter of China as well as the accuracy of her novel.

Kang charged that *The Good Earth*'s emphasis on romantic love ran contrary to the ideals of a Confucian society:

> Since Mrs. Buck does not understand the meaning of the Confucian separation of man's kingdom from that of woman, she is like someone trying to write a story of the European Middle Ages without understanding the rudiments of chivalric standards and the institutions of Christianity. None of her major descriptions is correct except in minor details.[23]

The editors of the publication appended a comment to the end of the review defending *The Good Earth*, stating that in their opinion, Kang "neglects the literary qualities of a narrative which, among those published during the past season, was one of the very few that aroused a lasting enthusiasm." They explained their decision to print the review by conceding, "because the story is so simple and effective that its accuracy has been taken for granted—*The Good Earth* deserves to be discussed from the standpoint of an Oriental [*sic*] familiar with the standards that underline Chinese life."[24] This editorial statement relies on an equation of racial identity with cultural authority, granting Kang's review a weighty relevance because of its origins. The editors clearly ignore the fact that Kang was Korean rather than Chinese and assume that the Confucian tradition is the same across East Asian cultures.

A longer and more sustained critique of Buck's work, including *The Good Earth*, appeared in the form of Kiang's "A Chinese Scholar's View of Mrs. Buck's Novels." Kiang's article turns on an analogy as well, but rather than using writing as his example, Kiang references Chinese painting—in particular, the ancestral portrait. These portraits adhere to very specific conventions and utilize particular techniques; Kiang argues that Westerners, whether writers or painters, work according to different kinds of representational guidelines than do the Chinese. Kiang also provides a detailed inventory of objections to details of *The Good Earth*, characterizing Buck's accounts of sexuality as "pathetic and unhealthy" and disapproving of what he sees as the undue influence of "coolies and amahs" on Buck. He allows, "There are, of course, among them many honest and good country folk, hard working and faithfully serving as domestic helpers," but he also believes, "Their idea of life is inevitably strange and their common knowledge is indeed very limited. They may form the majority of the Chinese population, but they are certainly not representative of the Chinese people." Kiang goes on to assert that "the great harm is that the reader would naturally be led to imagine China from this picture and to form his judgment upon it accordingly; the writer has thus consciously or unconsciously rendered a most unwelcome service to the country in which she was reared and still lives." He concludes by suggesting that Buck's talents might be better utilized in the translation of Chinese novels, and he offers his view that as long as Chinese coolies and amahs, rather than Chinese literature, are the main source of information about Chinese culture, Westerners cannot hope to understand China no matter how long they live in the country.[25] Kiang's challenge goes further than Kang's in that it questions not only Buck's knowledge of Chinese culture, including her sources, but also her choice of culturally specific aesthetic traditions and conventions. Kiang concludes by acknowledging Buck's long residence in China; however, while this experience functioned elsewhere as a guarantee of the truth of her writing, Kiang disputes the belief that the mere fact of living in a place can produce credible knowledge of it.

Buck's reply to Kiang was published along with his piece in the *New York Times Book Review*. Her impassioned response is instructive, not least for its skilled deployment of various guarantees of cultural authority. She begins by acknowledging that her representation does indeed depart from the conventional portraits of Chinese subjects, but she defends her version by suggesting, "Anyone who knows those portraits must realize how far from the truth of life they are."[26] She therefore concedes what Kiang calls her "failure" to conform to established conventions but justifies her method as a deliberate favoring of "the truth of life" over "the portrait with the official button." Buck also responds methodically to each of Kiang's charges of errors in the representation of Chinese culture and customs by recounting instances in which she personally witnessed the behaviors or actions in question. She further argues that the wide variation in local customs in China makes it difficult to generalize about "Chinese customs" in narrow and absolute terms. Each of her anecdotes confirms yet again Buck's real familiarity with Chinese culture, especially since all are written in the first person, but her most pointed remarks go even further, turning the tables of the debate to question Kiang's legitimacy as a representative of the Chinese people: "When [Kiang] says 'They'—meaning the common people of China—'may form the majority of the population in China, but they certainly are not representative of the Chinese people,' I cannot but ask, if the majority in any country does not represent the country, then who can?" She continues,

> But I know what Professor Kiang would have: there are others like him. They want the Chinese people represented by the little handful of her intellectuals, and they want the vast, rich, somber, joyous Chinese life represented solely by literature that is ancient and classic. These are valuable and assuredly a part of Chinese civilization, but they form only the official buttons. For shall the people be counted as nothing, the splendid common people of China, living their tremendous lusty life against the odds of a calamitous nature, a war-torn government, a small, indifferent aristocracy of intellectuals? For truth's sake I can never agree to it.[27]

Whereas Kiang questioned Buck's ability as a Westerner to represent China accurately, Buck situates Kiang within a "small, indifferent" intellectual elite, far removed from and certainly not representative of "the common people" of China, the majority of the population and the primary subjects of her novels.

Finally, although Kiang accuses her of doing a disservice to China in her work, Buck refrains from judging the influence of her writing, choosing to allow time to determine those effects. However, she mentions receiving numerous letters from readers attesting to the way in which her work aroused their interest in China and humanized the Chinese. She concludes,

> For myself, I have no sense of mission or of doing any service. I write because it is in my nature so to do, and I can write only what I know, and I know nothing but China, having always lived there. I have few friends of

my own race, almost none intimate, and so I write about the people I do know. They are the people in China I love best to live among, the everyday people, who care nothing for official buttons.[28]

Buck's assertions about the lack of motive or intent behind her writing and her choice of China as a subject are disingenuous, but rhetorically, they naturalize her work as spontaneous representations of her lived experience in China. Who can speak for China? Kiang, identified as a "Chinese scholar" in the title of his review, and as Buck's "Chinese critic" in the title of her reply, draws authority from his racial and national identity as well as his academic credentials, while Buck writes from a lifetime of experience among "the common people" of China. Buck was a white American woman. Yet as her response to Kiang demonstrates, she used the facts of her residence in China and the depth of her familiarity with Chinese culture and customs to hold her own as a representative of the Chinese people against the challenge of a "Chinese scholar," not an easy task.

Authenticity in Context

As a Hollywood product, MGM's film would not be evaluated by the same standards of accuracy as Buck's novel. In addition, as a fictional narrative, the film would be constructed according to very different principles than those governing either early cinema actualities or contemporaneous documentary films. At the same time, the studio not only hoped but also worked to ensure that their film would benefit from its associations with the accuracy and authority of Buck's representations of China. The challenges that MGM faced in determining a "factual and realistic approach" to a film set in a faraway land such as China were hardly unusual, except that the stakes were perhaps higher given the film's source material. In "A Veteran's View of Hollywood Authenticity" (1950), Louis van den Ecker explains the responsibilities of a technical adviser on Hollywood films, particularly in ensuring the authenticity of a film's portrayal of distant times, places, and cultures.[29] Although the article was published a decade and a half after the release of *The Good Earth*, van den Ecker's conception of cinematic authenticity was derived from films, incidents, and discourses dating back to the 1920s. The article therefore articulates many of the issues facing producers of films set in distant historical periods or faraway places that shaped how MGM understood and established authenticity in *The Good Earth.*

A brief introductory biographical statement informs the reader that van den Ecker had served in the Belgian army, the French Foreign Legion, and the Polish army; had seen action in World War I; and since 1923 had been employed as a technical adviser on more than forty feature films. This opening establishes his credentials and authority for writing the article, not an insignificant matter given the topic at hand. He attributes the desire for greater authenticity in films to Hollywood's hopes of avoiding the economic consequences of negative representations of "foreign subjects":

> For the greater number of producers in Hollywood, authenticity has become a byword. This has come about primarily because of the endless stream of letters that once arrived from all parts of the world protesting and criticizing misrepresentations, anachorisms [something out of place in or foreign to a country], anachronisms, and other blunders committed in the making of motion pictures. . . . The greatest danger in making pictures on foreign subjects is the possibility of giving offense to foreign nations. The misrepresentation of foreign mannerisms in earlier pictures, and especially the representation of unjustified cruelties by foreign characters in order, supposedly, to strengthen dramatic values, touched the dignity of certain groups and institutions abroad, with the result that certain pictures were banned in a number of countries. The consequent loss of income led to a decision to do things right. And the *technical adviser* was born.[30]

Ruth Vasey provides a more detailed version of the history of Hollywood's foreign relations, marking the beginning of industry awareness of the economic consequences of offending foreign nations with Mexico's 1922 decision to ban the entire output of companies that had been producing films with negative representations of Mexican villains. The Motion Picture Producers and Distributors of America addressed this issue at its first board meeting on April 13, 1922, resolving to "do everything possible to prevent the production of any new motion picture films which present the Mexican character in a derogatory or objectionable manner" and authorizing an industry representative to travel to Mexico.[31] To the extent that the association "initiated negotiations at a diplomatic level, and in its designation of film content as a site of negotiation between the industry and its foreign markets, this early Mexican episode

anticipated practices that would increasingly characterize the association's foreign policy in the 1920s and 1930s."[32] Such practices played a
critical role in the negotiations between MGM and the Chinese government over the production of *The Good Earth.*

Although van den Ecker's article initially foregrounds challenges to
Hollywood's stereotypes of foreign mannerisms and characters, it ultimately leaves behind these kinds of examples to discuss a broad range of
relatively straightforward and even somewhat banal issues. Since the inception of the technical adviser, van den Ecker proudly asserts, "The mistake of placing an obstetrical instrument on an operation table in a military hospital scene is a thing of the past."[33] Another instance in which a
technical adviser came to the rescue was noticing the presence of a basket-
ful of potatoes in a French marketplace. The problem was that the scene
was set during the reign of Louis XIII, but potatoes were not cultivated in
France until the era of Louis XVI.[34] At other times, van den Ecker, in his
role as technical adviser, was called on to verify the details of national military uniforms.[35] The work of a technical adviser is thus initially represented as a simple process of evaluating the diegetic world of the film according to the standards of reality and recommending any necessary
adjustments to bring the world of the film in line with the world itself.
Midway through the article, however, van den Ecker complicates matters
by adding, "Yet there may be exceptions to the rule of authenticity."[36]

While economic considerations were one of the primary motives behind the push for greater authenticity in Hollywood films, the considerable expenses that could be incurred in striving for authenticity also
called for flexibility. Van den Ecker recommends that technical advisers
"never interrupt the shooting of a scene unless the loss caused by the in-
terruption is smaller than the value of the mistake that is in the making."[37] According to this logic, some errors are literally not worth the
time and money necessary to correct them. This cost-benefit analysis offers an explicit reminder that film studios came to appreciate authenticity not because they aspired to reproduce reality more precisely but
rather because they hoped to avoid offense. Another significant con-
straint on the pursuit of authenticity is introduced in van den Ecker's insistence on the importance of narrative: "Technical advisers must possess enough of the dramatic instinct to sacrifice absolute authenticity
when it is in conflict with the values of a scene. As long as the action
seems logical and effective, license should be taken and a compromise established."[38] The technical adviser's responsibilities ultimately appear to

be best understood as defensive ones; the adviser acts as a bulwark against errors that might lessen the credibility of the drama in the eyes of the audience and lead to negative economic repercussions. What had at first seemed a clear-cut process of identifying and correcting mistakes becomes considerably more ambiguous.

Authenticity begins as an absolute term; historical and cultural details are either correct or incorrect. But when balanced against the cost of interruptions to the filmmaking process and the centrality of the all-important story, authenticity becomes a relative standard. In the end, a film needs merely to be authentic enough to pass muster among review boards, audiences, and critics. Nevertheless, van den Ecker concludes with a strong statement of authenticity's value: "A few directors may be impatient with the criticisms and suggestions of the technical adviser, but the majority welcome them and are eager to profit by them. As a result, most Hollywood scenes involving past history or strange places are presented with amazing accuracy so far as physical investiture and action are concerned."[39] The appearance of *amazing accuracy* in a sentence where *authenticity* might be expected is striking. The use of the word *accuracy,* which does not appear elsewhere in the article, implies that technical advisers enabled Hollywood to produce "precise, correct, and truthful" films, to recall a few common synonyms for *accurate.* However, van den Ecker shows how often truth and the details of reality must give way to economics and the demands of narrative, which makes his use of the phrase *amazing accuracy* hyperbolic.

Although the difference between *accuracy* and *authenticity* is not obvious, particularly since their meanings overlap to some degree and they are sometimes used interchangeably in popular discussions of films of "past history or strange places," it is useful for analytical purposes to distinguish between the two. In her study of the Hollywood historical epic, Vivian Sobchack notes the frequent appearance of concepts of accuracy and authenticity in the advertising rhetoric of the genre.[40] However, she explains, "*authenticity* and *accuracy* are not synonymous terms in relation to the Hollywood epic's system of equivalencies intended to generate a 'history effect.'"[41] She looks to the essays accompanying a Los Angeles County Museum of Art exhibition, Hollywood and History: Costume Design in Film, for examples:

We are told that "Max Factor supplied Twentieth Century-Fox with 4,402 period wigs 'authentic to the last curl.'" However, this authenticity is transparently invoked in an essay specifically indicating that women's wigs in Hollywood historical epics were *never* accurate representations. Similarly, we find out that perceived authenticity of costume depends only on *partial* accuracy.[42]

Although the issues surrounding the cinematic adaptation of *The Good Earth* revolve around representing another place rather than another time, this distinction between accuracy and authenticity remains relevant. In these examples and for my purposes, *accuracy* signifies a close proximity to "reality," whether of a distant time or place, whereas *authenticity* suggests a looser representation of "reality" that is nevertheless presumed to have some grounding in it. In the positive reviews of Buck's novel, an entity known as China was presumed to exist in stable form, and Buck's work was measured against this reality and deemed accurate because it was thought to closely approximate "China." What MGM needed to achieve in its adaptation of *The Good Earth* was not so much an accurate as an authentic representation. Their film would be measured not by its proximity to a given reality but rather by its credibility and legitimacy as a Hollywood version of China that had an identifiable basis in "China" even if certain elements of the film departed from this reality.

As van den Ecker implies, accuracy could be a matter of significant political import. In the early days of the industry, according to van den Ecker, "the general attitude was 'Who knows what is right or wrong, anyway?'" However, according to van den Ecker, "the number of letters proved that many knew."[43] During the 1930s, the Chinese government often acted as the arbiter of the truth of Hollywood's visions of the Chinese, expressing its objections in stronger terms than merely letters of protest. Given the history of Hollywood representations of China and the Chinese, the Chinese government had good reason to be vigilant. According to Vasey,

> Like Mexico, China had been sufficiently insulted by Hollywood's characterizations of its citizens to be suspicious of . . . claims that movies were agents of international amity. Hollywood's propensity to represent Chinese characters as vulgar stereotypes, combined with its historical preference for Chinese villains and the exacerbating factor of Britain's representational influence, gave Chinese diplomats in the United States sufficient cause to be on their guard.[44]

Vasey reports that Harold Lloyd's first talkie, *Welcome Danger* (Clyde Bruckman, 1929) was banned by the Chinese government in 1930 for its negative representations of San Francisco's Chinatown residents. Several other countries rejected the film following a Chinese diplomatic campaign.[45] Other films that faced censure by the Chinese government included *Shanghai Express* and *The Bitter Tea of General Yen*. *Shanghai Express* starred Marlene Dietrich, with Anna May Wong in one of her better-known roles. The story, which centered on a Peking-to-Shanghai train hijacked by a rebel army commander played by Warner Oland, provoked objections from the Chinese government.[46] The Film Censorship Committee in China threatened to ban all Paramount films from the country unless copies of *Shanghai Express* were removed from the worldwide market; the threat was withdrawn after the two parties reached an agreement. Paramount issued an apology and expressed its intent to refrain from producing future offensive characterizations of the Chinese.[47] The Chinese also criticized *The Bitter Tea of General Yen*, with the gentlemanly General Yen portrayed by Nils Asther and Barbara Stanwyck as his captive. The film proved controversial within the domestic U.S. market for its intimation of interracial romance, while in China what drew fire was its representation of the Chinese political scene. Eric Smoodin's careful examination of the negotiations among Columbia Pictures, the State Department, and Chinese officials over *The Bitter Tea of General Yen* concludes that "the American film industry may have controlled the world market, but the Hollywood studios simply could not impose their will on foreign theaters and viewers."[48]

This contentious history was not forgotten when MGM requested permission to film in China for *The Good Earth*. Filming on location commonly occasioned diplomatic contact between a studio and a foreign country's government. In Vasey's words, "The cultivation of official favor was important in these instances both because it expedited practical matters surrounding production and because it enhanced the American industry's prestige and trading status."[49] Charles Clarke, a cameraman with the MGM crew sent to China, reported that after arriving, the party waited three months for the official decision regarding whether they would be permitted to shoot. He attributes the government's hesitation to the history of cinematic representations of the Chinese: "The first necessity was, of course, to secure the requisite Government cooperation and permits. This proved a slow and involved process; the Chinese have so repeatedly been misrepresented in both American and European films that they have, quite justifiably, come to have a profound mistrust of motion picture people." However, according to Clarke, one evening Chiang Kai-shek "amused himself by going to the cinema, where he saw a film of the 'Dr. Fu-Manchu' school."[50] The negative stereotypes featured in the film, identified as *The Mask of Fu Manchu* (Charles Brabin, 1932) in Jay Leyda's account of the incident, supposedly persuaded Chiang to grant the necessary permissions to MGM.[51] (The studio presumably downplayed or otherwise evaded the fact that *The Mask of Fu Manchu* was an MGM production.)

Clarke speculates that Chiang reasoned, "If our group, who wished to film 'The Good Earth,' and to show the Chinese as the human beings they really are, were denied permission to photograph their scenes, surely . . . we would go home and continue to produce the objectionable 'yellow peril' films. Hence it was far better to help us, rather than to hinder."[52] Although Clarke's ability to know Chiang's thoughts is questionable, the story is still instructive because it reveals how the producers imagined *The Good Earth* as a different kind of film from its predecessors. Furthermore, it seems reasonable to assume that the decision regarding whether to allow MGM to film in China was conditioned to some degree by the government's sense of what kind of a film MGM would make. Presumably, a film like *The Good Earth*, produced by a cooperative studio, would be a welcome departure from the familiar Hollywood vilification of the Chinese. Clarke implies that this promise of producing a more positive kind of representation was then leveraged to obtain access to Chinese locations and more general cooperation from the government.[53]

In the 1930s, the Chinese Nationalist government under Chiang's leadership was struggling for legitimacy. Officials faced military uprisings from the nascent Chinese Communist Party and Japanese encroachment on Chinese territory. Without overstating the importance of film, at this critical historical moment, the government recognized the significance of the kind of representation of China presented by a Hollywood prestige picture, especially one based on a prizewinning and bestselling novel. By participating in the process of making *The Good Earth*, the Chinese government could influence the production of the film rather than only reacting to it after the fact. At the same time, Metro-Goldwyn-Mayer depended more heavily on foreign sales than did most other studios and was therefore particularly sensitive to the concerns of foreign governments that had the power to both directly and indirectly affect international sales.[54] This was especially true for a high-profile picture such as *The Good Earth*. By establishing and then maintaining contact with the Chinese throughout the making of *The Good Earth*, the studio avoided potentially damaging and expensive objections to the film after its release.

A 1937 report issued by China's Central News Agency describes some of the details of the negotiations between MGM and the Chinese government regarding *The Good Earth*, which ultimately extended far beyond permission to film in China. The Chinese vice consul in Los Angeles heard of MGM's plans to adapt Buck's novel and first expressed concerns regarding the film. (While the report does not mention specific objections, it is likely that the Chinese government viewed unfavorably the novel's depictions of extreme poverty.) Next, the Chinese embassy in Washington, D.C., was consulted, and finally, officials in Nanking reviewed the matter. The Ministries of the Interior and of Education eventually agreed to the production but stipulated that the film would be subject to the regulations governing the making of foreign films in China.[55] Talks between the studio and the Chinese government resulted in an unusual six-point formal agreement. First, "the film should present a truthful and pleasant picture of China and her people." The second through fifth points involved the government's degree of control over the film, including the ability to appoint a representative whose suggestions would be taken seriously by the studio, the possibility of adding a preface authored by the Chinese government, and the requirement that footage taken in China be approved by the Chinese censor. Finally, "the Chinese Government hopes that the cast in the picture will be all Chinese."[56] Although the cast ultimately was not entirely Chinese, the studio fulfilled most of its other obligations. For example, a government representative, General Tu Ting-hsiu (referred to as General Theodore Tu in many U.S. news reports), was indeed assigned to the picture, and he stayed with the production until almost the end.[57] The Chinese government approved the film for release in the United States in January 1937 and for release in China later that spring with some scenes excised. Deleted scenes included those showing deprivation and poverty, such as refugees fallen by the wayside and O-lan and her children begging in the southern city, as well as depictions of looting and the disciplining of the looters by soldiers. The scenes suggesting a relationship between Wang's son and Wang's second wife were also removed.

The agreement's first point reveals the difference between accuracy of

the kind at stake in the debates between Buck and her critics and that involved in the negotiations between MGM and the Chinese government.
Unstated yet understood was the government's preference for pleasant-
ness over truth when the two might conflict. MGM's willingness to accommodate official concerns led the Chinese government to cooperate
in the production of the film, including granting permission to film in
China, which was certainly conducive to *The Good Earth*'s protest-free
release and distribution and its reception as a legitimate representation
of China. As Vasey points out, "The 'property' for which producers were
prepared to pay such high prices was less the literary source itself than its
reputation and the attendant advance publicity, which could be secured
for the price of the movie rights. As in so many of Hollywood's business
dealings, the most negotiable factor in the transaction was film content."[58] But to win over audiences and to make the most of the reputation of the literary source, MGM would need to do more than simply
avoid offensive characterizations. The production history of *The Good
Earth* suggests that MGM took seriously the charge of representing
China. At various moments, studio officials considered but ultimately
rejected the possibility of shooting the film entirely on location in China,
of using an all-Chinese cast, and of employing subtitled Mandarin Chinese dialogue. The studio's claim that the film was an authentic portrayal
of China—apparently reinforced by the popular press—nevertheless remained a key factor in the promotion of the film and in the film's reception.

"China" in California: The Making and Selling of
The Good Earth

The theatrical adaptation of *The Good Earth* previewed in Philadelphia
before opening at New York's Nixon Theatre on October 17, 1932. The
play, adapted by Owen Davis and Donald Davis, starred Claude Rains as
Wang Lung, Alla Nazimova as O-lan, Henry Travers as the father, and
Sydney Greenstreet as the uncle. Buck's contract with the Davises gave
her the authority to determine "all points of racial and national accuracy
... a court of last resort in respect to any questions as to ... Chinese civilization, life, and custom."[59] Buck was, in effect, acting as a technical adviser of the type that van den Ecker promoted, though for a play rather
than a film. Despite Buck's involvement, the play received mixed reviews.

Privately, Buck expressed the opinion that European and American actors could not convincingly play her Chinese characters.[60] Many critics expressed similar opinions in their published reviews.

During the lengthy production of the cinematic adaptation of her novel, Buck did not act as an adviser regarding the details of Chinese culture, although she did offer fairly detailed suggestions to the studio early in the film's production history.[61] On August 24, 1932, Buck wrote to MGM's J. Robert Rubin: "My dear Mr. Rubin, I have been thinking over the making of the motion picture, THE GOOD EARTH, and especially how we could help you in the matter of its accurcay [sic]." Her letter detailed the best times of year to travel in China, suggestions for how to work with the Chinese government, potential Chinese motion picture company partners, particular cities and regions of China that might serve as appropriate locations for specific scenes, and pragmatic advice about allowing plenty of time and patience for working in China. She also advised that the studio ensure that "the men whom you send there be of such a personal character as not to make any unfortunate contacts with Chinese women, or you may find a great deal of trouble on your hands."[62] In light of these recommendations, shooting on location in China appeared to be a foregone conclusion. The only question was where in China, since many of the locations Buck had in mind while writing the novel had changed enough in the intervening years that they would no longer be suitable for the scenes that took place there.

Buck also supported using an all-Chinese cast, though she acknowledged that this decision lay with the studio: "The Chinese have such remarkable dramatic instinct and there are so many natural actors among them that I should think among those more trained such as you might find in a motion picture company, you would be able to choose suitable persons."[63] Trade publications and studio memos indicate that Irving Thalberg, the producer of the film, intended to shoot the film in China using Chinese actors.[64] MGM first sent personnel to China in mid-November 1932 to screen-test Chinese actors and obtain background footage. George Hill, the first director of the film, went to China in 1933 to oversee location shots and screen tests, and tests of Chinese actors in China continued through 1933 and early 1934. In addition, on November 6, 1933, Hill informed Ben Piazza of MGM's casting department of the decision to use Mandarin Chinese rather than some other Chinese dialect and to dub it in if necessary.[65] Surviving documents from the early stages of the film's production also include a detailed inventory of screen tests of Chinese actors, records of background footage taken of land-scapes and cultural activities, and a list of phonetic pronunciations of some basic Mandarin Chinese words and phrases. These traces of MGM's work and travels in China offer remarkable reminders of the se-riousness with which the studio approached this project and the scope of its early ambitions to represent China to U.S. and global film audiences.

Sometime in 1933, the decision was made not to shoot *The Good Earth* on location in China.[66] Instead, the film was shot on a five-hun-dred-acre location in Chatsworth, California, a short drive from Holly-wood, although some of the footage shot in China was used for back-grounds and as references for the art department, and an enormous number of objects were purchased in China for use in the film. Many Chinese and Chinese American actors were tested, but the lead roles went to European American actors. In retrospect, this casting decision appears almost inevitable given that, as Hye Seung Chung notes, "during the 1930s and 1940s, major Asian roles were played by Caucasian stars (such as Katherine Hepburn, Walter Huston, Boris Karloff, Peter Lorre, Paul Muni, Warner Oland, Luise Rainer, Edward G. Robinson, Myrna Loy, and Loretta Young) in yellowface, and only minor or character parts were available to real Asian American actors."[67] Yet the press coverage of the film's preproduction efforts and studio correspondence suggest that MGM at least entertained the possibility of casting Chinese actors as the leads, however improbable that idea might seem today. According to one account, Hill eventually became resigned to shooting the film in Califor-nia but remained committed to using an entire cast of Chinese actors. He apparently did not learn of the studio's interest in casting Caucasian ac-tors in the lead roles until he read of it in the MGM bulletin *Studio News*.[68] No evidence indicates that any Chinese American actors were considered for the role of Wang Lung, and Anna May Wong, who had hoped for the role of O-lan, was reportedly considered only for the role of Wang Lung's second wife, Lotus, a prostitute in the book who was transformed into a "sing song girl" in the film. In the end, she played nei-ther.[69] Chinese Americans ultimately received a number of minor roles, and they swelled the ranks of the extras. Along with the decision to use Euro-American actors as the leads came the choice to perform the dia-logue in English. Despite the film's departure from its improbably ambi-tious earlier plans, the publicity and popular discourse surrounding the film continued to insist on its authenticity, suggesting just how invaluable the idea was to this production yet also how malleable the definition of *authentic* could be.

If *The Good Earth* had been shot on location in China starring Chinese actors speaking Chinese, the studio might have used the views of China and the images and sounds of Chinese people speaking their native language (if they were Mandarin speakers) to establish the film's proximity to the reality of China—that is, its accuracy. Such a film could have taken advantage of the verisimilitude associated with the cinematic medium in a manner similar to early films despite the addition of the fictional narrative; the images of the country and its people captured by the camera and filmmakers on location would enable audiences to see China through a form of virtual travel. These glimpses of what might have been are certainly tantalizing given the final version of the film. However, as important as accuracy was, it could not be the only or even the most important consideration in determining where and how to make the film. The fascination of *The Good Earth* as an example lies precisely in this disjuncture between the demands and constraints of a studio-produced fictional narrative of the 1930s and the filmmaker's initial ambitions for the film.

Shooting a classical Hollywood film entirely on location in China in the 1930s would have been an immense undertaking. The fact that the studio even considered this possibility, along with using Chinese actors speaking Chinese, attests to the importance of the shooting location, choice of actors, and language in producing a legitimate representation of China. Perhaps, in line with the ideology of the China mystique, the studio even had a genuine desire to contribute to a better understanding of China among U.S. audiences, although this is difficult to gauge. Yet the costs of producing an accurate film had to be weighed against the film's ability to recoup the investment of the studio's resources. These calculations resulted in a film rooted in the reality of China yet constrained by Hollywood dictates. In other words, MGM would make an authentic film of China that was only partially accurate.

Once the studio decided to shoot principal photography in California and cast two Euro-American stars as the leads, it emphasized the travels and labors of the MGM crew on location in China as signifiers of the film's authenticity. Deprived of the direct, indexical link between film and place that shooting on location could provide, the studio used discourses of authenticity to emphasize a series of more mediated relationships between the reality of China and the images recorded on film. One definition of authenticity in a film such as *The Good Earth* was its approval for screening by the Chinese government. In a climate of heightened sensitivity regarding the kind of representation of a nation and its peoples a high-profile Hollywood film presented, the absence of official objections to the film not only facilitated the global distribution of the film but also tacitly signaled the government's acceptance of its characterizations and plot. Next, I consider how *The Good Earth* was promoted as an authentic film to audiences even though the studio departed from what would most straightforwardly constitute authentic methods of production. These promotional efforts were undertaken both by the studio and by other institutions such as the mass media that, while not direct instruments of the studio, nevertheless aided the studio in publicizing its films.

Although the trade papers reported on the tribulations associated with the production of *The Good Earth,* from negotiations for the rights to the novel to casting conundrums to MGM's lease of the location in Chatsworth, articles intended for a general audience were, as was typical, more selective in how they represented the film. Typically, these articles assured readers that the film was indeed authentic, as evidenced by a detailed report on the film's production history. How might knowledge of *The Good Earth*'s production shape how a viewer sees the film? Barbara Klinger offers a useful framework for analyzing how the texts surrounding *The Good Earth* encouraged viewers to accept the film as a form of knowledge of China.

Klinger argues that "digressions" in the reception of a film, understood as instances when the spectator "respond[s] to filmic moments in excess of their function within the narrative," are in fact important modes of intertextual engagement with processes of commodification.[70] She begins with Roland Barthes's and Umberto Eco's theories of the role of intertextuality in the process of reading and then further narrows her focus by turning to Theodor Adorno and the Frankfurt School for an understanding of how commodification affects the reception of mass culture. Klinger suggests that the film industry's promotional practices fetishize certain elements of a film to identify the film as a particular type of product. Following Stephen Heath, Klinger refers to such promotional texts as "epiphenomena" and includes among them such materials as posters, ads, trailers, features on the stars or director, specials on the "making of" a film, and objects such as toys and T-shirts.[71] She writes,

"The textual elements foregrounded through the process of com-modification are given to frequent reworking through specific promo-tional inter-texts devoted to extending a film into the social sphere as fully as possible."[72]

Certain elements of a film, according to Klinger, are especially subject to commodification: "characters/stars, subject matter/genre, and style, including mise-en-scène (the setting, costumes, etc.) and cinematogra-phy."[73] In these instances, "The single element in a film—the character a star plays, a scene created by special effects—is never just 'itself,' its func-tion in the narrative, but the source of polysemic extension, grist for other kinds of signification."[74] The "digressions" that take a viewer away from the text of the film therefore result from efforts by the film indus-try to affect the reception of the text: "The spectator who fragments the text according to his/her knowledge of 'mass media gossip' is not incom-petent for want of reproducing the proper reading of a text, but, on the contrary, highly competent in an intertextual sense; the good viewer so-licited by the commercial apparatus."[75] This theory of reception empha-sizes that the audience's interaction with a film involves not just the sounds and images on the screen but also an entire body of texts de-signed to promote the particular film.

In the case of films shot on location, the images of a place in a film (whether the film is fictional or nonfictional) not only provide the set-ting for the actions and events on screen but also result from the travels undertaken by the filmmakers to acquire these images. When the film is a narrative one, the setting functions within two narratives simultane-ously: that of the fictional diegesis and that of the film's production his-tory, a story that can be actively publicized to add value to the film. As Klinger notes, "The most significant aspect of stylistic hype lies in its pre-sentation of background stories on how a certain scene or effect was ac-complished. Promotion provides background stories, as it does in the case of the star, with an emphasis on a behind-the-scenes view of the making of a film that testifies to authorial and technical achievement."[76] Once again, if *The Good Earth* had been filmed on location in China, with Chinese actors speaking Mandarin Chinese, the promotion of the film as a virtual voyage to China might have been relatively straightfor-ward. The problem, however, was that *The Good Earth* was filmed pri-marily in California. As a kind of compensatory act, the publicity for the film highlighted MGM's various travels to and exchanges with China to establish the legitimacy of the film's representation of that country.

The Good Earth opens with a dedication to producer Irving Thalberg, continues with its credit sequence, and then offers an onscreen prologue: "The soul of a great nation is expressed in the life of its humblest people. In this simple story of a Chinese farmer may be found something of the soul of China—its humility, its courage, its deep heritage from the past and its vast promise for the future." In the next shot, the sun rises, creating the effect of a fade-in and gradually bringing light to an agricultural setting with a small stream, a dirt road, and a small house with hills in the background. A series of dissolves shows the community preparing for the day ahead. A farmer sets off for his fields; a woman draws water from a well; a man walks down a road with his ducks; and two water buffalo and one donkey, each yoked to a wagon, trudge over a small bridge along with their masters. A dissolve to the exterior of a modest dwelling is followed by the appearance of text superimposed over the setting: "It was Wang Lung's marriage day." The words remain as the image returns to the opening scene. Is this China or California? According to the film's promotional intertext, the answer is "Both."

A June 1934 article, "The Good Earth: With M.G.M. on Location," reported on the activities of the MGM crew in China at a time when it had already been decided that the film would be shot primarily in California. The article's author clearly appreciated the advantages of shooting a film about China on location in China: "Un-understandable to many is the policy of taking scenes here but having the central action filmed elsewhere." He cited practical reasons for the decision: "Every variety of weather will be used, and the studio equipment is more reliable than the weather man. All the backstage paraphernalia of developing and editing a film is likewise more conveniently located in Culver City." This author also believed in the pedagogical potential of the film, which could "bring to the Occidental an accurate as well as colourful portrayal of China's people, of her culture, of her needs and of her prospects—equally, it can falsify them."[77] Thus, the writer's sense of the film's ability to shape Western notions of China, which was shared by many commentators, was accompanied by concern about the kind of representation of China the film would offer. Such preoccupations, along with the presumption that filming on location in China would lead to a more accurate vision, cast an unusual amount of scrutiny on the decision to shoot most of the film in California.

The article assured readers that despite the fact that The Good Earth would not be filmed on location in China, the staff of the "Good Earth" which has been in China since January, has gone to much arduous labour and tremendous expense to gather authentic material in the assembling of properties and costumes, in the research for accurate details of the story and then supplementing them photographically, and in taking reels and reels of individual scenes.[78]

The article visually documents the presence of the film crew in China through a handful of accompanying photographs. One shows a technician, two cameramen, and a director sitting on the ground and eating, while another features two cameramen posing with their cameras. The first image identifies the members of the party but not their location. The latter image, however, is captioned "M.G.M. Cameramen, Charlie Clark and 'Newsreel' Wong, on location shooting background shots for farmer scenes." Another photograph suggests the film's spectacular potential by purportedly depicting four thousand extras hired at $1.50 per day to play refugees from a famine, in a scene set "30 miles outside of Peiping where the surrounding scenic effects nearest matched that of Shantung where the original story is laid." The text and images underline the crew's presence and immense labors in China as well as the authentic Chinese origins of props, costumes, "accurate details of the story," background shots, and the refugee scene. The article also notes that "at the time of writing the assembling of actors and actresses is in progress, they are uniformly to be Chinese, some taken from China, some students in America, and some who are available through regular studio resources."[79] The article seeks to convey that even though the most obvious guarantee of authenticity was not practical, the film's integrity as a legitimate portrayal of China was assured by the crew's work. The MGM staff's visit to China was hardly comparable to Buck's nearly forty-year residence in the country yet was critical to the promotion of the film since it provided the basis of the film's physical connection to the story's setting.

Information about the film's production history thus allowed for a double vision of the Chatsworth location, dressed as China for the film. Knowledge of MGM's immense effort to reproduce China in California, supported by evidence of the crew's travels to China, made it possible to see the film's setting as China as well as to appreciate the work that went into creating "China" in California. By the fall of 1936, shortly before the film's premiere, the "location" referred to in an article titled "On Location with *The Good Earth*" was no longer China but rather "the semidesert country twenty miles out of Hollywood," chosen because "it is one of the few spots in Southern California that closest resembles China."[80] The emphasis had shifted from *being* in China to *creating* China in California. As if to drive home the success of the makeover, an image of the Chatsworth location is captioned "China in California! Over 500 acres were transformed to represent a Chinese countryside."[81]

The article reports,

> The story behind those water wheels and mills and buffaloes is an interesting one. Almost as interesting as the Chinese vegetables we see growing close to the stream and the Chinese huts we see every so often on the hillsides. Practically every stick or stone or growing thing we see has been brought over from China by a crew Metro sent over when, three years ago, the decision to produce *The Good Earth* was made.[82]

Another article on the film's production pronounced MGM's efforts "one of the greatest location tasks ever attempted by Hollywood," in which "five hundred acres of rolling terrain have been transformed into a replica of the densely populated farm areas of North China."[83] A small section of China was, in effect, re-created in the San Fernando Valley based on photographic images of China but also featuring a plethora of material objects transported from China to California (fig. 3.1). Whereas the earlier article emphasized the MGM crew's travels in China, this one focuses on the importation of Chinese items to California. Trade paper accounts of the work of the representatives of MGM in China described their offers to purchase nearly everything that could be packed and moved. With such a convincing simulation of China, shooting on location in Chatsworth was very nearly as real as shooting on location in China itself. The place where the majority of the filming occurred may have been located in California, geographically speaking, but it was also in a sense Chinese, at least in terms of the authenticity of the features of the landscape and habitations.

The studio's official program for the film similarly emphasized the quantity of objects that traveled across the Pacific. The program for *The Good Earth,* similar in design to programs now distributed at symphony halls and theatrical performances though rarely in movie theaters anymore, included information about the more than 390 packing cases of objects purchased in China and shipped to California:

FIGURE 3.1   MGM Publicity still, *The Good Earth* (Sidney Franklin, 1937).
The accompanying text reads: "Detail of the huge location being constructed
for Metro-Goldwyn-Mayer's 'The Good Earth.' Entire hillsides were terraced
and planted in Chinese fashion, farms, villages, walled towns, a Chinese irri-
gation system, rice paddies, wheat fields, and garden patches were constructed for Irving G. Thalberg's production of Pearl S. Buck's epic of the
Orient. Paul Muni and Luise Rainer play the principal roles. Thousands of
Chinese players were recruited in San Francisco, Los Angeles, Sacramento,
San Diego, Portland, and Seattle for the undertaking. Victor Fleming is the
director. The five hundred [acre] location, with the Chinese city and replica
of the Great Wall of China, is one of the most extensive engineering and
agricultural projects ever attempted for a motion picture, and literally transforms a California countryside to North China." Courtesy of the Academy of
Motion Picture Arts and Sciences. THE GOOD EARTH © Turner Entertainment Co. A Warner Bros. Entertainment Company. All Rights Reserved.

Teakwood tables, China temple dogs, gongs, dishes, water pots, wooden plows, matting, baskets of every nature, colored joss papers, Chinese water wheels, a Chinese windmill, Chinese bone needles, a Chinese sundial, Chinese toys, a wedding sedan chair, rickshas, doors, windows and other parts of buildings, Chinese idols, cooking utensils, both for rich and poor, chop sticks for rich and poor, rugs, two thousand costumes, pictures, bronzes, earthenware jars, etc.[84]

This list gives the impression of a Chinese community being uprooted in its entirety and transported across the Pacific; indeed, the re-created China in Chatsworth is uncannily reminiscent of the ethnographic villages at world's fairs and international expositions.

Ethnographic villages, initially popularized at the 1889 Paris Exposition Internationelle, were in significant evidence for the first time in the United States at the Chicago Columbian Exposition of 1893. These villages provide a precedent for the notion of importing authentic materials to the United States to reconstruct a faraway place, thereby bringing distant lives and cultures to U.S. audiences. The irony here is that MGM's efforts to re-create China in Chatsworth were, in a way, a return to a protocinematic form that served as a model for the cinematic display of the spectacle of nonwhite Others.[85] Like ethnographic villages, MGM's "China" was created as a distillation of China, but unlike the earlier villages, it was intended from the start as a setting for a fictional narrative that would circulate on film. That is, rather than inviting Americans to travel to the Chatsworth site to witness the lives of the Chinese, as would have been the case in a world's fair, the filmmakers would stage for the camera the living of Chinese daily lives and the performance of their rituals; these images would then be circulated to audiences in their hometowns, for viewing at their local theaters. Like Burton Holmes, who viewed the exhibits of the 1893 Columbian Exposition as a way to travel the world within the fairgrounds and imagined his first illustrated travel lectures on Japan as an extension of and substitute for this virtual travel, MGM's film of *The Good Earth* was a way for U.S. audiences to see China and learn about the Chinese without leaving home.

The marvelous accomplishment of re-creating China in Chatsworth, however impressive in the way it used authentic Chinese crops and props, was still not quite complete. To truly come alive, this re-creation required inhabitants. World's fairs usually brought over "natives" to live in the ethnographic villages; for *The Good Earth*, two award-winning

Austrian-born Hollywood stars were cast in the lead roles, supported by scores of Chinese American extras. Paul Muni, who portrayed Wang Lung, was an accomplished screen actor who became a star after playing the title role in *Scarface* (Howard Hawks, 1932) and won his first Academy Award for *The Story of Louis Pasteur* (William Dieterle, 1936). Luise Rainer, chosen for the role of O-lan, received an Oscar for her work in *The Great Ziegfeld* (Robert Z. Leonard, 1936). Although critics of the theatrical adaptation of *The Good Earth* found the actors' Euro-American identities an obstacle to the successful adaptation of Buck's novel, film critics applauded Muni's and Rainer's performances, and Rainer received the best actress Oscar for her work in the film.

In the opening sequence, following the images of the community awakening and the text informing the viewer that it is Wang Lung's wedding day, the camera slowly tracks back from a crude window overlooking the scenic setting into a small home, panning right and tilting downward to come to rest on a medium close-up of a bare-chested man lying awake in bed. The sunlight increasingly illuminates his face as he says to himself, "This is the day!" For today's viewers, the image of Muni as Wang Lung is jarring. Muni is obviously not a Chinese or Asian actor but a Caucasian actor in yellowface makeup, and contemporary audiences feel this distinction keenly since such casting decisions are no longer acceptable.[86] The decision to feature two well-known European American actors in the lead roles clearly subordinated the desire for authenticity to the need for stars in a prestigious Hollywood film. But even for audiences in the 1930s, for whom Warner Oland as Charlie Chan may have been the most familiar "Chinese" in the movies, the choice to use Euro-American stars in this film rather than having an all-Chinese cast required an accommodating shift in the definition of authenticity.

Stars are, of course, one of the most recognizable and thus promotable elements of a film. But in the case of historical epics, and especially in an example such as *The Good Earth,* in which the stars are to portray characters of a different racial and cultural background, there exists a tension between the traits that make a star a valuable commodity and the temporal or cultural specificity of the role. Alicia Annas notes,

> When a star was cast in a period film, the studio faced a dilemma. While it was desirable that moviegoers believed that the historical image presented on screen was indeed authentic, it was economically vital that the star's

image was not sacrificed to history. In looking at how Hollywood moviemakers reconciled these two conflicting demands, one can see a systematic approach to the way they handled makeup and hair, combining stars' modern images with illusions of historical accuracy.[87]

Background stories about the production of *The Good Earth* make explicit this dialectic between the star's image and historical (or in this case racial and cultural) accuracy. Muni and Rainer relied on the work of MGM makeup director Jack Dawn to transform their facial physiognomies using a system of "facial inlays" that one reporter touted as "the most realistic make-up ever used for Chinese roles."[88] Paradoxically, this text celebrates the reality of the artifice of yellowface. Thus, audiences are encouraged to see Muni as the European American star that he is but also to remark on how extraordinary makeup techniques make him appear to be Chinese. Viewers are not meant to mistake Muni for a Chinese man. To learn behavior and gestures, both Muni and Rainer reportedly spent some time with Chinese families in California: "Muni lived on a Chinese farm near Sacramento to absorb the mannerisms and characteristics necessary for his role. Miss Rainer lived for a time with a Chinese family in San Francisco."[89] Reports regarding Muni's and Rainer's efforts to prepare for their roles thus served the dual functions of burnishing their star images while insisting on the authenticity of their appearances and performances.

Chinatown in Chatsworth

One of the most insidious effects of U.S. orientalism's efforts to define Asia and America as two distinct entities is the difficulty of asserting an Asian American position or subjectivity. While *The Good Earth* presents a vision of China that seems entirely independent of and separate from the United States, this opposition is contradicted by the realities of its production, including its origin in the observations of an American missionary woman and the participation of Chinese Americans in the making of the film. A number of prominent Chinese American residents of California appeared in the film as extras, along with hundreds if not thousands of Asians (most though perhaps not all Chinese) recruited from up and down the Pacific Coast. Their presence in the film was widely reported in the press, and in many cases, as in the discussion of

their role in Muni's and Rainer's education in the lifeways of the Chi-
nese, they became the standard-bearers for Chinese authenticity. In a
film widely seen as having the potential to educate U.S. audiences about
China and the Chinese yet filmed almost entirely in the United States,
Chinese Americans from all walks of life were called on to stand in as
Chinese peasants and farmers, to perform a Chineseness scripted by
Hollywood, and to make China in Chatsworth come alive. As ethnic Chinese, they fulfilled the superficial imperatives of authenticity, yet as residents of the United States their life experiences were distinct from those
of the Chinese farmers on whom Buck based her characters. MGM
found enough Chinese in California and on the West Coast to fill all the
required spots in *The Good Earth* only because Chinese people had been
immigrating to the United States for almost a century. However, their
roles required them to act as if they had never come.

While some Chinese Americans may have served as unofficial consul-
tants, offering opinions about particular customs or practices, just as often their presence and appearance were all that was required of them.
For one reporter who visited the Chatsworth location, the local Chinese
lent an ethnic authenticity to the scene, but he did not deem their work
real acting as much as simply being:

> The Chinese were allowed to act typically Chinese such as they do down-
> town on Chinese New Year. . . . The scene was taken without their knowl-
> edge and it was a perfect "shot." Director Sidney Franklin knew what he
> wanted and got it. . . . He wanted a natural scene and he knew how to get
> it out of the shy Chinese.[90]

For this reporter, the extras were a part of the feel of China he so admired
of the production, on the order of the fields of Chinese crops and the water buffalo. From this perspective, Muni and Rainer were skilled profes-
sionals who achieved authenticity through study and hard work (and
"facial inlays"), while the Chinese American extras merely carried on
with their lives, serving as a living backdrop for the picture.

Another piece on the film stated,

> More than 2000 Chinese are used in the picture, hundreds of them often
> appearing in a single scene. They were recruited from as far north as Seat-
> tle and as far south as Mexico. About 80 percent of them speak almost per-
> fect English. Many of them are from the Chinese quarter in Los Angeles

and are veterans in pictures. True to intra-city tradition, the San Francisco and Los Angeles Chinese quarrel a great deal about their respective "home towns." William Law, one of the rotating presidents of the famous "Six Companies" and chief of the bay cities contingent, grumbles about Los Angeles' "high fog," and Keye Luke, an Angeleno, retaliates with barbs about San Francisco's "low fog." Of course, this quarreling isn't really serious enough to promote any tong wars.[91]

This description contains an uneasy recognition of these individuals as both Chinese and American. Indeed, observers often found the Chinese Americans surprisingly American, as in the reference to their almost-perfect command of English. The debate over the relative virtues of Northern and Southern California is familiar, yet hometown is placed in quotes, as if to suggest that Law's and Luke's respective claims to San Francisco and Los Angeles as their places of origin were somewhat tenuous. The reference to tong wars, however humorously intended, serves as a reminder that Chinatown had a reputation for lawlessness, particularly as it had been portrayed in numerous films of the preceding decade. This account is symptomatic in its ambivalence toward Asian immigrants in the United States, even at a time when Americans were being encouraged to view the Chinese in China with newfound identification and empathy.

Reports of the number of Chinese American extras employed by the film functioned as indicators of the authenticity of the film, much like the detailed inventories of objects imported from China. Most viewers of *The Good Earth* probably saw nothing more than Chinese faces in the background, which were consistent with the Chinese dwellings and the Chinese cooking implements in the film. Yet for some of the Chinese American extras, participating in this film was a meaningful education in how Hollywood constructs authenticity and an occasion to consider Chinese American identities in the context of Hollywood's version of the Chinese. In a wonderfully entertaining essay on his experience as an extra in *The Good Earth*, Charles L. Leong offers rare insight into the production of the film (fig. 3.2). While the novel and the film were consistently applauded for their accuracy and authenticity, Leong makes evident the artifice behind Hollywood's vision of China. Although film scholars have long taken for granted the constructed nature of any Hollywood text, Leong's reminiscences stand out because they reveal the specific contradictions involved in filming an authentic version of *The Good Earth* in California. Even more significantly, Leong's essay repre-

FIGURE 3.2   Charles L. Leong, ca. 1936. Courtesy of Russell Leong.

sents how some of the Chinese American extras on the set understood authenticity very differently than did those who produced and sold authenticity to the film's audiences.

To play a peasant in prerevolutionary China, Leong had to allow the studio barber to shave away his hair, his "luxurious matting of crowning glory."[92] Later, in the makeup department, an artificial queue was fastened to his shorn head. As the barber did his work, Leong remembered an old racist rhyme, "Ching chong chinaman, sitting on a rail . . . along came a white man and chop off his tail," and considered the irony of the fact that he is getting paid to wear a queue for this film.[93] He writes, "The year was 1936, the scene a Hollywood studio, twenty-five years after the banishment of the old Manchu regime in China, and with it, the banishment of queue—and a bunch of young American Chinese, all of whom have never been to China, learning how to braid pigtails, just like their fathers did years and years ago."[94] The queue, once a sign of the unassimilable foreignness of the Chinese man, is now just a Hollywood prop, and instead of being harassed, Leong will be financially compensated for attaching one to his head. But even as an artificial element of a Hollywood costume, the queue still generated memories for him of the history of the violent physical harassment the Chinese experienced in the United States.

Hollywood's China was a site of disequilibrium for Leong, full of paradox as well as unexpected moments of real poignancy. Some of the contradictions of the movies were familiar, such as the fact that Oland, a Swede, was the most well-known "Chinese" in Hollywood. Others might have been predicted—for example, the sterilization of the dirty costumes worn by the peasants and farmers in *The Good Earth* at the end of each day and the fact that Chinese interpreters translated the director's English commands even though the majority of the cast spoke English. But who would have guessed that the "unofficial mayor of Chinatown," the man to see if a studio needed Chinese actors for its films, would be Tom Gubbins, a Chinese-born Irishman? These details show something of what was involved in bringing China to California as an intermediate step in bringing China to U.S. audiences. However, working on the set provided more than insight into how the dream factory spins out its fantasies. Given that the film often required large numbers of extras at one time, the making of *The Good Earth* allowed members of the Chinese American community to gather and interact. Among Leong's warmest memories was lunchtime on the set. "Probably years ago some Mrs. Wong brought slices of rare Chinese roast duck to eat at the studio during the lunch hour," he hypothesizes, "and a Mrs. Lee or Mrs. Sing, as women of all nationalities, would bring something better than Mrs. Wong's to eat and offer. And so this fine old Chinese custom is firmly established in the studios. We young extras love it."[95] According to Leong, the lunch hour provided not only an opportunity to delight in delicious food but also a social scene, as these gatherings allowed mothers to draw attention to the positive qualities of their daughters in front of many members of the Los Angeles Chinatown community. Participating in the film thus incidentally became an exercise in community building. The wry reference to "this fine old Chinese custom" of eating Chinese food during lunch hour on the set shows how Chinese Americans could create new customs in their U.S. context, specifically in the moviemaking world of Southern California. While the extras were helping to simulate an authentic, faraway China in California, they were also bringing a little bit of Chinatown to Chatsworth.

For the Chinese Americans on location in Chatsworth, working in the facsimile of China sometimes called forth complex responses. In Leong's account, the older generation, who had firsthand knowledge of China, felt nostalgic for the past: "It was natural that the old folks reminisce, speaking of old times, friends, and things in faraway China. Somehow, these synthetic, plaster and frame movie sets did something to them. Hollywood created a nostalgic mood for them."[96] Those who were born and raised in the United States, like Leong, listened "eagerly, absorbing of the China we have not yet seen. Everyone is transplanted, through the animated magic carpet of 'back home' food and talk, to the land of his love."[97] These responses to the China of *The Good Earth* remind us of how the film's production of China for its U.S. audiences could have different effects for different viewers. For most non-Chinese American audiences, the magic carpet was the film itself, a form of virtual transport to a foreign world that provided the opportunity to learn about a distant culture, its people, and their customs. In the production of the film, the careful reconstruction of China in Chatsworth evoked memories of another time and place among the older generation of Chinese Americans and allowed the younger generation to reflect on what might have been, to imagine what growing up in China would have been like.

Curiously, Leong pronounces the set in Chatsworth "too authentic," and although he never loses sight of the camera recording his every move, as he toils in the fields he allows himself to feel, if only for a moment, as if he actually were in China:

> I was barefooted and hoeing a thin row of rice shoots. I felt the warmth of the soil. I was in China. And back of me, a camera followed my every action. Twenty other young brown bodies gleamed in the California sun, tilling the rice fields. Glistening, actually working and covered with more sweat than clothing. Here we were, twenty young American-born Chinese, trying to simulate, to reenact, for the movies, a scene which was part of the national fiber of our forefathers. My mind was far from the usual prosaic things. Was this a dream, a fantasy, realism? Was this China or Hollywood? "This, but for the grace of God," I thought, "I might actually be doing."[98]

"Is this China or California?" is inflected quite differently when posed by a Chinese American extra on the set of the Chatsworth location and by a generic audience member addressed by the film's promotional intertext.

Neither the trade press nor the popular press reports of the film covered the experience of being a Chinese American actor playing a Chinese farmer, shopkeeper, street performer, or teahouse patron or any of the other multitude of Chinese roles in *The Good Earth*. But given the large numbers of Asian Americans who appeared in this film, stories about the production of *The Good Earth* might well have circulated among Asian American communities on the West Coast in more informal, verbal accounts or in community-oriented publications.[99] Leong's valuable account of his experience on the set provides insight into how discourses of authenticity surrounding *The Good Earth* could have a very different resonance for Chinese Americans who worked on the film. His unique perspective, while not necessarily representative, reminds us of the many narratives of the film's production history that were not publicized or promoted as defining elements of the film's commercial identity but that nevertheless formed part of the history of the film itself.

Chinese Lessons

MGM's simulation of Chinese farmland in Chatsworth was, by all accounts, convincing. The Chinese American extras on location could reminisce about China or imagine themselves there, while journalists marveled at the feat of re-creating China in California. But however impressive the transformation of the Chatsworth location may have been, it was only part of the film, the setting for the action. What of the story itself and the characters within it? The film's narrative followed the novel in its broad outlines, reproduced some dialogue verbatim, and offered a number of literal depictions of scenes described in the book. The film also introduced several changes that made it a more familiar text on the model of a Hollywood spectacular of the 1930s, usually at the expense of accuracy. Both the novel and the film begin on Wang Lung's wedding day. However, the romantic aspects of the relationship between Wang Lung and O-lan that Kang found so troubling were heightened in the film, as is apparent in the film's ending. The final scene takes place shortly after O-lan's death, with an image of Wang Lung beside the peach tree O-lan had planted on the evening of their union. He utters, "O-lan, you are the earth" as the orchestral music reaches a crescendo, just before the film fades to black.

In addition, the film elevates O-lan's importance and pays correspondingly less attention to the sympathetic but flawed character of

Wang Lung. The filmmakers choose to end the film at O-lan's death rather than tracing the ascent of the Wang family to landlord status. Because of this decision, the film replaces the novel's cyclical narrative of rise and fall, implied by the sons plotting the sale of some land after Wang Lung's death, with a story of Wang Lung and O-lan's struggles to raise their family and prosper. As Buck put it, in the film, "O-lan gets the pearls, the second wife is dismissed, Wang returns to the land—the American romance in other words."[100] Along with these shifts in narrative emphasis, the film softens or omits some of the novel's more difficult and potentially controversial details. The novel's uncle, a parasitic, amoral, and vicious character who was pacified only through opium, is transformed into a greedy, lazy, but comic buffoon. The film glosses over the specifics of Wang Lung's obsession with Lotus, his eventual second wife, and ignores his dalliance with young Pear Blossom (a logical omission, since this episode takes place long after O-lan's death). By editing out these more unsavory aspects of the story, the filmmakers may well have been conceding to the demands of prevailing censorship codes, both U.S. and Chinese; still, the changes resulted in a less complex, more idealized, more two-dimensional portrait of Chinese life. Buck's commitment to portraying "the splendid common people of China, living their tremendous lusty life" was transformed into an effort to represent China and the Chinese in a sympathetic manner, as a people and a nation worthy of U.S. sympathy and support.

The film also intensifies the significance or effect of certain scenes from the novel. The images of the land itself, including a handful of background shots from China, have a vastness that is more spectacularly shown on the silver screen than described in words. The film's depiction of O-lan caught up in the looting of the great house in the southern city is harrowing. The sheer number of rampaging looters creates a visceral reaction in the viewer, especially when O-lan falls to the floor and the crowd tramples her. The rousing defense against the locust plague is the climax of the film, the moment when Wang Lung finally returns to the land, yet it is a relatively minor event in the novel. Each of these examples takes advantage of the medium of cinema to draw the viewer into the narrative by using the scale of the screen to create greater emotional engagement. But overall, the film retains most of the major narrative events of the novel up to O-lan's death. The fidelity of the adaptation, combined with the careful construction of China in Chatsworth, brought accolades to the film from all quarters. The film hewed closely enough to the original story to be accepted as a skillful, high-quality translation of the novel while taking full advantage of the engaging spectacle that the cinematic medium could achieve. The rare challenges to the novel's accuracy that Buck faced, as in Kang's and Kiang's critiques, never materialized in relation to the film.

Accuracy was, above all, what Buck's novel purportedly offered and was the quality for which it was celebrated. Therefore, it was a necessary ingredient in the cinematic adaptation of the novel, particularly if it was to be seen as offering its audiences credible knowledge about China and the Chinese. At the same time, the film's authenticity was relative rather than absolute. Authenticity was defined by conventions and expectations and was subject to change, as the shifts in its discursive construction throughout the production of the film demonstrate. What is perhaps most remarkable about *The Good Earth* is how successfully Buck's authority was reinforced despite the fact that the film starred two Euro-American actors speaking English in Southern California. The promotion of the film's production history played a significant role in this achievement. All of this effort apparently sufficed to give audiences the illusion of filmmakers present on the scene, bringing viewers to China, much as Buck educated Americans about China by simply writing of what she knew from her experience of everyday life there.

The seriousness with which *The Good Earth* was received as an educational text about China, including as a form of virtual travel to China, is nothing short of astounding. *The Good Earth* begins with a preface that suggests that the film provides an insightful view of the past heritage and future promise of China. Reviews, testimonials, and various ancillary materials produced in relation to the film demonstrate a willingness to view *The Good Earth* in just the way the studio suggested. The foreword to a 1937 study guide published by Educational and Recreational Guides praises not only the entertainment value of the film but also its pedagogical effectiveness: "Possibly one could travel in China for a year and not learn more of its problems and significance than one obtains from the selected details of the photoplay, conscientiously based on extended researches in China as well as on Mrs. Buck's novel."[101]

This guide to *The Good Earth* was one of a series of film discussion guides that originated with the efforts of the National Council of Teachers of English to promote film appreciation in high schools. The council's research was summarized in a general work, *Photoplay Appreciation in American High Schools*,[102] and then followed by the production of a series of study guides "intended to train judgment and appreciation with reference to specific photoplays."[103] The choice of films for which to produce study guides leaned heavily toward those that adapted well-known literary works or focused on important historical events or figures. Although the guides were initially intended for use by English teachers, the organization also had ambitions to create guides with a broader appeal:

> To those who have participated in the new development of this program thanks are extended for their assistance in a project that, we all hope, may prove of benefit in bringing our schools and other educational agencies closer to the needs and actualities of everyday life. We may hope, too, that the training of good judgment that these Guides are intended to effect will result in the encouragement of finer, more artistic photoplays.[104]

The twin ambitions of these guides are thus made explicit: to make education more relevant by engaging with an immensely popular mass cultural form, the cinema, and to encourage the production of high-quality films that could be studied as art by treating select films as texts worthy of rigorous intellectual scrutiny.

Given the history of this series of study guides, the selection of *The Good Earth* as a subject is significant because it recognized the film as worthy of serious and extended study. The guide's purpose and intended audience are apparent in its subtitle, *Suggestions for Reading and Discussion in Classes of Older Students, Women's Clubs, and Community Forums*. In this study guide, representations of the film are supplemented by rationales for learning about China that conform fully to Karen Leong's "China mystique"; these rationales range from the country's cultural achievements over the centuries to its important role in contemporary international politics. The thirty-two-page guide is divided into five parts: "China, Old and New," "Author of the Novel," "Related Reading," "The Production of the Photoplay," and "Analysis of the Photoplay." These sections provide a cursory overview of Chinese culture and customs, a one-page summary of Buck's life, and an introduction to film analysis using *The Good Earth* as a case study. The short bibliography of related readings lists several fiction and nonfiction books about China, including a work by Burton Holmes. A series of miniature stills is also included, with images from the film and from the making of the film accompanied by questions about Chinese history, culture, or customs, such as an image of Wang Lung and O-lan prostrating themselves before

FIGURE 3.3   Miniature Stills for Notebooks: *The Good Earth*—Series
3. "C-1: What is the Chinese habit of kow-towing? (Be sure you can
pronounce the word.)" Courtesy of the Academy of Motion Picture
Arts and Sciences. THE GOOD EARTH © Turner Entertainment Co.
A Warner Bros. Entertainment Company. All Rights Reserved.

the Old Mistress of the Great House followed by the question, "What is
the Chinese habit of kow-towing? (Be sure you can pronounce the
word)" (fig. 3.3).[105] In other words, the study guide uses the film as a
point of departure for a fully developed lesson regarding not just *The
Good Earth*, but also China and the Chinese.

In the conclusion, the author invites readers to judge the authenticity
of the film based on the information provided in the earlier sections of
the guide:

> Vividness, illusion of reality, and authenticity are the pictorial qualities
> that mark excellence in costume pictures. Your preliminary study of China
> and the Chinese has probably given you a sufficient basis for judging the
> value of these factors in this film. . . . Let us select one scene and review the
> details that combine to produce the effect of reality.[106]

The author then considers the representation of Wang's farmhouse and clothing. Not surprisingly, they are found to be impeccably authentic. This exercise further underlines the status of the film as a quasiethnographic text. Equally extraordinarily, this exercise implies that reading approximately thirty pages about China and the Chinese qualifies one to determine the "vividness, illusion of reality, and authenticity" of *The Good Earth.* Ignoring the quality of the information relayed in the discussion guide for the moment, it is notable that the text not only provides information about China but also encourages its readers to use this newly gained knowledge in their evaluation of the film, as if they were now adequately informed to be capable of such critique. Finally, in something of a self-fulfilling prophecy, the film is found to be authentic according to the standards of the study guide, which further certifies the film as a source of knowledge of China. The tone of this discussion guide is conversational, with a relatively accessible level of discourse. Other guides had more ambitious agendas in terms of the analysis and knowledge of China they required and produced.[107] Despite their differing degrees of sophistication, all of these texts share the unstated assumption that audiences could learn about the realities of Chinese life from viewing and then discussing *The Good Earth.*

To Harold Isaacs, the film elicited sympathy for the Chinese in their ongoing conflict with the Japanese, by giving "the quality of individual recognition to the figure of the heroic Chinese peasant or peasant-soldier who offered battle to the Japanese against such great odds in the years just before Pearl Harbor."[108] James Thomson Jr. also links the film to heightened American awareness of China in relation to the Sino-Japanese War: Buck "would be lucky again when the movie version of the novel, released in 1937, coincided with Japan's all-out effort to conquer China. By then, millions of Americans knew whom the Japanese tanks and planes were slaughtering; it was Wang Lung, O-lan, and all the rest."[109] It is unlikely that the Chinese victims of Japanese aggression were individualized to quite this degree, but the film did help to create a more sympathetic portrait of the Chinese that contrasted with the increasingly negatively stereotyped Japanese. Sympathy is not, however, the same thing as knowledge. The film may have turned the attention of millions of viewers to a far-off conflict, but it offered little in the way of historical, cultural, or political context to aid audiences in achieving a greater understanding of the ongoing events. The film did offer U.S. audiences the feeling of knowing the Chinese to be human beings struggling to live off the land, with sorrows and triumphs similar to those of Americans.

As an adaptation of Buck's novel, the film was a critical and commercial success, but was it an accurate or even an authentic depiction of China? For many reasons, this question is impossible to answer definitively; it is also beside the point. The initial interest in Buck's novel and the later excitement over the film resulted in part from a *lack* of knowledge about China on the part of most U.S. audiences, accompanied by a desire to learn more about the country and its people. Because they had so little knowledge of China, the majority of the readers of the novel and viewers of the film could evaluate the authenticity of *The Good Earth* only by distinguishing it from previous representations that had been deemed stereotypical and inaccurate. It is revealing that efforts to adhere to authentic representations of China in *The Good Earth* were not extended to the film's advertising campaign. The studio's publicity and marketing for *The Good Earth,* known as "exploitation and ballyhoo" in the 1930s, unabashedly relied on the clichéd orientalist imagery the film itself mostly tried to avoid, suggesting that older orientalist visions of China continued to exist alongside new perceptions of the country and its people. (The one obvious exception is the depiction of Lotus, Wang's second wife, by Tilly Losch.)

In the film's press book, a catalog of advertising ideas intended for theaters showing the film, promotions involving the participation of young, attractive Asian women were legion, and novelty accessories available to hand out to viewers included Chinese Magic Fortune Incense, Chinese Lucky Coins, and a Chinese Rice Envelope. In addition, a nationwide personal appearance tour by Hii, "the Chinese Bull," was reportedly enormously well attended. Buried near the back of the catalog, under the photograph of "Another jinrikisha street stunt," is a brief explanation of the general tenor of the publicity on offer:

> Some Road-Show engagements started out with the idea of avoiding Chinese exploitation tricks so that their public would not think "The Good Earth" was just another Chinese picture. However, most of them soon found out that people responded more quickly to the many and varied Oriental color effects in house dress and street crowds assembled more quickly when attractive "Chinese" girls distributed novelties and a jinrikisha traveled the streets.[110]

In other words, even if the film was conceived as an authentic picture suitable for people with an interest in learning more about the "real" China, Oriental exotica still sold tickets most effectively. The strategies involved in the studio's selling of *The Good Earth* point to the tradition of Hollywood films about the mysterious and exotic Far East. The notion of "avoiding Chinese exploitation tricks" typical of "Chinese pictures" was well and good, but apparently, without the stereotypical signs normally associated with the Chinese, audiences seemed slow to recognize the subject of the film.

Peter Conn attributes the novel's phenomenal success in part to the fact that its story of the challenges faced by a farmer and his family belonged to a well-established American literary tradition that resonated strongly with Americans in the years following the Depression.[111] If this is true, then *The Good Earth*'s success in humanizing the Chinese resulted from its ability to make the Chinese seem more familiar to Americans, more like Americans. Read or seen as a mirror of U.S. national myths, neither the novel nor the film could acknowledge the common humanity of the Chinese and the Americans while still adequately recognizing the differences between the United States and China. Furthermore, according to Karen Leong, the "positive images" of *The Good Earth* may have altered the content of U.S. orientalist conceptions of China yet still maintained the hierarchical relationship between the United States and China. Leong elaborates,

> Buck engaged American orientalism in ways that normalized China and made China more familiar and comfortable as a concept for the public. . . . At the same time, Buck's articulation of American nationalism in constant reference to China also contributed to a new mythology of the China mystique, presenting China as a reflection of American values and society.[112]

This image of China's potential would shift dramatically in slightly more than a decade, as the Chinese communists became the feared enemy, while the Japanese, after their defeat in the Second World War and the ensuing U.S. occupation, became the most important U.S. ally in Asia. Yet Americans still envisioned the United States as the bringer of freedom and democracy to the world, even as the specific identities of its Asian friends and foes changed with unfolding international events.

CHAPTER FOUR

At Home in the World

Occupied Japan and the American Century

From *The World Is Mine* to *The World Is My Home*

In James Michener's autobiography, *The World Is My Home: A Memoir,* he attributes his success as a writer in part to fortuitous timing:

> I published my books at the precise time when Americans were beginning to look outward at the entire world rather than inward at themselves. They were spiritually and intellectually ready and even eager to read the exploring kind of books I wanted to write.... Had I come along fifty years earlier, when America was isolationist, I doubt if anyone would have bothered much with my writing.[1]

Fifty years before Michener's first novel, *Tales of the South Pacific* (1947) was published, however, illustrated travel lecturer Burton Holmes was just embarking on his career. Holmes's fond recollections of the first two decades of the twentieth century in his autobiography, *The World Is Mine,* suggest that his efforts to present "the world, outside of America" to U.S. audiences were met with great enthusiasm.[2] Holmes's career demonstrates that Americans in fact showed substantial interest in representations of the "entire world" long before Michener appeared on the scene.

Holmes and Michener embody contrasting ways of being an American at two different times in U.S. history. A consideration of their very similarly titled autobiographies and their careers provides a useful point of departure for this chapter about U.S. films shot on location in Japan following the conclusion of the Second World War. In 1947, Irving Wallace rated Holmes's greatest challenge in the upcoming season as "a new audience of travel-sated and disillusioned ex-GIs. Many of these men, and their families, now know that a South Sea island paradise means mosquitoes and malaria, and not Melville's *Fayaway* and Loti's *Rarahu*."[3] Holmes's brand of travel lecture could not continue to exist unchanged after the Second World War. As Christina Klein notes, "Hundreds of thousands of Americans flowed into Asia during the 1940s and 1950s as soldiers, diplomats, foreign aid workers, missionaries, technicians, professors, students, businesspeople, and tourists."[4] All of these Americans had particular experiences of Asia; Holmes was no longer in the position of representing a largely unfamiliar world to his U.S. audiences.

Although Holmes's autobiography was published in 1953, the book concludes with his travels to England, France, and Italy during the First World War, leaving out more than three decades of his life and work. Perhaps Holmes was aware that the war marked the end of the period during which he would have his greatest influence. Michener began his career as a professional author at the same time as Holmes was in the twilight of his career as a travel lecturer. Despite garnering relatively little attention when it was published, *Tales of the South Pacific*, based on Michener's time as a U.S. Navy lieutenant, won the Pulitzer Prize in 1948, became a successful Rodgers and Hammerstein Broadway musical, and was then remade in 1958 as a lavish, colorful, widescreen cinematic spectacle directed by Joshua Logan. Although Michener's autobiography does not mention Holmes (nor does Holmes write of Michener), the timing of the publication of *Tales of the South Pacific* and its subsequent success made Michener a challenger to Holmes; in their professional lives, both men represented the outside world to U.S. audiences.

In Holmes's lectures, he was always a traveler, merely passing through, and he always strictly maintained the distinction between (white) Americans and native Others. Michener, in contrast, prided himself on his ability to feel at home in the world, to go beyond merely visiting to living in a place:

> This concept that the people of all geographical areas and civilizations are my brothers and sisters has created a never-ending problem for me: if I'm so closely bound to them, does it follow that I owe allegiance to all nations? Or do I owe a special debt of patriotism only to my homeland? I have never been able to answer such questions categorically, for obviously I have been a citizen of the world, at home everywhere, at ease in all cultures, with all religions, and with all kinds of people living under almost every conceivable form of government.[5]

Michener's claim that the world was his home derived from the power of being an American abroad, as did Holmes's sense of entitlement in traveling and representing the world to his fellow Americans. However, the differences between these two men's attitudes reveal significant changes in how the United States related to the world. Holmes's detached, amused, observational perspective is as appropriate for the birth of U.S. overseas imperialism at the turn of the twentieth century as Michener's all-embracing citizen-of-the-world humanism is suited to the midcentury establishment of U.S. global hegemony in the era that saw the coining of the term *American Century*.

Given these dramatically different historical contexts both in international relations and in the development of cinema as an art and an institution, traveling to Japan to shoot a film on location after the Second World War was not the same enterprise as it had been at the turn of the century. Holmes started his career with two lectures based on an 1892 visit to Japan, which he described as "like living in a land of exquisite old Japanese prints."[6] These lectures, which were illustrated with hand-painted photographic slides, showed a country in the midst of selectively adapting certain Western habits—of dress, for example. Around the turn of the century, the United States viewed Japan with grudging admiration not only for its embrace of Western ways but also for its military victories. In the published version of "Japan—The Cities," Holmes writes, "Now for the first time in the history of nations a dark-skinned people has assumed and is bearing worthily the 'white man's burden.'"[7] By the time of Michener's *Sayonara* (1954), Japan's imperial ambitions had come to a disastrous end, and Japan had been subjected to a seven-year U.S. military occupation. The cinematic adaptation of Michener's *Sayonara* was photographed in color and in a widescreen format, and U.S. audiences witnessed in an especially spectacular fashion the "reality" of Japan the film crews captured on location. In the six decades between Holmes's first lectures on Japan and the cinematic adaptation of Michener's novel, nearly everything about Japanese–U.S. relations, including the form and style of the visual representations of this topic, had changed.

Following the bombing of Pearl Harbor on December 7, 1941, discourses about Japan and the Japanese proliferated in every medium. A *Life* magazine article gave readers tips on "How to Tell Japs [*sic*] from Chinese."[8] Noted anthropologists such as Ruth Benedict worked for the Office of War Information to produce Japanese national character studies. Hollywood made openly racist fictions, while Frank Capra's wartime propaganda documentary helped soldiers to *Know Your Enemy: Japan* (1945).[9] Americans were bombarded with negative images and narratives of Japan and the Japanese. During and after this period, films as a form of knowledge of Japan had a dramatically different function than that of works like *The Good Earth*. There was a surfeit rather than a lack of knowledge of Japan during the war, and as historian John Dower observes, "To people at war, after all, the major purpose in knowing one's enemies is to be better able to control or kill them."[10] At the conclusion of the war, Americans had been exposed to several years of wartime propaganda about the Japanese. But the project of the postwar occupation and reconstruction of Japan as well as the looming Cold War required a rather different set of attitudes.

The issue was less the need to educate Americans about a little-known country, as in the previous chapters, but rather the desire to manage and reshape U.S. perceptions of Japan as its status changed from hated enemy to trusted ally. Dower describes the U.S. occupation of Japan as "the last immodest exercise in the colonial conceit known as 'the white man's burden.'"[11] The reference to the "white man's burden" recalls the Philippine-American War, the context in which the phrase originally appeared, yet the kind of overt imperial domination that characterized the U.S. presence in the Philippines at the turn of the century did not suit the image the United States hoped to project of itself at midcentury. The representation of Japan and U.S.–Japanese relations was particularly important at this historical juncture because the realities of the U.S. occupation of Japan contradicted American efforts to construct a national identity as a "nonimperial world power in the age of decolonization," in Klein's terms.[12] In the face of the perception of the global threat of communism and the growth of anticolonialist nationalism, the United States needed to construct an image of itself as a liberal democratic state that believed in racial equality and was suited to world leadership.

The American missionary was the emblematic figure behind *The Good Earth*, the one whose knowledge of China made telling the story possible. All of the films discussed in this chapter are linked to the presence of the U.S. Army in Japan, initially in practical terms (in allowing access to Japanese shooting locations), then as the foundation for their narratives and the identities of their main characters, and finally in more complicated ways involving the ideological requirement to repudiate, renounce, or rearticulate the history of the United States in Japan during and after the war. While *The Good Earth* focuses entirely on the everyday people of China, never acknowledging the U.S. origins of the novel and film, the four films of Japan discussed in this chapter foreground international relations: they all feature white Americans in stories of interracial, intercultural interactions with the Japanese, set more or less in the present. Correspondingly, although *authenticity* remains an important term in the promotional texts surrounding these films, the experiences of the director, cast, and crew on location in Japan, as real-life examples of Americans in Japan, were far more important to the publicity campaigns. As material instances of U.S.–Japanese relations, the production histories of these films shot on location in Japan were publicized as events that reinforced the ideologies of the films themselves. At the same time, the films' images and narratives offered an imaginary vision of Japan within a world that welcomed and appreciated U.S. leadership. This chapter therefore considers in particular the interplay between the material productions of these films and the imaginary geographies they project. Intertextuality will remain important, as I rely on studio promotional texts, popular press articles, and film reviews to identify the discourses that framed the reception of these films. However, I also include a far greater emphasis on the texts of the films themselves than I did in my discussion of *The Good Earth,* given the degree to which the narratives of shooting on location in Japan are tied to the films' narratives of being an American in Japan during and after the Second World War.

The four films examined in detail in this chapter were released over a period of eleven years; I selected them because they express the shifts that occurred in the relations between the United States and Japan during that time. They will be examined in chronological order, which puts into relief most clearly the changes in U.S. national identity vis-à-vis Japan. Two of the films are relatively popular and well known. *The Teahouse of the August Moon* (Daniel Mann, 1956) depicts U.S. occupation forces in Okinawa as bumbling, good-natured soldiers eager to accommodate cultural difference. *Sayonara* (Joshua Logan, 1957) plays out a story of interracial love conquering racial prejudice during the Korean War and has already been the subject of significant scholarly inquiry. My discussion of these two films therefore focuses on the lesser-known aspects of their production histories and promotional strategies. The other two films of the chapter are less familiar but are well worth examining. *Tokyo File 212* (Dorrell McGowan and Stuart McGowan, 1951), made during the last year of the occupation, folded scenes of a thriving Japan virtually free of occupation forces into its anticommunist spy story. *My Geisha* (Jack Cardiff, 1962) focuses on racial and gender relations and racial impersonation, blurring the boundary between (white) American and Japanese. The film fulfills Michener's ideal of white Americans at home in the world while simultaneously suggesting that the real Japan may be endangered by the overwhelming influence of American culture, a process set in motion in large part by the U.S. occupation. Taken together, these films demonstrate a new U.S. attitude toward Japan that was symptomatic of the role the United States saw for itself in the American Century.

In Occupied Japan

Tokyo File 212 was, according to news items of the period, the first American feature to be shot entirely on location in Japan.[13] The film originated with George Breakston, a Paris-born actor who arrived in the United States as a child and appeared in American films from the 1930s to the 1940s before turning his attention to directing and producing. Breakston worked with the U.S. Signal Corps in Japan during the war and at the time of the production of *Tokyo File 212* was living in Japan with his American wife.[14] He was able to interest Dorrell and Stuart Mc-Gowan in producing and directing the film, and the seven-hundred-thousand-dollar cost of the production was covered in large part by Melvin Belli, a San Francisco–based lawyer with Hollywood clientele, and the Japanese company Tonichi Enterprises (associated with the newspaper *Mainichi Shimbun*), which contributed approximately one hundred thousand dollars because, "according to the producers, the picture will show that Japanese can be good democrats."[15] On April 23, 1950, the *New York Times* announced, "Japan will be 'invaded' by a Hollywood troupe in June, it became known the other day, to make a film, entitled 'Tokyo File 291' [*sic*]."[16] The film was shot in Japan over thirty-six days beginning on August 5, 1950. Hollywood studio RKO distributed the independently produced film.

 Tokyo File 212 was released in 1951, the year before the end of the U.S. occupation of Japan and the year after the start of the Korean War. The film, which was reportedly based on an actual U.S. military file, follows the efforts of a U.S. intelligence agent, Jim Carter (Robert Peyton), to track down old college friend Taro Matsudo (Katsuhiko

Haida), who is thought to be aiding the communists in Japan. Jim goes undercover in Tokyo as an American journalist and is aided in his investigation by Steffi Novak (Florence Marly), a mysterious Eastern European woman who is familiar with Japan and offers to act as his guide and assistant.[17] Jim learns that Taro was completing his training to become a kamikaze pilot at the moment of Japan's surrender and was so distraught by this unexpected turn of events that he became involved with the communists. After initially rebuffing Jim's efforts to reach out to him, Taro realizes the error of his ways and sacrifices himself to save Jim, his father, and Steffi and to unmask Oyama (Satoshi Nakamura) as the villainous communist leader. The film concludes as Jim says good-bye to Steffi at the airfield before returning to the United States, his mission accomplished.

The film opens with an onscreen acknowledgment that gives the audience some sense of the political and historical context of the production: "This picture was filmed entirely in Japan with the approval of: The United States Department of Defense, The United States Army, Far East Command, The Japanese Government, The Tokyo Metropolitan Police. For their cooperation, we gratefully express our thanks." Press coverage of the film often emphasized U.S. governmental approval, highlighting the film's identity as a postwar feature filmed on location in Japan at a time when the country was still under U.S. occupation. The film's story line, which was well suited to the ideological goals of the reconstruction, was undoubtedly helpful in securing official consent for the production. One article also implies that Breakston's connections to the U.S. military in Japan helped to make the film possible: "Through certain military and diplomatic associations [Breakston] was able to secure the initial permissions. The McGowans carried these to completion in Washington."[18] Another piece suggests that the man in charge of the U.S. occupation of Japan, General Douglas MacArthur, supported the picture by allowing filming in Japan, providing facts taken from intelligence files for the story, assigning interpreters to the production, and letting officers and men appear in the film as themselves.[19] This article underlines the film's anticommunist message and its relevance to current events, though with a certain tongue-in-cheek tone: "The movie industry's contribution to the convoys of planes, tanks and men we're sending to Japan was rushed off today. It's an airlift of falsies . . . to turn size 30 Japanese girls into size 38. [Dorrell McGowan] needs those misses for extras and sub-roles, and there's nothing like a few size 38s to add interest to a picture."[20] Beyond the film's predictable anticommunist message and its use of some of the typical attractions of a low-budget drama, *Tokyo File 212* also offers its audience unexpected pleasures directly related to its ability to shoot on location in Japan.

The film's images of occupied Japan offer rare glimpses of a particular time and place, with an almost documentary-like allure. These scenes and the historical context of their production make *Tokyo File 212* a significant text, distinguishing it from scores of other B movies of the time also set in the exotic lands of the Far East but filmed on studio back lots. The posters available to exhibitors in the RKO press book for *Tokyo File 212* emphasize the film's identity as a "spy thriller" and the fact that it was shot on location in Japan with the cooperation of the U.S. and Japanese governments. The poster reproduced on the cover of the press book, for example, has the movie's name and the words "Filmed on the spot in Japan" and "Dangerous spy net in the powder-keg Orient!" as well as a jumble of images drawn from the world of pulp fiction covers, most prominently of a beautiful white woman's face (fig. 4.1). This promotional text effectively calls attention to the major selling points of the film—that is, its genre identity and shot-on-location production, particularly in the absence of a well-known director or famous actors. The studio's publicity and marketing thus reinforce the themes emphasized in the press coverage of the film, emphases that continue throughout the film itself.

After the opening credits, the film segues into the story as Jim narrates, in a voice-over during a pan of a cityscape, "This is Tokyo, Japan, as it looked from my hotel window. A city of six and one quarter million, the last outpost of democracy in the Far East." He continues, after a cut to a shot of a busy intersection, "To most of the people going about their business here in the Ginza, it was hard to believe that a war was raging in Korea, only six hundred short air miles away." The next shot shows a nervous Japanese man with a suitcase walking down a crowded sidewalk as Jim intones, "But even here, death was on the march, and it was headed straight for me," over an image of himself exiting a car with a woman. Throughout this narration as well as in the opening credits, the audience's attention is drawn in two different directions. While the film has a realist veneer produced by the audience's knowledge of the dual U.S. and Japanese governmental approval of the film and the images of contemporary Japanese life seen at the outset, it also follows the most hackneyed conventions of B-movie thrillers set in the Orient: the clichéd "Chop-

FIGURE 4.1   Black-and-white reproduction of the one-sheet poster
for *Tokyo File 212* (Dorrell McGowan and Stuart McGowan, 1951).
Courtesy of the Academy of Motion Picture Arts and Sciences.

stix"–style font used for the names and titles in the credits, the overly dramatic "Oriental" musical score that opens the film, and Jim's ominous voice-over narration. The result is a strange juxtaposition of the plotting, dialogue, and acting typical of a low-budget spy thriller with intriguing documentary scenes of Japan in 1950. In fact, these views wield an undeniable visual interest that is arguably more compelling than the story. In this opposition between story and setting lies both the fascination and the failure of the film.

The use of location shooting in this film is in a sense unnecessary, given that the story of *Tokyo File 212* is fairly conventional and could easily have been produced on a studio back lot. *Blood on the Sun* (Frank Lloyd, 1945), for example, shares a great deal with *Tokyo File 212* in terms of tone, characters, and narrative structure. *Blood on the Sun* is set in Japan in 1929 and stars James Cagney as Nick Condon, an American newspaperman working in Tokyo who helps to smuggle the infamous Tanaka Memorial out of the country, thereby revealing Japan's militarist plans to the world.[21] In mid-October 1944, when the film was produced, shooting on location in Japan would have been impossible. However, the film hardly needed location shooting for a narrative in which Condon encounters various operatives in hotels, restaurants, and bars; learns information; is betrayed; fights back; and has a final showdown on a street in front of the American embassy. Similarly, location shooting would have been wasted on *First Yank into Tokyo* (Gordon Douglas, 1945), most of which takes place in a Japanese prisoner of war camp. In this film, Tom Neal plays Major Steve Ross, an American pilot who undergoes plastic surgery and becomes "Sergeant Takishima." His mission is to infiltrate the prisoner of war camp to rescue an American scientist who holds the key to the atomic bomb. *Tokyo File 212* similarly did not require location filming, and audiences would not have expected it. Yet it was filmed in Japan, with a relatively large number of Japanese cast and crew members.

For many reviewers, the glimpses of Japan and the Japanese that the film offered were far more valuable than the story. According to a *Variety* reporter, *Tokyo File 212* "is an atmospheric melodrama, filmed entirely in Japan, with good exploitation values. However, colorful and interesting atmosphere is bogged down by very routine spy plotting that keeps it on a pulp fiction level despite presumably factual story source." A few sentences later, the reviewer reiterates, "A Cook's tour of Tokyo streets, celebrations, theatres, clubs and seamy nightlife provides the colorful background for the tale and had scripters come up with a story equally as interesting, 'Tokyo File 212' could have been sock."[22] The *Box Office* reviewer agreed:

> Probably the film's most potent asset is the fact that it was produced entirely in postwar Japan with the approval of the U.S. defense department and other agencies. Such authentic backgrounds, the employment of a largely Japanese cast and some fairly interesting glimpses of Nipponese customs and scenery find the going a bit rough, however, in view of the confusing and labyrinthine story supplied by Dorrell and Stuart McGowan.[23]

The *New York Times* was even less generous:

> "Tokyo File 212" has the unique distinction of being the first Hollywood feature to be filmed in Japan. But, financial reasons aside, it is difficult to discover from the proceedings unveiled at the palace yesterday why the long trip was made.... Say this for the producers, however. They did manage to capture some of the sights in the teeming metropolis, including the busy populace, theatres, night clubs and street celebrations. . . . But the story, which gets in the way of this sight-seeing tour, is something else again.[24]

The fact that all three reviewers evaluated the atmosphere and background of the film apart from its plot or story is significant. That they also unequivocally deem the Japanese customs and scenery more interesting than the story suggests a symptomatic split between the film's mise-en-scène and the film's narrative.

Many scholars have noted the contradictory impulses of spectacle and narrative in film. Tom Gunning, for example, cites early French filmmaker George Méliès's insistence that the "tales" of his films are of little importance other than as pretexts for "tricks" and tableaux. This assertion supports Gunning's conception of early cinema as a "cinema of attractions," designed to present views to the audience rather than to tell stories.[25] Gunning also notes two studies related to his analysis of early film: Laura Mulvey's discussion of "the dialectic between spectacle and narrative" in classical cinema, and Donald Crafton's study of slapstick comedy, "which did a balancing act between the pure spectacle of gag and the development of narrative."[26] In Mulvey's essay, the spectacle of the woman threatens to arrest the narrative, while Crafton writes of the spectacle of physical comedy. In *Tokyo File 212*, we see another example of how the pleasures of the sights that film can provide—this time of a touristic type—are distinct from and apparently far more compelling than the story of the film. The images we see of Japan and Japanese culture in *Tokyo File 212* are detailed and varied, including the bustling Ginza district of Tokyo in the opening of the film; the imposing governmental National Diet Building, also in Tokyo; a festival in the seaside town of Enoshima; the hot springs resort town of Atami; a performance by Ichimaru, a celebrated geisha; and a brief glimpse of the Takarazuka Revue performing at the Imperial Theater in Tokyo. The presence of these sights in the film is not, however, strongly motivated by the story. In fact, in many instances in *Tokyo File 212*, the narrative strains to justify the setting, inverting the usual relationship between background and foreground.

Jim's visit to Enoshima is one example of when the scenery diverts attention from the story. Jim travels there at the suggestion of a mysterious telegram. The sequence begins with a brief scene at a railway station in Tokyo showing Jim evading a man sent to follow him. The next scene, our first view of Enoshima, does not show Jim disembarking from the train, as might be expected, but displays the festival he is to attend. We are shown his arrival only after several views of the street festival and the celebrants. He initially appears on a crowded sidewalk in a long shot that allows a glimpse of the nearby coastline. Jim makes his way to the festival, and as the parade passes by, a man in a mask tells him to be at the shrine in ten minutes. When he finally encounters the mystery man at the shrine, he sees that it is Taro, whom Jim has been seeking. Jim extends his hand and exclaims, "Taro!" but Taro does not reciprocate. The scene fades out on a medium shot of Taro with a stern look on his face that is visually rhymed in the impassive demeanor of a statue in the background.

There is no indication of whether Jim and Taro speak during this encounter until the following scene, when Jim is ambushed and abducted by a group of men who question him. Only during this interrogation and Jim's later report of the incident to his superiors do we learn of his conversation with Taro. Atypically for a classical narrative, the film does not depict on-screen this important confrontation between the main character and the man he was assigned to find, which includes information key to the plot.[27] Although the film shows various aspects of the town of Enoshima and we know that Jim's trip to Enoshima ends with a meeting with Taro, we learn little of the encounter itself except in retrospect. Judged by the standards of narrative clarity, the Enoshima sequence favors sightseeing over storytelling. Other sequences, such as Jim's meeting with Oyama in Atami, show evidence of a similar tension between mise-en-scène and narrative. The initial bird's-eye view of Atami, along with Steffi's explanation that the city is "celebrated for hot springs, honeymoons, and romance," appear as a touristic introduction to the site. In the hotel at Atami, Ichimaru's performance offers an intriguing view of Japanese culture. However, the narrative events of this segment, in which Oyama tries to discover whether Jim is an intelligence agent or really just a journalist, seem laborious, and the supposed suspense over the threat of poisoned food is stilted and unconvincing.

Most of the important events of the story take place in interiors, on stage sets. The crucial scene in which Naniko (Reiko Otani), Taro's former girlfriend, tries to convince him of the benefits that have accrued to Japan during the U.S. occupation takes place in Naniko's hospital room, where she is recovering from injuries sustained during an attempted kidnapping. Naniko asks Taro, "In the old Japan, did a farmer ever own his land? Could workers demand fair treatment? Was the voice of the lowest as strong as the highest? Things are good. Why do you want to destroy them?" Her words and evidence that his comrades were responsible for the injuries that led to her hospitalization and eventual death convince Taro to change sides. Before he can act, however, Oyama summons him. The climax of the film takes place in a studio set of an office with what appear to be painted cityscapes in the windows. In the office, Oyama reveals his nefarious plan to murder Jim, Steffi, and Taro's politician father with a bomb. In an act of desperation, Taro jumps out of the office window to his death. Taro's spectacular suicide simultaneously saves Jim, Steffi, and his father by drawing them away from the bomb site and implicates Oyama in his death, thereby exposing him as the head of the communists in Japan. Taro sacrifices his life not for the emperor and the old, militaristic Japan, as he had originally been trained to do, but for the new Japan, "the last outpost of democracy in the Far East." The political implications could not be clearer: democracy is an ideal worth dying for. From pledging his life to the emperor to renouncing communism and giving his life for democracy, Taro Matsudo demonstrates the path that the Japanese are meant to follow under the tutelage of their U.S. overseers.

Although the conclusion of the film does not mention the Korean War, the film obviously looks forward to Cold War politics. Despite the transitional historical moment of the film's production, its narrative erases almost all traces of the Second World War and the U.S. occupation to emphasize the confrontation occurring in Japan between democracy (represented by the United States) and communism (linked to the Russians). A number of news reports concerning the production emphasized the timeliness of the subject matter, noting, for example, that the scene of the railroad strike in the film was based on a recent incident in Japan. Dorrell McGowan also boasted of the film's realism: "No movie producer knows what realism is until he has made a picture in Japan."[28] But one of the examples he cites reveals more than he probably intended about the "real" conditions of the production of the film. For the explosion at the conclusion, the Japanese crew planted fifteen bombs in the interest of creating a more believable effect, whereas McGowan had only planned on using six. Through some miscommunication, the U.S. air patrol was not informed in advance of the planned explosion and reacted as if it were the beginning of an actual riot, surrounding the scene with military police, fire engines, and riot squads.[29] McGowan recounts this episode to demonstrate the Japanese commitment to verisimilitude, but it is equally revealing of the reality of the historical context of the film's production. The Americans were in charge and were determined to maintain order, even using military force if needed to suppress labor unrest and minimize communist influence. The narrative of *Tokyo File 212* illustrated why such policies and actions were in the best interests of the Japanese as well as the United States and the world.

We might ask why the filmmakers chose to incorporate images of Tokyo city life, Japanese resort towns, and geisha performances into a film with such an overt, even simplistic, political message. The filmmakers had received permission to film their fictional narrative on location in Japan, and if the press coverage is any indication of its importance, this in itself was a newsworthy event. Were the documentary images merely an attempt to make the most out of an established attraction and potential selling point for the film, regardless of its narrative? Did the travel views have any function beyond serving as a decorative background for the story? I believe that the film had a dual identity and double lesson, since it offered U.S. audiences a contrast in images of Japan just after the war and Japan five years later. The first photographs and newsreels of Japan after the surrender showed Americans the extent of the devastation U.S. forces had visited upon the country. As thinly motivated as the trips to Enoshima or Atami were within *Tokyo File 212*'s narrative, these scenes showed audiences a side of the country that emphasized natural beauty, cultural heritage, and leisurely pursuits. Similarly, the Tokyo street scenes show a city going about its business, a dramatic contrast to the recent scenes of wartime destruction. On a narrative level, *Tokyo File 212* offered a ponderous lesson in the evil character of the communists; on another level entirely, the film functioned as a sightseeing excursion into contemporary Japan. While Taro Matsudo's ultimate sacrifice confirmed the value of the ideals of democracy, an ideological argument made most easily through the dialogue and narrative, the street scenes and other documentary-like views within the film could serve as evidence of the achievements of the U.S.-led postwar reconstruction. Caught between these two separate but interwoven ideologies as well as between the generic conventions of a B-grade spy thriller and the enchantments of on location travel views, *Tokyo File 212* ends up a divided text that comes up short in the area of cinematic unity and coherence but does so in a way that makes it a uniquely revealing historical work.

In Occupied Japan: The Cold War Version

The Allied occupation of Japan from August 1945 until April 1952, in practice a primarily American endeavor under the command of General MacArthur, was an unprecedented undertaking. "In those years," writes Dower, "Japan had no sovereignty and accordingly no diplomatic relations. No Japanese were allowed to travel abroad until the occupation was almost over; no major political, administrative, or economic decisions were possible without the conquerors' approval; no public criticism of the American regime was permissible." He also describes the general attitude and behavior of the American occupiers in terms of a well-intentioned but nevertheless imperial presence built on hierarchy and practices of domination:

> [The Americans'] reformist agenda rested on the assumption that, virtually without exception, Western culture and its values were superior to those of "the Orient." At the same time, almost every interaction between victor and vanquished was infused with intimations of white supremacism. For all its uniqueness of time, place, and circumstance—all its peculiarly "American" iconoclasm—the occupation was in this sense but a new manifestation of the old racial paternalism that historically accompanied the global expansion of the Western powers.[30]

Dower carefully notes, however, that not all individual interactions between the Americans and the Japanese were so clear-cut and that the Japanese had expressed similar attitudes of superiority and paternalism in their imperial ambitions vis-à-vis other Asian nations. The Japanese were not merely the victims of American domination, and not all Americans saw the Japanese with imperial hauteur. Nevertheless, the Americans ruled Japan for nearly seven years, turning Tokyo's financial district into Little America and rewriting the Japanese constitution. However, regardless of the degree to which the U.S. occupation of Japan may have resembled the earlier U.S. occupation of the Philippines or China, in the Cold War context the film industry provided U.S. audiences with a rather different representation.

Films that took the occupation as their explicit subject and setting were not produced until after the end of the occupation itself. This temporal lag led to stories that focused on the U.S. occupation but were framed within the politics of the Cold War and the establishment of U.S. global hegemony. In *Cold War Orientalism,* Christina Klein's wide-ranging study of popular U.S. representations of Asia in the postwar era, she argues that the texts she examines "helped to construct a national identity for the United States as a global power." However, she adds, "The task of national identity formation was complicated by the fact that this rise to global power took place at the very moment when nationalist leaders throughout Asia were in the process of throwing off Western domination."[31] Klein identifies three characteristics such imperatives created in the texts: Cold War politics were fundamental to their narratives, whether implicitly or explicitly; the focus was on Americans in Asia rather than Asia itself; and the texts promoted an ideal of racial tolerance and inclusion.[32] Although my focus is different from Klein's, her argument is relevant to the films I discuss in this section.

During the Cold War, films that addressed the U.S. occupation within their narratives stressed intercultural encounter and exchange between the Americans and the Japanese. For example, they showcased Americans willing to look past the racial hatreds of the war and to learn to work with and learn from their former enemies. Discourses surrounding the production of the films shot on location further reinforced this theme; traveling to Japan and filming there became small-scale examples of successful and harmonious international relations. *The Teahouse of the August Moon* is probably the most well known of these films today. Other films focusing on U.S. occupation forces in Japan and released in the United States in the mid-1950s include *Three Stripes in the Sun* (Richard Murphy, 1955), *Navy Wife* (Edward L. Bernds, 1956), and *Joe Butterfly* (Jesse Hibbs, 1957).[33] All of these films were shot at least partly on location in Japan, with the exception of *Navy Wife*, for which I have not been able to confirm shooting locations.

The difference between occupation-era politics and Cold War politics—in particular, the development of U.S. national identity as a global leader—can be strikingly illustrated by comparing *Tokyo File 212* and *Three Stripes in the Sun*. Where *Tokyo File 212* shows the transformation of a former Japanese soldier, *Three Stripes in the Sun* demonstrates how an American soldier overcomes his wartime hatred of the Japanese to become a benefactor for Japanese children and the fiancé of a Japanese woman. The film begins with an onscreen prologue that relates the real-life basis of the narrative: "In December, 1949, this plane was carrying a group of servicemen to occupation duty in Japan. With the co-operation of the United States Army and working in the original Japanese locations, we have tried to show you what happened to one of them. This is the story of Master Sergeant Hugh O'Reilly." O'Reilly (Aldo Ray) initially hates the Japanese, but he eventually changes his opinion, raising money for a Japanese orphanage, and even proposing marriage to his Japanese interpreter. The main character of *Tokyo File 212*, in contrast, encounters "good" democratic Japanese and "bad" communist Japanese while carrying out his work of ensuring that Japan remains "the last outpost of democracy in the Far East." His closest personal and professional associate is a mysterious Eastern European woman, and once the villain is apprehended, he returns to the United States, untouched by his sojourn in Japan. *Three Stripes in the Sun*, however, emphasizes the evolution of O'Reilly's view of the Japanese from the enemy to human beings committed to rebuilding their war-torn society. This shift in perspective was, of course, the same one that the U.S. public and the army itself were asked to make in the years after the Second World War.

The film *The Teahouse of the August Moon* was an adaptation of the Pulitzer Prize–winning play by John Patrick, who also penned the screenplay. Patrick based his work on a novel by Vern Sneider that was inspired by his experiences as a member of the U.S. military government in Okinawa in 1945, where he served as commander of a small village, Tobaru.[34] *The Teahouse of the August Moon* presents a comical and essentially benign vision of the U.S. "democratization" of Okinawa. However, the extremely broad, nearly farcical tone of the film, along with the suggestion that the Okinawans, headed by Marlon Brando as Sakini, really have the upper hand, makes *The Teahouse of the August Moon* the most fantastical of the four films this chapter considers.[35] It is useful to examine *The Teahouse of the August Moon* in greater detail because of its exaggeratedly humorous version of intercultural exchange; its popularity as a representation of the U.S. occupation of Japan, first as a theatrical production and then as a major Hollywood film; and the discourses of friendship, understanding, and cooperation that accompanied the film's on-location shooting.

After establishing the setting as "Okinawa 1946," the film begins with a prologue taken verbatim from the play that situates the U.S. occupation of Okinawa within a longer history of foreign occupations:

> Lovely ladies, kind gentleman: Please to introduce myself. Sakini by name. Interpreter by profession. Education by ancient dictionary. Okinawan by whim of gods. History of Okinawa reveal distinguished record of conquerors. We have honor to be subjugated in fourteenth century by Chinese pirates. In sixteenth century by English missionaries. In eighteenth century by Japanese war lords. And in twentieth century by American Marines. Okinawa very fortunate. Culture brought to us. . . . Not have to leave home for it. Learn many things. Most important that rest of world not like Okinawa. World filled with delightful variation.[36]

The film then introduces Colonel Purdy (Paul Ford), a self-important bureaucrat whose main concerns are maintaining hierarchical divisions between the natives, the enlisted men, and the officers and advancing his career within the U.S. Army. Captain Fisby (Glenn Ford), a former professor of the humanities who has had a less-than-successful army career, enters the scene and is immediately sent to administer the village of Tobiki. Amiable, earnest, and well-meaning but also ineffectual and easily swayed, Captain Fisby is manipulated by Sakini and the villagers at every turn. He agrees to a variety of requests, beginning with taking an army jeep overloaded with passengers and their belongings to Tobiki via a very roundabout route and ending with building a teahouse for the village rather than the pentagon-shaped schoolhouse called for in the Army handbook's "Plan B." Along the way, Fisby comes to appreciate the comfort of a kimono (even if his is actually a bathrobe), the ministrations of a geisha, and the pleasures of watching the sun set each evening from the pine grove. The villagers, for their part, enthusiastically appoint a chief of police, a chief of agriculture, and a president for the ladies' democratic club. They willingly produce handicrafts to sell, as Fisby instructs, but then switch to a sweet-potato-based brandy when their original wares fail to find buyers. Their new enterprise meets with almost instant success, until Purdy learns of it and orders it shut down. Despite the apparent destruction of the teahouse, when word comes from Washington that Tobiki is to be cited as an example of "American get-up-and-go," the villagers quickly reconstruct the teahouse.

John Patrick's play opened on Broadway on December 10, 1952. Three years later, the play was still earning rave reviews, as in a 1955 *Los Angeles Times* article that described the work as "the most satisfactory drama to emerge in the postwar American theater," adding, "No play of the modern theater has had such universal appeal."[37] The reporter describes the play as concerning the "efforts of the American Army of Occupation to bring democracy to the Okinawans. Instead of Americanizing Okinawans, it manages adroitly to Okinawa[n]ize Americans."[38] Patrick attributed the success of his work to the "universal quality . . . which must stem from the eternal tale of the little man turning the tables on the great, of the failure who comes to terms with himself." The playwright further speculates, "The gentle fun it pokes at American efforts to fit western culture on the Orientals must particularly delight people of occupied countries."[39] Whether this drama could bring pleasure to people of occupied countries is an open question. Regardless of the play's reception elsewhere, its critical and commercial success at home suggests that this representation of the American occupation certainly appealed to U.S. audiences, who could envisage their representatives abroad as honest, well-meaning men who were willing to learn about and even adopt foreign customs while generously sharing American know-how and get-up-and-go.

The lessons the Americans learn from the "Orientals" are made most explicit near the conclusion of the play and the film, just when it seems that all of Fisby's efforts in Tobiki have been for naught. Fisby tells Sakini, "I used to worry a lot about not being a big success. I must have felt as you people felt at always being conquered. Well, now I'm not so sure who's the conqueror and who the conquered." Fisby continues, "It's just that I've learned from Tobiki the wisdom of gracious acceptance. I don't want to be a world leader. I'm making peace with myself somewhere between my ambitions and my limitations."[40] However, Fisby's "failure" to carry out the generic Plan B and his willingness to work with the villagers and take into consideration their needs and concerns are precisely what lead to his success in leaving Tobiki a better place than when he arrived. Although Colonel Purdy, Captain Fisby, and Captain McLean are in charge in Okinawa, their largely ineffectual efforts to govern the natives raise the question of who really has the upper hand. Much of the comedy of the piece derives from this upending of the expected balance of power. As occupiers, the Americans could not be more benevolent. Who could object to such efforts?

The media coverage of the film's production in Japan reinforced this narrative theme of Japanese-American amity with the power to blur the distinction between conqueror and conquered. The film's producer and the director arrived in Japan in February 1956; the cast and crew followed in April. MGM constructed the fictional village of Tobiki near the real Japanese town of Nara with the intention of using it as the primary shooting location. Heavy rainfall disrupted the production, however, and the studio was forced to ship the village to Culver City, California, to complete shooting.[41] Despite the fact that the weather permitted only a few days of exterior shooting in Nara, the trip to Japan was deemed worthwhile. According to director Daniel Mann, "Just the fact of being in Japan enriched all of us. The warmth, generosity, capacity for work of these people have given us a specific feeling, an attitude about them. And that, after all, is the theme of our story—that peoples can learn about each other and thus to accept each other. This we LIVED."[42] More specific examples of the friendly relations between the filmmakers and the Japanese appeared in reports of the cast on location. For example, the MGM press book describes the efforts of Eddie Albert, who portrayed the army psychiatrist, and his wife, Margo, to learn Japanese while on location. According to the studio, "By the time the picture was completed they were able to ask for directions, order food, and feel at home in Japanese shops."[43] The most prominent of this type of coverage were the reports of Brando's behavior in, reactions to, and experiences of Japan (fig. 4.2).

The film's producer, Jack Cummings, had proposed sending Brando to Japan early to prepare for his role as Sakini, but the studio declined to do so because of the extra expense.[44] Despite being denied the additional preparation time, Brando reportedly made considerable and widely publicized efforts to learn about Japan and the Japanese. A brief article in *Collier's* magazine reported, "Marlon Brando is one who believes, 'When in Japan, do as the Japanese do.' On location there for the first time to star in M-G-M's *The Teahouse of the August Moon,* Brando spent all of his spare time studying both the country and her people."[45] The article

FIGURE 4.2   MGM Publicity still, *The Teahouse of the August Moon* (Daniel Mann, 1956). The accompanying text reads: "Play time in Japan . . . during the location filming of MGM's 'The Teahouse of the August Moon' finds Marlon Brando, in make-up as the Okinawan interpreter, 'Sakini,' showing co-star Glenn Ford and Japanese extras a tricky hand game. The Japanese, Brando and Ford learned, were enthusiastic participants in all such games during spare moments in the filming near Nara, ancient capital of Japan." Courtesy of the Academy of Motion Picture Arts and Sciences. THE TEAHOUSE OF THE AUGUST MOON © Turner Entertainment Co. A Warner Bros. Entertainment Company. All Rights Reserved.

also describes how Brando greeted the Japanese press with a carefully memorized speech in Japanese, and "after that, it was love at first sight between Marlon and Nippon."[46] Brando described shooting the film as "a great emotional experience. Before I went to Japan, I had a completely false picture of the Japanese. I thought of them as cold, inscrutable. I found them to be warm and friendly, and more emotional even than the Italians."[47] One writer saw Brando's efforts to prepare for the role, in-

cluding the quality of his yellowface makeup, as exemplifying the "unit-
ing of two cultures," a process that "spread from the star to the entire
production."[48] In contrast, press accounts of the Metro-Goldwyn-Mayer
crew's travels to China to shoot backgrounds and purchase props for *The
Good Earth* made little mention of the Chinese who participated in the
process. While MGM's travel to China was valued as evidence of the studio's efforts and intentions to produce an authentic representation of the
country, Mann's description of the time his cast and crew spent in Japan
values the experience itself rather than the end results. Although studio
publicity for and press coverage of *Teahouse* still focused on the film's
stars rather than the Japanese people, the studio promoted and reporters
admired above all the American movie stars' efforts to learn Japanese
language, customs, and culture.

In fact, the promotional usefulness of the experiences of the cast and
crew in Japan most likely outweighed the aesthetic contributions of the
on-location footage to the completed film. The scenes shot in Nara in
this Cinemascope and Metrocolor film are visually distinct from and su-
perior to the Culver City studio scenes, which lack depth and detail in
the backgrounds. But given the agricultural and rural landscapes featured in this narrative, the studio might have achieved very similar effects by shooting *The Teahouse of the August Moon* entirely in California.
Critics did not remark in detail on the beauty or fascination of the Japanese backgrounds, as they did in the reviews of *Tokyo File 212*. Mentions
of the setting typically were positive but quite general, as if an appreciation of the backgrounds was de rigueur when a film had been shot on location in a distant country. The *Hollywood Citizen-News* coverage of the
film's premiere at the RKO Pantages Theater dutifully noted, "MGM
filmed a good part of this picture in Japan. The setting is Okinawa, and
the lovely backgrounds, in color and wide screen, give a rich feeling to
the celluloid canvas."[49] The *Los Angeles Times* reported that representatives of the Japanese government were present at the film's premiere
since it was filmed in part in Japan, and briefly remarked on the film's
"unusually colorful Oriental background."[50]

In what might well be the exception that proves the rule, according to
a June 1956 article filed from Nara, Japan, but published after the cast and
crew had already left for Hollywood, "Authenticity was the main reason
Mr. Mann wanted to shoot the entire $2,000,000 production in Japan."[51]
However, this rhetoric of authenticity, although central to *The Good
Earth* and relevant to many of the films discussed in this chapter, ap-

peared very rarely in articles about *The Teahouse of the August Moon* except, ironically, in reference to Brando's portrayal of Sakini. Most reviews of the film commented on the farcical nature of the comedy, suggesting that critics saw it as the opposite of a realistic or authentic film. Bosley Crowther of the *New York Times* was particularly forceful on this point, proposing, "Even if anybody were so literal-minded as to want to believe that this is the way Okinawans and American Army officers behaved, the performers would quickly disabuse them, for the acting is extraordinarily broad." Despite his many criticisms, Crowther allows that the film was meant as entertainment, not as a history lesson: "It was made for the purpose of amusement, not to teach geography or give a serious, accurate picture of American occupation in the area of Japan. And it fairly succeeds in that purpose. It is a funny, good-natured show, which looks pretty good in color and broad-beamed CinemaScope."[52]

Crowther's review was unique among the mainstream press reports of the film because it began with a brief discussion of Akira Kurosawa's *The Seven Samurai/Shichinin no samurai* (1954), which was currently playing in New York City.[53] Crowther notes that although Kurosawa's film is set in a village in sixteenth-century Japan, its characters and narrative form are very much like those of an American Western. Crowther sees a similar "striking opposition between geography and form" in both films.[54] Whereas *The Seven Samurai* is in some ways a Western set in Japan, *The Teahouse of the August Moon* purportedly takes place in Okinawa but is clearly a Hollywood production in form and in sensibility. Although Crowther does not use the term, the spirit of his review suggests that *The Teahouse of the August Moon* situates Japan within an imaginary geography according to Hollywood.

The MGM press book for the film further extends the history of this imaginary vision of Japan with a brief notice about how even though the village of Tobiki was fictional, the Japanese government decided to grant it a material status: "Future maps of Japan will show a new village, 'Tobiki,' although visitors to the spot will find nothing there but rice paddies. . . . In recognition of the first picture to be filmed by M-G-M in Japan, Governor Ryoza Okuda of the Nara Prefecture ordered Tobiki officially placed on all maps."[55] This official recognition of Tobiki points to some of the disturbing implications of the film's dislocated or deterritorialized representation of Okinawa and Okinawan and Japanese history. Although Tobiki is supposed to be an Okinawan village, Nara Prefecture is more than fifteen hundred kilometers northeast of Okinawa.

This reordering of Japanese geography pales in comparison, however, to the village's relocation to Hollywood for most of the film's production. Finally, Tobiki's appearance on Japanese maps with a corresponding physical site that boasts nothing but rice paddies serves as a fitting metaphor for the tenuous relationship between the historical and geographical realities of Japan and their representation in *The Teahouse of the August Moon.*

The Teahouse of the August Moon obviously offers an idealized, entertaining version of U.S. occupation rather than a serious investigation into real historical events. This was, undoubtedly, part of the appeal of the text. But the choice of Okinawa as the setting for such a story is especially significant. Okinawa occupies a key strategic location and is infamous for a horrific battle there late in the Second World War that claimed the lives of ninety-five thousand civilians.[56] In 1951, a U.S.-Japanese peace treaty gave the United States complete administrative control of Okinawa for an indefinite period of time, and not until May 15, 1972, was administrative authority transferred back to Japan. During this time, the United States turned the island into a massively fortified military base. Despite Okinawa's reversion to Japan, a contested event given the historical relations between Japan and the formerly independent kingdom of Ryukyu (which was annexed by the Meiji government of Japan in 1879), the island retains a significant U.S. military presence. The vast disparity between the actual place and the fictional version of it on stage and screen is truly remarkable, even by the standards of Hollywood fiction. For the inhabitants of Okinawa, the differences between the conquerors (both Japanese and American) and the conquered would certainly be painfully apparent. As for audiences around the world, it is difficult to say whether they associate Okinawa with the comical exchanges of Captain Fisby and Sakini rather than with the Second World War battle and U.S. militarization in the postwar period, but Fisby's good deeds in Tobiki clearly provide a better public relations story for the United States as a nonimperial world power than do memories of the Second World War and the reality of the postwar occupation of Japan.

Rest and Rehabilitation in Japan

One year after filming *The Teahouse of the August Moon,* Brando returned to Japan to shoot *Sayonara* with director Joshua Logan. Based on

Michener's novel of the same name, the film's story of interracial love set in Japan during the Korean War is a more fully articulated vision of an ideology of racial tolerance than that expressed by *Teahouse*'s comical U.S. occupation forces and Okinawan villagers.[57] Logan reportedly had a long-standing interest in Japan but did not have the opportunity to visit the country until 1951. While there, during a conversation with Michener at the Tokyo Foreign Correspondents Club, Logan brought up the idea for a story set in Japan that would show off modern Japanese culture, especially the theater, and Michener responded by writing *Sayonara*.[58] Logan wanted to make a film of *Sayonara* because he believed that the narrative promoted cross-cultural understanding: "I had been looking for years for a story that would try to explain something of the East to the West, and vice versa. James Michener's novel had struck me as one that contained a lot of fascinating information on both cultures."[59] However, Logan chose not to explore the recent history of the West in the East. Although the main character of the film is a member of the U.S. military, the importance of past and present U.S. military engagements in Japan and Korea are less significant than the romance at the center of the film. As Gina Marchetti notes, "*Sayonara* is another entry in a long Hollywood tradition of social problem films that use melodrama and romance to make concrete (but also personalize, individualize, and often trivialize) broader social or political concerns."[60] Because the filmmakers refused to recognize imbalances of power at various levels and along various axes of difference, the cross-cultural understanding the film espoused remained limited to the terms of a heterosexual romantic relationship. Yet since this interracial relationship was controversial at the time the film was produced, the relationship between a white American man and a Japanese woman could be seen in broader terms—specifically, the multiple contexts of race relations in the United States in the 1950s, U.S.-Japanese relations after the Second World War, and the role of the United States as a world leader during the Cold War and after. In this highly charged atmosphere, *Sayonara* attempts both to acknowledge the existence of racism in the United States and to show the possibility of change, one person at a time.

The novel and the film both turn on Major Lloyd Gruver's change of heart about (white) American servicemen marrying Japanese women. The film, like the novel, begins with Gruver's opposition to the impending marriage between an enlisted man, Kelly (Red Buttons), and a Japanese woman, Katsumi (Miyoshi Umeki). But as Gruver's relationship with his fiancée, Eileen Webster (Patricia Owens), becomes increasingly strained, he finds himself being drawn to the extraordinary Hana-ogi (Miiko Taka), the star of the all-female Matsubayashi troupe (a fictionalized version of the famous Takarazuka Revue). Hana-ogi and Gruver embark on a secret affair, knowing that most of their colleagues, families, and friends would disapprove, while Kelly and Katsumi get married and happily set up house. The relationship between Gruver and Hana-ogi is uncovered, and Kelly receives orders to return to the United States in a blatant effort to separate him from his Japanese wife, who cannot enter the United States under current immigration laws. Rather than face separation, Kelly and Katsumi commit a double suicide.

In Michener's novel, the final pages find Gruver contemplating the tragic ending of Kelly's and Katsumi's lives and regretfully bidding *sayonara*, or goodbye, to Japan and his relationship with Hana-ogi. He tells himself, "Even as I said these words I knew that I had to put them out of mind, for I was forced to acknowledge that I lived in an age when the only honorable profession was soldiering, when the only acceptable attitude towards strange lands and people of another color must be not love but fear."[61] In contrast, the final scenes of Logan's film show Hana-ogi stepping outside the Tokyo theater and dramatically announcing her acceptance of Gruver's proposal of marriage to a waiting crowd of fans, reporters, and Gruver himself. An American reporter asks Gruver, "Major, the big brass are going to yell their heads off about this, and the Japanese aren't going to like it much either. Do you got anything to say to them sir?" Gruver replies, "Yeah. Tell 'em we said sayonara." By having Gruver bid good-bye to the army and to those in Japan who would disapprove rather than to Hana-ogi and Japan as a whole, the film symbolizes a different age than does its literary predecessor.[62] The studio's production notes for the film emphasize that *Sayonara* is a new kind of story about East-West relations, describing its conclusion as "a smashing climax dedicated to the belief that the old saw of 'East Is East, and West Is West, and Never the Twain Shall Meet' is as passé as the Madam Butterfly romances of yore."[63] If the studio is to be believed, *Sayonara* practically ushered in a new era of racial harmony. However, *Sayonara* was not alone in proposing a new embrace of the East. *Sayonara*'s happy ending is reminiscent of *Three Stripes in the Sun*, which ends with Sergeant O'Reilly proposing to his Japanese interpreter. But unlike *Three Stripes in the Sun*, which focused on an individual soldier's change of attitude, *Sayonara* indicts the racial attitudes of a broad swath of U.S. society, including the army, federal immigration legislation, and individuals such as Colonel Crawford and General Webster and his wife.[64]

Brando was Logan's first choice for the role of Gruver. At their initial meeting, Brando objected to the book's representation of the Japanese and what he saw as its general attitude of white supremacy.[65] In Michener's novel, Gruver's cringe-inducing views of the Japanese certainly deserve criticism. Gruver finds Hana-ogi appealing because of her unusual nature; she is exceptionally beautiful, exceptionally talented, and completely unlike the other Japanese women he has seen in the streets of Japan. The book never examines Hana-ogi's thoughts, and Gruver treats her with condescension, especially regarding her English language abilities. The novel underlines how emasculating Mrs. Webster is and contrasts the Websters' marriage to Gruver's relationship with Hana-ogi. In Japan, Gruver learns a masculinist ideal of heterosexual romance, particularly in comparison to the marriage of duty and obligation lived out by his parents and the Websters and promised by his union with Eileen. Gruver also sees his affair with Hana-ogi as transcending racial and cultural difference, yet despite the supposed strength of their bond, the novel ends with the two people going their separate ways.

The initial motivations of the producer, director, and star in making *Sayonara* suggest that the main players responsible for this film were operating fully within what Klein calls "Cold War orientalism," a rearticulation of Edward Said's theory that takes into account liberal discourses of race within postwar U.S. global expansion.[66] Klein writes,

> The United States thus became the only Western nation that sought to legitimate its world-ordering ambitions by championing the idea (if not always the practice) of racial equality. In contrast to nineteenth-century European imperial powers, the captains of America's postwar expansion explicitly denounced the idea of essential racial differences and hierarchies.[67]

At the second meeting with Logan and producer William Goetz, Brando objected to the end of the novel, saying, according to Logan, "I can't do a picture where the American leaves the Japanese girl like the arrogant ending of *Madame Butterfly*."[68] Logan called Paul Osborn, the writer, asked if he'd agree to change the ending, and then informed Brando that his character could marry the Japanese girl at the end. Brando agreed to take the role. The pronounced southern accent with which Gruver speaks in the film was said to be Brando's invention, to which the director agreed because "the race prejudice would come through nastier that way, and race prejudice was really the basis of our story."[69] Goetz felt that with the accent, "You don't have to explain to audiences WHY he's prejudiced."[70] Thus, several features situate the film squarely within Cold War–era attitudes of liberal tolerance: the film's implicit references to the struggles regarding race relations in the United States; Logan's understanding of the story as one that "would try to explain something of the East to the West, and vice versa"; and Brando's insistence on a more positive portrayal of the Japanese and a less racist and tragic ending. This perspective of liberal tolerance, however, also coexisted with older views of an exotic Japan that did not differ radically from turn-of-the-century attitudes.

Soon after deciding to make the film, Logan and Goetz went to Japan to study the culture. Again, as in the example of *The Teahouse of the August Moon,* representations of the filmmakers' preproduction and production visits to Japan aligned with the basic ideology of the film's narrative. This time, the filmmakers emphasized the charms of an essential and timeless Japanese landscape and culture; this focus allowed them to sidestep any serious acknowledgment of the history of the U.S. war against and subsequent occupation of Japan. Goetz and Logan visited Takarazuka, home of the all-female performance troupe about which Michener had written, attended Kabuki performances, and searched for appropriately photogenic settings. Logan and Goetz were looking for something quite specific in their pursuit of possible shooting locations:

> Kyoto, the ancient capital of Japan, was the principal location. There Logan and Goetz found the "true" Japan locations they needed. It s[t]ill is the land of the kimono, the wooden shoes (geta) and the ricksha. It was in Kyoto and environs that the awesome Japanese scenery used as a backdrop was found.[71]

This description implies a distinction between the "true" Japan and some other Japan.

Cinematographer Ellsworth Fredricks echoes this belief that the film shows a particular version of Japan to audiences, claiming that "from a purely photographic standpoint, 'Sayonara' presents a different view of Japan than has been revealed in American-made films which have preceded it."[72] At the request of Logan and Goetz, Fredricks and certain other members of the production staff, including the entire camera crew, arrived in Japan two weeks before shooting was scheduled to start. They spent the time "study[ing] the country, its manners and customs, and its people."[73] This effort, Fredricks believes, resulted in "an intangible quality to the finished picture that might otherwise not be there."[74] It is indeed difficult to discern how their quasianthropological study affected the film, but the effort and expense budgeted for the purpose of familiarizing the crew with Japanese culture is notable, especially when contrasted with MGM's refusal to send Brando to Japan early for similar purposes for *The Teahouse of the August Moon.* Whatever knowledge the production staff may have gained, however, was relegated to the background. Very little of Japanese life or customs is represented in the film, which focuses, in narrative terms, primarily on the culture and customs of the American military. *Sayonara* indeed presented an image of the country that differed from that of either the Second World War era or occupied Japan but did so by returning to an older vision of Japan as an exotic land, a place remarkably similar to the country that Burton Holmes had found so enthralling. Despite Logan's purported desire to "explain something of the East to the West, and vice versa," his interest in Japan, like Holmes's, was primarily aesthetic.

Logan's appreciation for Japanese scenery and culture, which Fredricks represented spectacularly through Technicolor and the relatively new Technirama widescreen format, underpins the visual impact of the film and marks a significant difference from the novel.[75] But this admiration for Japan, which turns out to differ little from a fetishization of exotic difference, also demonstrates the limits of liberal tolerance. Japan is, quite emphatically, the setting for the narrative, as the location footage strikingly and dramatically illustrates. A number of reviewers pronounced the film's visual imagery remarkable. Wrote Philip Scheuer, Logan's "Japan, in Technirama and Technicolor, becomes breathlessly lovely, a series of translucent prints, in the camera of Ellsworth Fredricks."[76] According to Crowther,

> In a frame of handsome Japanese surroundings—outdoor gardens, graceful, sliding-paneled homes, bare-walled theatres and delicate tea-houses, shown in colors of exceptional taste and blend—[Logan] has pictorially justified the jangle and the harmony of cultures in his tale. There are scenes that are visually poetic, and that's as good as can be said for such a film.[77]

Most intriguingly, in a gushing review of the film for the *L.A. Examiner,* Ruth Waterbury finds that the real star of the film is "Japan herself, in all her exquisite, understated, deliberate loveliness." Waterbury adds that although *sayonara* means "good-bye," "the film means 'hello' to Japan, shown here in a manner which only the most fortunate tourist could see it. Here you see its temples and its towns, its fabulous Kabuki and Matsubayashi theaters—and mostly its people."[78] Her article concludes, "'Sayonara' often has the quality of a dream. . . . Make it your journey of the New Year—a journey into pleasure, and better understanding of human beings, and into the continual romance that all human hearts seek.[79] While Waterbury is unusual in explicitly describing the film as a virtual voyage, this discourse is present implicitly in the majority of the reviews of the film.

Unlike *Tokyo File 212*, the spectacular settings of *Sayonara* effectively support the film's narrative without overcoming it. The location scenes and cultural performances of *Sayonara* are crucial to the film not because they convey information about Japan but because they motivate Gruver to fall in love. In *Three Stripes in the Sun*, Sergeant O'Reilly's transformation begins with the empathy awakened by the sight of a ramshackle home for Japanese war orphans. Major Gruver, in contrast, changes his opinion of the Japanese when he first sees Hana-ogi cross the bridge from the dorms to the theater where she will perform. The choice of a bridge for this scene received much attention from the filmmakers. Logan and Goetz found the real bridge in Takarazuka disappointing, with Logan characterizing it as "a metal arch with side rails of wire netting" that "offered no hint of young love or sexual suspense."[80] On the island of Shikoku, they found a more suitable bridge—"A high arch, a graceful, humpback bridge, it was lyrical, photogenic, and obviously something that would be beautiful for the girls to walk across."[81] But taking the cast, crew, and equipment from Kyoto to Shikoku Island would have added considerably to the film's cost, so the filmmakers settled on a bridge in a royal enclosure in Kyoto, normally open only to visiting dignitaries. Getting permission to use the bridge, which required a formal dinner with the appropriate Japanese officials and the producer, director, and cast, including Brando, was worth the time and effort. The resulting scene is eye-catching, with crowds of young women in color-coordinated dress crossing the lengthy bridge, which spans the entire width of the screen when it is introduced in an extreme long shot.

Gruver's admiration for Hana-ogi deepens as he watches her perform. The sequence showing the Matsubayashi Girls Revue onstage is elaborate, featuring about half a dozen song-and-dance numbers with sumptuous production values, all with colorful costumes and intricate sets shown off to great effect by the Technirama and Technicolor technologies of the film. The film also showcases Kabuki and Bunraku performances, along with a range of Japanese interior and exterior settings. Although the Gruver in Michener's novel was largely repulsed by Japan, the film Gruver and the members of the audience (both within and outside the diegetic world of the film) are treated to a beautiful and extravagant vision of Japanese women and Japanese culture intended to arouse aesthetic and erotic appreciation. (In a parallel but minor plotline, Eileen Webster carries on a mild flirtation with Nakamura [Ricardo Montalban], a celebrated Kabuki artist who first captivates her with his performance of a lion dance on stage.) In learning to appreciate this world, as Gruver does, viewers become reacquainted with a nation that has been returned to its former status as a source of exotic, erotic difference and fascination, leaving behind its associations with the Second World War and postwar occupation.[82] Such images of Japan could have been captured only on location, yet the images of Japan the filmmakers chose to utilize were also highly selective and representative of a very particular view of the country and its people. Robert G. Lee comments that the opening of the film, "shot against the serene background of a lush Japanese garden, with gracefully arched footbridges and a watercourse," is "the classically Orientalist image of Japan—aestheticized, unchanging, pastoral, and ahistorical."[83] Lee thus demonstrates the ways in which the film's "Cold War orientalism" builds on the older orientalist form of geographical and cultural distinction. As the film attributes to Japan an essential, timeless difference, it therefore denies historical complexity and contradiction.

The imminent union of Gruver and Hana-ogi at the film's closing credits, which replaces the resigned defeat at the conclusion of the novel with a happy ending, also had broader implications for discourses of race within the United States. Since the film suggests that Gruver will take Hana-ogi back with him to the United States after their marriage (and the necessary changes in U.S. immigration law), their union represents the possibility of integrating the former wartime enemy into the U.S. body politic. Caroline Chung Simpson argues that Japanese war brides symbolized a hopeful new cultural pluralism in the United States precisely because they were Japanese, not Japanese American (or any other U.S. minority) and therefore outside of the historical discriminations faced by racialized citizen-subjects in the United States.[84] For *Say-*

onara to effectively condemn racial prejudice and promote its vision of a newfound understanding between East and West, it had to repress the history of Asians in the United States—in particular, the relocation and internment of Japanese Americans during the Second World War.

Therefore, the fact that Miiko Taka, the female lead of the film, was Japanese American required a selective publicity and marketing campaign that would concede the star's U.S. origins but emphasize her Japanese ancestry. At the same time, the campaign could not acknowledge the grave consequences this ancestry had for her, her family, or her community during the Second World War. This project of selectively publicizing Taka's background was challenging and convoluted. As Simpson argues, "Throughout the postwar years, the potential of interned Japanese Americans' presence in the body politic to disturb the problems of American identity remained a perpetual threat, an irrepressible part of the negotiations between the needs of national history and the 'incommensurabilities' of racial memory."[85] Not only did Taka have the requisite beauty and performance abilities, but her American childhood and upbringing were most likely advantages in that she would be able to perform the English-language dialogue easily and could communicate effortlessly with the filmmakers and her fellow cast and crew. However, her Japanese ancestry also posed a challenge to the message of the film, as it provided a pointed reminder of the nearly 120,000 people of Japanese ancestry who were forced to leave their homes to be incarcerated in internment camps during the war.

Before her part in *Sayonara,* Taka had been working at a travel agency, and she lacked prior acting experience. The choice of an unknown and inexperienced actor to play opposite Brando was news. Coverage of the film frequently included the story of her discovery, although different sources offer different versions. The studio's production notes recount that a talent scout invited Taka to the studio to audition after spotting her at the annual Nisei Festival in Los Angeles, a story that was frequently repeated in the popular press.[86] In an interview published in the *Los Angeles Times,* Goetz tells of searching in Japan for a female lead for *Sayonara* and then searching in West Coast U.S. cities with large Japanese American populations before almost deciding on Shirley Yamaguchi, an established Japanese actor. According to Goetz, Taka was first seen at the studio on December 15, when she accompanied a friend who was auditioning for a part; he does not mention the Nisei Festival at all. He also maintains that he and Logan knew immediately that she was the one they were looking for. Less than two weeks later, Taka departed with the company for Japan.[87]

Some of these narratives note the irony of searching in Japan for an actor to play the part of Hana-ogi, only to find her in Los Angeles, though a handful of reviews mistakenly describe Taka as a Japanese actor. Reviewers generally agreed, however, that Taka was beautiful, graceful, and enchanting. In virtually all of the articles about and reviews of the film that acknowledge Taka's U.S. citizenship and residence, the reporters take care to add that she was nevertheless reared "in strict Japanese tradition": "During her childhood she was taught the gracious art of the tea ceremony, flower arranging and odori dancing."[88] Taka herself confirmed such representations by identifying herself as "a Japanese girl" and assuring readers and audience members, "While I was born in Seattle and brought up in Los Angeles, I know the native Japanese mind and traditions."[89] Only one of the articles mentioned the relocation of Taka and her family to Gila Bend, Arizona, during the Second World War.[90] While *Sayonara* leveled criticisms of racial prejudice against individuals, army policy, and immigration legislation, it did not recognize the mass incarceration of Japanese Americans during the war. To do so would have called into question the foundations of its message of liberal tolerance and its implicit representation of the United States as a liberal democratic state committed to racial equality.[91] Thus, the studio, seeking to promote Taka as a talented and beautiful American actor of Japanese ancestry, emphasized her familial and cultural ties to Japan and acknowledged her U.S. nationality while skirting the persecution of Japanese Americans like her in the United States a little more than a decade earlier.[92]

In the film, when Hana-ogi meets Gruver in person for the first time, she tells him, "My father was killed by [an] American bomb dropped on my country. You have been my enemy. I have hated Americans. I have thought they were savages. There has been nothing but vengeance in my heart." Gruver replies, "Miss Ogi, there were an awful lot of Americans who were killed too. I think it would be best if we forgot about that." Hana-ogi implicitly agrees with him when she tells him that he does not appear to be a savage and that she wishes to apologize for her mistaken assumptions. With this exchange, the film banishes to the past the troubled history of Japanese-American international relations and prepares for a new beginning. Also forgotten, or more accurately, repressed, was the enmity against Japanese Americans in the United States, which was precisely what Taka, as a Japanese American, could not be allowed to voice. The film ends with Gruver and Hana-ogi in a car on the way to the U.S. embassy in Tokyo to begin the paperwork for their marriage; it offers little sense of the challenges yet to come. As a counterpoint to this conclusion, King Vidor's *Japanese War Bride* (1952) gives some indication of how the incarceration of Japanese Americans during the Second World War might figure in Gruver's and Hana-Ogi's future in the United States. The film, about a white Korean War veteran who brings his Japanese wife home to Salinas, California, explicitly addresses the Japanese American internment within its narrative but paints it as a historical event that is best left in the past in the interests of moving on to a more tolerant future. Yet history is not so easily dismissed. Regardless of how enchanting Japan appeared in *Sayonara* and how effectively the film transported its viewers to this exotic dreamland, audience members could hardly be expected to revise their views of Japan and the Japanese as quickly as Gruver did. Nor would the wartime treatment of the Japanese and Japanese Americans by the U.S. government be so easily forgiven or forgotten.

Although Brando was skeptical of *Sayonara*'s sentimentality, the film's liberal views of interracial marriage and its more positive representations of Japan coincided with his political perspectives at the time of the film's making. Just before shooting *The Teahouse of the August Moon,* Brando traveled to the Philippines, Thailand, Indonesia, and other countries in Asia studying the role of industrialized nations in the developing world in hopes of making a film about United Nations aid workers. In interviews with the press about his journey, he criticized his fellow Americans for their lack of knowledge of Asia, saying, "Our understanding of Asians will never improve until we get out of the habit of thinking of the people as short, spindly legged, buck-toothed little people with strange customs."[93] He felt that his chosen line of work offered an opportunity to help improve international relations, and he criticized films that countered this aim: "The Asians are looking to us for signs of friendship. You have no idea the amount of harm that a picture like 'House of Bamboo' can do."[94] According to the article, "Brando is all fired up to make a film that will bring Americans closer to an understanding of Asians. His present plan is to portray an American worker for the UN in Asia and depict his reactions to Asian culture and people."[95] The desire to promote better understanding of Asians and Asia in the United States motivated Brando to campaign for the role of

Sakini in *The Teahouse of the August Moon* and to accept the starring role in *Sayonara*, films he later criticized. Yet the sincerity of his desire to facilitate intercultural understanding is evident, as is its function as an element of Cold War orientalism.

Brando came away from his research trip to Asia more critical of the role of westerners in Asia than when he began it, but the film he envisioned making out of what he saw and learned never materialized. He had the opportunity to express some of these views, however, in his role as Harrison Carter MacWhite, the newly appointed U.S. ambassador to the fictional Southeast Asian country of Sarkhan, a thinly disguised Vietnam, in *The Ugly American* (George Englund, 1963), which was filmed in Thailand. The film's representation of U.S. policy in Asia gave voice to a sharply critical view of the role of Americans in Asia. Somewhat unexpectedly, changing opinions of the figure of the American in Asia can be seen in the trajectory of Brando films on this topic from the mid-1950s to the early 1960s, from the benevolent occupiers of *The Teahouse of the August Moon* to the enlightened believers in ethnic liberalism in *Sayonara* to the Western imperialists represented by the arrogant ambassador in *The Ugly American*.

At Home in Japan

The Ugly American signaled the geographic shift of the scene of American intervention in Asia from Japan to Vietnam, yet Japan remained of interest to U.S. audiences in the early 1960s. As a film about a Hollywood film being shot on location in Japan, *My Geisha* (Jack Cardiff, 1961) can be seen as a metacommentary on Americans in Japan, particularly if we consider the promotional texts connected with the film. *My Geisha* stars Shirley MacLaine as Lucy Dell, a successful Hollywood actor, and Yves Montand as her husband, film director Paul Robaix. The back of the videotape cover describes the film as a "delightful, gorgeously filmed comedy of mistaken identities" and asks, "Who's that mysterious Oriental beauty? It's Shirley MacLaine!" The film begins with Paul firmly refusing to cast his wife in his upcoming cinematic adaptation of *Madama Butterfly*, Giacomo Puccini's 1904 opera about the ill-fated romance between Cio-Cio San, a young geisha, and Lieutenant Pinkerton, an American naval officer. For the sake of authenticity, Paul is intent on shooting the film on location in Japan and casting a Japanese woman in the lead role. The studio, however, questions Paul's plan to use a Japanese woman for the role when his popular wife is perfectly willing to play the part. (Paul objects to her fame, which would overshadow his work as the director of the film, as was the case in their previous collaborations.) As a compromise solution, Sam (Edward G. Robinson), the film's producer, agrees to aid Lucy in her secret transformation into Yoko Mori, a Japanese geisha whom Paul subsequently hires for the part of Butterfly. Lucy initially transforms herself into a "traditional Japanese woman" as a simple acting challenge, but she comes to realize that as her Japanese alter ego, she offers her husband the support and understanding that he needs but that she, as an outspoken, strong-willed, self-centered (white) American woman, denies him. This insight, which depends on the same intersection of race, gender, and sexuality seen in *Sayonara*, allows Lucy to incorporate aspects of an idealized Japanese femininity into her personality, exemplified in the proverb, "No one before you, my husband, not even I," to become a better wife and to save her marriage.

The choice of *Madama Butterfly* as the film within this film is significant. *Sayonara* was publicized as the antithesis of this very well known narrative. Why was *My Geisha* reviving this age-old tale of Japanese-American relations? To answer this question, we must have some knowledge of the people behind the film. *My Geisha* was produced by Steve Parker, Shirley MacLaine's husband at the time. The Paramount production notes for the film devote a considerable number of words to emphasizing Parker's familiarity with Japan, describing him as, "doubtless the American with more expertise and affection for the orient [*sic*] than any other showman." The studio establishes that Parker was fluent in Japanese, had studied at Kyoto University, and had made two prizewinning documentaries about Japan, *Onsen* and *Geisha*. By shooting on location in Japan, he sought to show it "as a country of 'warm and breathing people, not as a series of cliché postcards.'"[96] Parker had lived in Japan when his father was sent to work there.[97] After the Second World War, Parker returned to the country to work for the U.S. occupation forces. Parker and MacLaine wed in 1954, but, dissatisfied with his work and life as MacLaine's manager in Hollywood, Parker left for Japan sometime around 1956 and set up a theatrical production company while MacLaine continued to pursue her career in Hollywood. In 1959, the company sent a touring stage show, *Holiday in Japan,* to the United States. In 1961, it produced and imported to the United States a "Philippine Festival" consisting of "wonderful, magnificent songs and native dances that were dying out among the natives themselves because of the popularity of our own raucous rock 'n' roll."[98] By 1963, Parker had offices in Tokyo, Hong Kong, Seoul, and Hollywood.

Parker's familiarity with Japan distinguishes him from the filmmakers discussed previously; in fact, his knowledge of Japan is reminiscent of, though hardly equivalent to, that of Pearl Buck's about China. Buck came out of a long history of American missionaries in China. Parker established himself as an expert on Japan in the postwar, increasingly internationalized realm of popular culture. Although his knowledge was based on lived experience, as Buck's was, Parker was concerned not with changing Japan or improving the lives of the Japanese, as a missionary might be, but with exporting Japanese culture to the West. He was a showman, and the value of his facility with Japanese language and customs lay in the insider's perspective and access it could provide.

The production notes for *My Geisha* as well as several reviews point out that Parker chose an experienced Japanese cinematographer, Shunichiro Nakao, for the film, and the production notes add that half of the crew was Japanese, with the remainder from England or the United States.[99] It was a point of pride for Parker that the production of *My Geisha* differed from other U.S. films shot in Japan:

> You can antagonize the Japanese by bringing in a whole studio, such as the "Sayonara" and "Teahouse of the August Moon" companies did. If you use all or mostly all U.S. personnel, you don't get the co-operation you must have from them. We used people from both countries, and were well covered with a dozen interpreters. Everything worked beautifully.[100]

Parker's representation of the ease of the production may have been exaggerated to support his reputation as an insider in Japan. Jack Cardiff, the director of the film, publicly criticized the Japanese for impeding the production, accusing them of manufacturing customs delays to take apart and photograph the film equipment for the purposes of copying it.[101] A few days after Cardiff's inflammatory statement, Parker, along with Paramount executive Martin Rackin, held a press conference to refute the charges, with Parker insisting, "Cooperation couldn't have been better."[102] Regardless of the degree to which the Japanese cooperated with Parker, he incorporated his criticism of earlier American film productions shot on location in Japan into *My Geisha* in a subtle yet pointed exchange directed at *Sayonara* and its director's claim to be "explaining something of the East to the West."

Early in *My Geisha,* soon after Paul and his cast and crew have arrived in Japan, they spend an evening at a teahouse, where they are entertained by geisha. Lucy, who has come to Japan without her husband's knowledge, bets Sam one hundred dollars that she can fool her husband into thinking she is a geisha. Dressed and made up to look like a geisha, she enters the dining room to serve the guests. Paul is apparently none the wiser as he inspects Lucy's powdered face and pronounces the shy young geisha more photogenic than Lucy. At the end of the evening, Paul turns to her and asks, "How do you say good-bye in Japanese?" Without missing a beat, Lucy responds, "Sayonara." Paul laughs as he realizes that *sayonara* is the only word of Japanese he knows. "It's the only word of Japanese that most people know," says Sam. Bob (Bob Cumming), who is to play the American naval officer in *Madama Butterfly,* mutters "Marlon Brando" on his way out. The joke, of course, is that Paul was on the verge of unmasking Lucy by asking her how to say something in Japanese. The word he picked, however, was the one word she knew—the one word that everyone knows—because of the film *Sayonara.* Since the point of this scene is to show that Paul cannot distinguish between a real Japanese geisha and his white American wife who has been made to resemble a geisha, this intertextual reference implies that most people (most Westerners, that is) who think they know Japan through the famous Brando film actually know very little.

Paramount billed *My Geisha* as "an American comedy of love and marriage," and indeed, the film puts the problems of the Euro-American couple squarely at the heart of the story.[103] Japan is the setting for the film, but unlike *Tokyo File 212, Sayonara,* and *The Teahouse of the August Moon,* there are no central Japanese characters outside of Yoko Mori, Lucy Dell's alter ego. However, because of the film-within-a-film story line and the racial and cultural impersonation at the center of this comedy of mistaken identity, knowledge of Japanese culture and customs is central to the plot. Learning about Japanese culture occurs both within the narrative of *My Geisha* and in the publicity and marketing of it, especially in interviews with MacLaine and Parker. The earlier films promoted their location shoots in Japan as exemplars of the current state of Japanese-American relations. *My Geisha* goes one step further by suggesting through its publicity and promotional texts that the film arose from the reality of the trans-Pacific and bicultural lives led by Parker, MacLaine, and their young daughter, Sachiko. Whereas Paul Robaix knows so little about Japan and Japanese women that he cannot tell the difference between his wife and a real geisha, Parker had an established reputation as a Japan expert. Furthermore, it was widely reported that Parker was a resident of Japan who spent the majority of his time in Tokyo in a home described as "Japanese in construction, but with the conveniences of Western architecture."[104] MacLaine, for her part, was labeled "Hollywood's number one Japan-commuter."[105] Thus, although all of the films discussed in this chapter are set in Japan, only *My Geisha* is presented from the perspective of Americans who actually live at least part of the time in Japan. MacLaine and Parker therefore represent a different version of the binaries of home and abroad, the United States and Japan; for this couple, the division between the two countries is much less absolute than for the filmmakers discussed earlier.

Unlike, for example, *Tokyo File 212, My Geisha* offers relatively few exterior location scenes even though the film was shot entirely in Japan over a period of three months. With the notable exception of a montage sequence approximately midway through the film that shows Paul and his cast and crew working in various outdoor sites while shooting *Madama Butterfly*, most of the action takes place in relatively everyday interiors. In this film, therefore, shooting on location is associated not with the recognizably exotic spectacles seen in earlier films but with the more modest spaces of Japanese hotels and teahouses, homes and offices. As the production notes proclaim, "'My Geisha' shows off-beat, off-hand, old and new Japan without reference to clichés. 'My Geisha' will neither open nor close with a shot of Fuji looking like a postcard."[106] But if viewers do not see many of Japan's familiar sights—what Parker repeatedly referred to as postcard clichés of the country—they have ample opportunity to observe Japanese culture and customs.

The narrative setup in *My Geisha* provides an opportunity for viewers to learn about Japan along with Lucy and especially about what being a geisha involves. Confusion about the exact nature of geisha was already a comic staple in U.S. films set in Japan. In *The Teahouse of the August Moon*, Fisby vehemently refuses to accept Lotus Blossom as his gift and is outraged by the prospect of "geisha lessons" for the women of the village until he realizes that he has a mistaken view of what a geisha does. When *Cry for Happy* (George Marshall, 1961) was released, Bosley Crowther began his review of the film, "Misunderstanding of the service

a Japanese geisha performs has been pretty well played out as the basis
for soldier-sailor comedies and tourist jokes."[107] The game of insinuating
that geisha offer sexual services only to insist indignantly that they are
respectable entertainers was thus already fairly well established in U.S.
films. But if they are not prostitutes, then what exactly do they do? *My
Geisha* seeks to take advantage of this curiosity as it fills in this gap in
knowledge.

When Paul informs his producer that he wants to make a film of
Madama Butterfly, shot in color and on location in Japan, he explains
that he wants to capture the real, traditional Japan. He also wants to use
a real Japanese woman in the lead rather than an actress so that the film
is real, not just an opera. It seems that whenever Paul speaks of his film,
he can be counted on to use the term *real* over and over again. Once in
Japan, however, Paul has difficulty casting the role of Butterfly. As he explains in frustration to Sam,

> I've seen thirty girls—ukulele acts on bicycles and rock and roll singers.
> They're more Western than the girls at home. I knew there was an Ameri-
> can tendency, but they're making a fetish of it. They're not Japanese any-
> more. Look at them. I felt this problem when I got off the plane and saw
> the neon signs. That's just why I want to do this picture. I want to capture
> that other spirit of Japan while it still exists.

Paul clearly finds the contemporary reality of Japan disappointing, and
his search for "the real, traditional Japan" is suffused with a strong sense
of nostalgia. Ironically, the process of Americanizing the Japanese that
began in earnest during the U.S. occupation, which *Tokyo File 212* and
The Teahouse of the August Moon celebrated, seems to have been all too
successful.[108] Despite having his pick from a room full of real Japanese
women, the only woman who fulfills Paul's criteria for the role is the one
designed with them in mind.

Paul realizes that the star of his film is none other than his wife relatively late in the narrative and, as fate would have it, through watching
her on screen. Near the end of the shoot, after what would presumably
have been weeks of working with the cast of the film, Paul is called to the
lab to review film from the past day's shoot. When he arrives, the technicians inform him that they will be screening the negative, in which all the
colors are reversed. As they view the film, the technicians remark again
on the odd coloring of the print. This repeated emphasis on color finally

reaches fruition when the image of Yoko appears on the screen and the technical details of the processing are such that her eyes appear blue and her hair red, revealing Lucy's true colors. At this moment, Paul recognizes that his wife has fooled him. "You shouldn't have done it, Lucy," Paul laments. "You're a clever girl—too clever for me." The audience, having been in on the ruse from the start, is spared the same embarrassment. As Paul learns a little too late, appearances can be deceiving, though apparently it is more difficult to fool the camera than the human eye. Because *My Geisha* critiques Paul's willingness to accept Yoko Mori for what she seems to be, the film suggests that Paul's vision of a traditional Japanese woman is incorrect, outdated, or both. Paul's blindness to his wife's deceit reflects his astounding lack of knowledge of the Japanese, a criticism that could also conceivably be extended to those who, like Paul, consider *Madama Butterfly* and *Sayonara* true representations of Japan and the Japanese. Not surprisingly, the film does not risk alienating its audience with such an overt critique. However, it does try to educate its viewers.

Earlier in the film, Lucy and Sam discover that cultural authenticity requires more than superficial resemblance. Lucy and Sam meet with an elderly geisha teacher in the hopes that he can instruct Lucy on how to be a geisha in a week or so. The teacher disabuses them of this notion by pointing out that the tea ceremony alone has ninety separate and exact steps and would take months to master. He then launches into a two-minute monologue about what a geisha is, telling them of one woman in particular who started her geisha apprenticeship at the age of seven; is able to speak French, English, and Chinese; plays excellent golf and tennis and is a ski champion; knows the closing prices of the franc in Geneva and the pound in London; can converse with almost any man about his profession; and may very well marry a cabinet minister one day. Geisha are, in his words, a "flawless combination of womanly graces and skills." He concludes that these characteristics cannot be learned in one week. Lucy agrees: "You couldn't teach me that in two lifetimes." The remarkable geisha, Kazumi Ito (Yoko Tani), happens to be visiting the teacher that day and agrees to work with Lucy for the duration of the filming in Japan to help her appear as much like a geisha as possible, even if she cannot actually become one.

The elderly teacher's lecture is almost identical to Parker's lengthy disquisition on the subject of geisha in "Operation Kimono," a *Cosmopolitan* article that offers a detailed interview with Parker and

MacLaine about the making of *My Geisha*. (The article's title also subtly reminds readers of the history of the U.S. military presence in Japan and the "infiltration" into Japanese life that this film purports to offer.) Parker compares the education of a geisha to the education of a doctor, noting that young girls often start their geisha education at the age of six or seven. Geisha can talk with businessmen about the closing prices in Geneva or the pound in London and may marry prime ministers, bankers, and professional men. Parker, like the teacher in the film, also explains the practice of *kangeko* (winter discipline), meant to promote mental discipline in apprentice geisha. In addition, Parker bemoans the decline of the profession because young girls in Japan no longer wish to submit to the discipline or long years of study required to become real geisha, the only opinion of Parker's that the geisha teacher does not voice onscreen.[109]

Through a kind of ventriloquism, Parker's knowledge is verbalized by the geisha teacher in *My Geisha* for the benefit of Lucy and the viewers of the film. Parker also shares this information directly with MacLaine as she prepares for her role; this sharing parallels the way that the accomplished Kazumi Ito helps Lucy Dell to construct the fictional Yoko Mori. Thus, Parker, the Japanese expert, both produced and guaranteed the authenticity of MacLaine's and Lucy's geisha or the double reality of Yoko Mori both within and outside of the film. He accomplishes this feat with the help of his onscreen surrogates, Kazumi Ito and the elderly geisha teacher. Aside from the lesson about geisha, viewers are also treated to an introduction to sumo wrestling, the rules and rituals of which Yoko explains to Paul and Bob after a quick briefing from Kazumi. It also falls to Yoko to inform Paul and Bob that coed bathing is not inherently scandalous but a question of different cultural norms.

Articles about the film frequently noted MacLaine's real-life connections to Japan, from her part-time residence in Tokyo in her "half-Western, half-Oriental home"[110] to her marriage to "the American with more expertise and affection for the orient [*sic*] than any other showman."[111] As the subheading of the *Cosmopolitan* article stated, "Shirley MacLaine has finally gone totally Asiatic by playing a geisha girl in her new movie."[112] As the star of the film, MacLaine was naturally the subject of most of the publicity surrounding *My Geisha*. Yet it was Parker who had really "gone totally Asiatic." In the promotional texts surrounding *My Geisha*, reporters sometimes asked Parker why he lived and worked in Japan, thousands of miles away from MacLaine. In *My Geisha*, Paul complains of being known as Mr. Lucy Dell, and he sees his film of *Madama Butterfly* as a way of making a name for himself. Drawing together the real world and the world of the film, Parker responded to queries about his and MacLaine's unusual living arrangement by saying, "I felt I was a second-class citizen here [in the United States]. I was beginning to be called 'Mr. MacLaine.' It was a situation I couldn't accept, so I left. Shirley understood, and she let me go."[113] *My Geisha* functions for Parker as *Madama Butterfly* does for Paul, as a way to establish himself as a film-maker and to communicate the real, traditional Japan. Parker, however, really does know Japan, whereas Paul has a naive and uninformed view of the country based on an early-twentieth-century Italian opera.

Parker was truly at home in Japan, stating "[Japan's] my country, I've got a real bug on it,"[114] and it is from this point of view that *My Geisha* attempts to educate audiences. If viewers of *My Geisha* gained insight into Japanese culture and customs by attending carefully to Parker's film, it was no more than what he offered to other Americans visiting Japan. The story for the film, written by Norman Krasna, came about during the time Krasna spent in Japan with Parker. According to Parker, during Krasna's first visit, "I took him all over the place. From the first night—when I introduced him to a teahouse, got his shoes off, and poured him some sake—he never stayed at a Western-style hotel. For four months he sat on the floor and soaked up atmosphere."[115] Parker also acted as a guide to Japan while he was in the process of booking *Holiday in Japan* in Las Vegas. In Parker's words, "I made a trip to Las Vegas and sold Bill Miller, of the New Frontier, on my idea. Japan was a blank to him, so I brought him over here and took him on a round of geisha parties, tea-houses, and night clubs. When he left, he said, 'This is it, send me the show.'"[116] Based on this example at least, Parker was an assured and confident host and an extremely effective tour guide.

Goetz and Logan, the producer and director of *Sayonara,* spent a considerable amount of time in Japan learning about the culture and customs, and they asked Fredricks, the cinematographer, to do the same. But in the case of *My Geisha,* no such trips or preparations were necessary, since Parker was already living in Japan and familiar with the language and culture. Furthermore, he chose an established Japanese cinematographer to shoot his film. Thus, rather than traveling to Japan with Parker and the cast and crew, viewers of *My Geisha* are invited to visit Japan by Parker, who graciously acts as their host and conducts them around the country and into the culture. More than merely visiting

Japan, working with the Japanese, or marrying a Japanese person would allow, Parker claimed the mantle of an expert in traditional Japanese culture who was comfortably ensconced in Japan. This claim was the ultimate expression of the privileges of being an American abroad, at home in the world at the height of the American Century.

Although their productions of Japan were separated by some seven decades, Burton Holmes and Steve Parker felt a similar affinity for Japan, and both men lamented westernization's effects on traditional Japanese culture. Holmes fondly reminisced, "I doubt if I have ever been happier than during the four months I spent in the as yet unspoiled *Japanese Japan* of 1892."[117] Speaking of the Japan of 1961, Shirley MacLaine told an interviewer, "Japan is still old-fashioned and still not quite with it, but the changes are speeding up. All this picturesque, naïve stuff will be gone, Steve and I are convinced, by the next generation."[118] These Americans abroad did not seem to acknowledge, however, that the same forces that brought them to Japan, that allowed them to travel across the Pacific and to enjoy the privileges of being welcomed into the culture, were also responsible for eroding the traditions that they found so distinctively, delightfully, Japanese. Herein lies the paradox of U.S. orientalism, as it continually attempts to fix the United States and Asia as separate entities, with essential qualities and traits, all the while finding in these differences the rationale for further border crossings.

Conclusion

Despite all of the information about geisha that *My Geisha* shares with its audiences, the film clearly was not the last word on the subject. Popular interest in and curiosity about geisha has continued unabated to the present day, as is evidenced by the 2005 film *Memoirs of a Geisha* (Rob Marshall), based on the 1997 novel by Arthur Golden (in another act of racial and gendered masquerade). *Memoirs of a Geisha* was shot in part on location in Kyoto, for some of the same reasons given by Joshua Logan in his decision to film *Sayonara* there. This recent film demonstrates the persistence of many of the rationales that motivated earlier U.S. filmmakers to produce films about the Far East and to travel across the Pacific to make these films. However, this is to say nothing more than that a certain type of U.S. orientalism remains profitable in Hollywood. Rather than cataloging the many instances of orientalist images and narratives in contemporary popular films, I conclude this study with a brief examination of a film that challenges the Western fascination with the geisha girl as well as established conventions of filming on location in China: David Cronenberg's 1993 adaptation of David Henry Hwang's play, *M. Butterfly* (1988).[1] Cronenberg's unusual approach to filming in China departs considerably from the typical strategies of on-location shooting. This film thereby raises the questions of what difference being on location makes and of whether U.S. films shot on location in Asia necessarily present visions that conform to the imaginary geography of U.S. orientalism.

The title of Hwang's play refers to Puccini's opera, *Madama Butterfly*, so central to Paul Robaix's sense of the spirit of traditional Japan in *My Geisha*.[2] The opera opens with American naval officer Benjamin Franklin Pinkerton preparing to marry fifteen-year-old geisha Cio-Cio San, also known as Butterfly. However, he intends to honor the commitment only for the duration of his stay in Japan. Cio-Cio San has such faith in her husband that after he sails away, she waits patiently for three years for his ship to reappear in the harbor, and she turns down a marriage proposal from a Japanese nobleman. When Pinkerton finally returns to Nagasaki, he brings his (white) American wife. Butterfly, who comes to understand that Pinkerton has forsaken her, agrees to give up their son to be raised by Pinkerton and his wife in the United States. In the climactic finale, Butterfly commits suicide. Hwang restages *Madama Butterfly* as *M. Butterfly*, the story of Rene Gallimard, a sexually insecure, socially inept French diplomat stationed in Beijing in the 1960s. Gallimard meets and falls in love with Song Liling, whom he believes to be a female opera singer. In their affair, he imagines himself as the cruel American sailor Pinkerton from Puccini's opera, with Song as his Butterfly. Two decades later, while on trial for treason, Gallimard learns that Song is not only a man but also a spy. This knowledge leads Gallimard to realize that all along, he had been Butterfly, the one who had given his love to a completely unworthy man.[3] The politics of Hwang's play have led to charges of didacticism and a defensive statement by the playwright that his work was not meant as an "anti-American" play. The play, however, clearly critiques certain fantasies of the Orient and Oriental women.

Cronenberg has bluntly stated that he found the play too schematic and its politics too obvious for his tastes.[4] In adapting the play for the screen, he elected to focus on the psychological aspects of a story of love and deception. Cronenberg dispenses with many of the broad comedic elements of Hwang's play as well as with much of the explicitly polemical, often sarcastic, dialogue. He acknowledges these differences when he notes, "The play is more overtly political than the movie. And it's conceivable someone might accuse me of depoliticizing it."[5] Cronenberg downplays Hwang's antiorientalist politics in favor of examining the strange workings of desire, fantasy, and sexuality. As a result, the political critique of the play, made at the expense of character development, is relatively absent from the film, which presents a more interiorized portrayal of a love affair. In short, the two versions of *M. Butterfly* differ in politics, narrative, dialogue, and staging.[6] In outlining the points of convergence and divergence between Hwang's play and Cronenberg's film, I am not arguing for the superiority of one version over another. Hwang's artistic concerns differ from Cronenberg's. What I am primarily interested in is the question of what happens to *M. Butterfly* as Cronenberg transforms it from a play into a film. As a cinematic adaptation, Cronenberg's *M. Butterfly* naturally invites comparisons to Hwang's play, drawing attention to what film as a medium brings to the story. In the context of my critique of film as a form of virtual travel and a source of knowledge of cultural difference, *M. Butterfly* provides another perspective on the mechanisms through which visions of Asia are constructed by film as a technology and shooting on location as a practice.

The distinction between theatrical and cinematic representation has a long and complex history in film theory. Generally speaking, scholars characterize film as a more "realistic" medium than theater. For example, the close-up is celebrated for allowing a degree of scrutiny that is simply not available to the theatergoer. In addition, the mobility of the camera, cast, and crew allows the use of a range of settings that cannot be reconstructed easily on a stage, including those shot on location in far-flung locales. *M. Butterfly* was shot on location in Hungary, China, France, and Canada but in a manner contrary to the conventions established over the course of the past century or so of cinema.[7] This departure was one of the primary reasons for the negative reception of *M. Butterfly* and the dismissive evaluations of the film's realism.

Existing scholarly analyses of Cronenberg's *M. Butterfly* have been based largely on textual analysis. In particular, some of the most intriguing readings of the film have relied on the psychoanalytic concept of fantasy.[8] However, few critics have considered the reception of the film. As I have done throughout this study, I consider not only the film's images and narratives but also its material production, promotion, and reception. Especially in the case of *M. Butterfly,* this type of analysis can tell us something about popular discursive constructions of the technology of cinema, shooting on location, and racial and cultural difference that a textual analysis of the film alone would not reveal. Thus, my object of study is not primarily the film itself, although I analyze one key scene from the film that I believe offers insight into the source of the negative reviews of the film. Following Janet Staiger's outline of a methodology for historical reception studies,[9] I analyze the reception of Cronenberg's *M. Butterfly*—in particular, the critical emphasis on close-ups in the film—along with the suggestion that the film was a less successful text than the Hwang play. My analysis also addresses the promotion of the film through its trailer and compares it to the publicity for earlier films shot on location. This compare-and-contrast approach demonstrates how the similarities and differences between *M. Butterfly* and the other fictional narrative films analyzed in this book highlight the motivations for and expected objectives of filming in distant and exotic locales.

Although popular press reviews measure the reception of a film only imperfectly and certainly cannot substitute for an empirical or ethnographic study of audience, they can reveal some of the discourses that shaped viewings of the film at the time of its release. Reviews of Cronenberg's film repeatedly referred to the text's theatrical origins and explicitly used the difference between film and theater to address the play's adaptation into cinematic form. Many critics focused on the camera's ability to show close-ups to the audience, singling out the close-ups of John Lone as Song Liling as a significant factor in the film's failure. In contrast, critics paid surprisingly little attention to *M. Butterfly*'s images of China. Janet Maslin begins her relatively sympathetic evaluation for the *New York Times* with a common refrain: "The film version of 'M. Butterfly' introduces a critically important new element into David Henry Hwang's play: the camera. The artifice that was possible on stage . . . is simply out of the question on screen."[10] John Simon, who had previously reviewed the play for *New York* magazine, wrote of the film, "The camera must come closer to the heroine than the eye of a spectator to an onstage character, and John Lone, good actor though he is, is far less convincing as a woman than some who have played the heroine on Broadway." Simon reiterates his belief that the cinematic close-up presented difficulties that the film failed to surmount, concluding that "this Butterfly was broken on the prism of the lens."[11] Reviewers repeatedly took exception to what the close-ups purportedly revealed: stubble on Lone's face. Richard Corliss complains, "His 5 o'clock shadow gives him away,"[12] while Todd McCarthy notes the existence of "the moustache stubble beneath the makeup."[13] Terry Pristin simply summarizes, "Several reviews said the shadow on Lone's upper lip makes it hard to accept the idea that the diplomat . . . could believe that his lover has borne him a child."[14] Discourses of race, gender, and sexuality were essential to how these reviewers saw the film. Yet it is also striking that the specificity of cinema was so frequently invoked. Equally intriguing is the near exclusive focus on the close-up.

The way Cronenberg approached the production of the film bears on the way the critics saw it. *M. Butterfly* was Cronenberg's first foreign location shoot. Comparing Cronenberg's approach to shooting on location to that of David Lean and Bernardo Bertolucci, Chris Rodley underlines the degree to which *M. Butterfly* departs from the familiar treatment of a setting such as China:

> At times, the backstreets of Beijing feel no more real than the backstreets
> of Tangiers [created on a set in Toronto] in *Naked Lunch*. Even the Great
> Wall of China might have been constructed by production designer Carol
> Spier. . . . Lovers of the David Lean school of location movie-making—or
> latterday Bertolucci—may legitimately wonder why Cronenberg bothered
> going there in the first place, so tantalizingly glimpsed are the wonders al-
> most on view.[15]

What indeed is the purpose of traveling to China to film on location if
not to capture the reality of China? The images of the film do not appear
to answer this question. Rodley's description conveys both the possibilities offered by filming in China and Cronenberg's refusal to embrace
them. As Cronenberg explains, "You always see Tiananman [*sic*] Square
or the Forbidden City. I didn't want to be a tourist."[16] By offering spectacular views only rarely and by using few of the recognizably Chinese
settings that being on location in China might have afforded, Cronenberg dramatically denies both established cinematic conventions and
perhaps even more importantly audience expectations.

At the time of the release of *M. Butterfly,* audience expectations for
films shot on location in China had been honed through nearly a century of film history. In refusing both realism and touristic spectacle, Cronenberg works against deeply ingrained rationales for shooting on location in exotic, distant lands. Around the turn of the twentieth century,
when Burton Holmes and the Edison filmmakers traveled to China,
Japan, the Philippines, and Hawai'i, they intended to capture life as it was
lived in these faraway places. As an element of Holmes's illustrated travel
lectures, films augmented the illusion of travel by being projected "at
moments when movement is essential to complete and vivify the impressions produced by the spoken words and colored illustrations."[17]
The Edison filmmakers similarly emphasized the novel technology's capacity to capture movement and thus life itself and to bring the world to
U.S. audiences. These early filmmakers traveled the world with their
cameras and produced on location films that would allow their audiences to see the world at home; their efforts seemed an almost obvious
utilization of what defined cinema as a technology.

By the time *The Good Earth* was produced, the popularity of fictional
narratives had long since surpassed that of actuality films; still, filming
on location retained the indexical association with reality that defined
the early travel film. Even more, travel to distant locations itself came to

be valued as an effort to lend greater reality to made-up stories. Thus, despite the fact that *The Good Earth* showed very little of China compared to the reconstruction of China in California, the film's claims to authenticity still rested largely on the MGM crew's travels to China. Similarly, the postwar travels of American filmmakers in Japan and their interactions with the Japanese anchored their works in the reality of Japan and in a particular version of U.S.-Japanese relations. The studios and the popular press promoted their experiences of travel as narratives that coincided with the diegetic narratives of the films, which imagined a new U.S. identity in the world. Whether at the turn of the twentieth century or decades later, what remains consistent in the practice of shooting on location is that filmmakers expended resources in the ostensible effort to record the reality of a place, whether this reality was an end in itself or a setting for a fiction. As *The Good Earth* so clearly demonstrates, a fictional film could produce "China" as an object of knowledge almost independently of the truth of its content through the operations of the cinematic apparatus and the deployment of particular discourses of travel, presence, and authenticity. Against this historical backdrop, it seems inexplicable that Cronenberg would turn away from the reality of China while shooting on location there.

One of the few scenes not a part of Hwang's play but invented solely for the film offers considerable insight into Cronenberg's approach to *M. Butterfly*. In this shot-on-location scene, Gallimard and Song bicycle to the Great Wall of China, one of the most iconic landmarks of the country, for a picnic. The sequence begins with an extreme long shot of a country road in the daytime, surrounded by fields on either side. The shift from the dark interiors and alleyways of Beijing, which have dominated the film to this point, to an outdoor, rural, sunlit setting is dramatic and literally requires the viewers' eyes to adjust to the sudden explosion of light. As the bicycling couple approaches, the camera cranes down to capture them passing by. The next shot shows a bicycle abandoned alongside the pathway at the top of the Great Wall. We then see Song approach Gallimard. An establishing shot depicts Song and Gallimard sitting across from each other on the Great Wall of China with their picnic spread before them, with the wall winding its way through the mountains in the background. The remainder of the scene consists of medium close-ups and medium shots of Gallimard and Song in conversation.

Cronenberg is quite explicit about his aims in this scene:

The audience gives a little gasp when you first cut to the shot of René and Song by the Great Wall of China. But it ends with a big close-up of Song and that's what it is. There's no 360-degree pan showing you that landscape. The wall isn't window dressing. Gallimard is being seduced by the combination of the Wall and being there with Song, but he feels it more than the audience. It's for him to be overwhelmed more than the audience.[18]

Cronenberg clearly grasps how Gallimard's views of China shape his view of Song. But the director seems determined to withhold this insight from the audience. The conversation between Gallimard and Song in this setting emphasizes how their attraction to each other is based in time-tested stereotypes of China and the West. Song asks Gallimard, "There is a mystery you must clarify for me. With your pick of Western women, why did you choose a poor Chinese with a chest like a boy?" Gallimard replies, "Not like a boy, like a girl—a young innocent schoolgirl waiting for her lessons." Song goes on to criticize Chinese men for oppressing Chinese women and expresses her excitement at loving a Western man who is not threatened by "his slave's" education. Gallimard heartily agrees: "Certainly not. Especially when my slave has so much to teach me." As he speaks, the camera shows Song in a medium close-up, gazing adoringly at Gallimard, the Great Wall an unfocused patch of tan in the background.

If this conversation rankles the viewer, it is surely because it employs some of the most offensive stereotypes of romantic liaisons between all-knowing white male saviors and the docile, grateful Asian women who love them. But Song is not what she seems, and Gallimard does not know nearly as much as he thinks he does. The fact that this scene is sandwiched between two other scenes that bring up questions of false knowledge and its consequences further highlights the irony of their exchange. Just prior to the Great Wall sequence, we see Gallimard at work at the French embassy, sitting stiffly at his desk as the newly appointed vice consul. He lectures his staff, "We French lost our war in Indochina because we failed to learn about the people we sought to lead. It's natural then, correct even, that they should resent us." Following the conclusion of the conversation between Song and Gallimard at the Great Wall, the film cuts to a close-up of a small mechanical device in the office of the French ambassador, Toulon. He enunciates clearly, "Tomorrow afternoon at 1700 hours we will detonate six atom bombs over the Forbidden

City." The technician standing nearby then disconnects some wires and assures the ambassador that they have now removed the last of the bugs, as Toulon chuckles, "That should give those Reds a thing or two to worry about!" In all three examples—the failure to understand the natives in a colonial context, the misperception of the identity of one's native mistress, and the gathering of false information through espionage—knowledge is incomplete or inaccurate, with potentially serious consequences. The juxtaposition of the interpersonal with the international implicitly plays on the connection between intersubjective stereotypes and foreign policy missteps that Hwang highlights in the afterword of *M. Butterfly*: "The neo-Colonialist notion that good elements of a native society, like a good woman, desire submission to the masculine West speaks precisely to the heart of our foreign policy blunders in Asia and elsewhere."[19] More subtly, in the context of the history of filming on location, these scenes also challenge the notion that seeing China on film is equivalent to traveling to China or learning anything about the country or its people. However, by refusing to be a tourist and showing the audience some of the spectacular views that filming in China makes possible, Cronenberg also avoids implicating viewers in the drama of seduction and stereotype that the play emphasizes so strongly.

My examination of cinema as virtual travel and as a form of knowledge of cultural difference has depended on a particular understanding of film as an indexical medium whose capabilities have been discursively constructed in terms of realism and verisimilitude. However, Cronenberg's unusual approach to filming in China requires a reconsideration of this perspective. Films shot on location in Asia can claim an ontological distinction from films shot in a studio back lot: they have a physical relationship to the geographical space of Asia, whereas films shot in the United States do not. But what significance, if any, does this ontological difference have? In the introduction, I suggest that films shot on location most fully exploit cinema's ability to bring the Far East to U.S. audiences. In addition, films shot on location in places corresponding to their narrative settings offer a special access to the reality of that place at the same time as they shape that reality by enveloping it within the conventions of cinema. To account for *M. Butterfly*, however, these statements require some revising.

What a filmmaker chooses to frame within his or her field of vision makes a difference. Cinema has the ability to bring the Far East to U.S. audiences yet need not necessarily make use of this ability. Films shot on location can offer a view of the "reality" of a place, but this place need not be constructed according to preexisting conventions of representation.[20] At the risk of romanticizing early film, I believe that some, though not all, of the films in the Occidental and Oriental Series provide glimpses of Asia and Asians that had not yet been determined by racially charged conventions of representation. This is not to say that the films were not racialized in some fashion. One need only look to the title of the series to see how the steamship company and the filmmakers saw the world's divisions. In addition, we do not know the precise conditions of the films' exhibition and reception, and we therefore lack information about how audiences of the time saw these films. But in setting up the camera to emphasize movement in public spaces, James White and Frederick Blechynden incidentally produced images of Asians that were less mediated than almost all existing representations of Asians of the time period. Viewing *Theatre Road, Yokohama* (Edison, 1898) today provides an almost magical window into another time and place that comes closer to the reality of a small corner of Yokohama than virtually any other form of representation. However, over time, shooting on location in Asia has become so strongly articulated with a tradition of orientalist discourse and imperial visions that the practice has become nearly synonymous with a particular perspective and politics. Edward Said observes how orientalist works are affiliated with other works, audiences, and institutions in an analyzable formation, "for example, that of philological studies, of anthologies of extracts from Oriental literature, of travel books, of Oriental fantasies"; this observation also applies to U.S. films shot on location in Asia.[21] Cronenberg's efforts to deny his audiences the type of virtual travel they might expect thus has the salutary effect of breaking away from orientalist practices of shooting on location in China. Yet given the film's narrative, his decision can also be criticized as one that protects rather than challenges his viewers.

Cronenberg describes Gallimard as "seduced by China." But the director deliberately chose not to represent China as a visual spectacle in the film despite the fact that, as he acknowledges, "the structure of the piece is so perfectly set up for that because Gallimard is really falling in love with China."[22] Cronenberg's unconventional stylistic decision to privilege a close-up of Song's face over an image of the Great Wall undercuts the setting's importance in constructing Gallimard's fantasy of the Orient. In terms of mise-en-scène, one would think that going to China would result in a more concrete sense of place. But Cronenberg manages to make the on-location image of the Great Wall appear almost as if it were a rear-screen projection, a special effects technique used in older films precisely to avoid the extra cost of taking the cast and crew on location. Rey Chow describes the production design of *M. Butterfly* as minimalist, a distinct departure from the predisposition toward "a sensational and extravagantly colorful approach whenever a non-Western culture is represented."[23] This means, though, that Cronenberg does not allow audience members a clear view of the seduction by the combination of the Wall and Song. They are thus left with the question of how Gallimard is seduced by Song alone.

By emphasizing Song's features from Gallimard's point-of-view, the camera in the Great Wall scene directs attention to Song's body as a legible text and places China at the margins of the frame. The cinematography of this sequence thus mobilizes the verisimilitude of the cinematic medium in the service of uncovering the "truth" of Song's/Lone's gender; the revelation of his real identity became the focal point of most of the reviews of the film, particularly in light of the release of Neil Jordan's *The Crying Game* (1992).[24] The symptomatic critical obsession with the close-ups of Song's face can therefore be explained in part by the directorial decision to emphasize the human drama of the narrative and to avoid exploiting the possibilities of an "exotic foreign shoot."[25] (Such responses also suggested, in many instances, a barely disguised homophobia that insisted on the critic's ability to tell the difference between a man and a woman.) The critical focus on the film's close-ups thus foregrounded discourses of race, gender, and sexuality that dominated the terms of the reading of the film. The resulting absence of interest in the film's traveling images minimized attention to or even awareness of questions of colonialism and the history of Western intervention in Asia.

The publicity for *M. Butterfly* further underlines the film's difference from other U.S. films shot on location in China. The initial Warner Brothers trailer, made before the film was completed and targeted to exhibitors for the purpose of generating theatrical bookings, represented the film as a large-scale epic. According to Rodley, "Maximizing the film's location shots and crowd scenes, Cronenberg appears to have made a movie of epic proportions and vision."[26] It is unclear whether the preview that played in theaters is the same as the exhibitor trailer to which Rodley refers, but the theatrical trailer opens with the image of the abandoned bicycle on the Great Wall of China. A voice-over narration explains the political situation: "After a century of foreign influence, Asia was about to reclaim herself." The French ambassador is then shown reading a memo detailing the growing threat represented by the Red Guard as scenes of street demonstrations and a labor camp flash on the screen. Only after the political situation has been established is the central romance of the film introduced.

David Geffen, whose company produced the film, reacted to the trailer with concern, asking Cronenberg, "Is this stuff in the movie? Are we selling something we don't have?" Cronenberg reassured Geffen that all of the images in the trailer were indeed part of the film but emphasized that the film was "not like a David Lean picture."[27] The exchange between Geffen and Cronenberg pinpoints precisely the contradiction of *M. Butterfly.* For the publicity and marketing department at Warner's, the location shots and crowd scenes must have been seen as the most easily commodifiable elements of the film. Understandably enough, the trailer attempted to promote *M. Butterfly* by capitalizing on its most visually striking and spectacular sequences. However, the images chosen for the promotional intertext gave the erroneous impression that *M. Butterfly* was an exotic epic, when the film was actually more of a psychological drama. Perhaps the marketing team could not imagine any other kind of film based on the presence of such images. This lack of correspondence between the film and its publicity and marketing campaign suggests that the studio not only had difficulty selling a film that works against established expectations but also could not even envision a film shot on location in China that would not make use of visual spectacle. Resisting familiar images and approaches was, however, Cronenberg's intention from the start.

Cronenberg's determination to avoid making *M. Butterfly* into a film like *The Russia House* (Fred Schepisi, 1990) is revealing:

> I didn't think [*The Russia House*] was very successful artistically because there was this obsession with showing you the real streets of Leningrad and so on. The camera was drifting to show you what was outside the window when really you just wanted to see the actors' faces. I couldn't believe how often the camera would just steadicam its way over to see the nice onion domes and stuff. I thought, "God, I don't want to make that mistake."[28]

Such images may or may not have been detrimental to the character development, narrative, or aesthetic achievements of *The Russia House,* but this statement unquestionably demonstrates Cronenberg's absolute refusal to turn *M. Butterfly* into a virtual voyage for the audience, an opportunity to see the real streets of China, the temples and palaces of the Forbidden City, or the Great Wall from the comfort of the theater or their living rooms. As Cronenberg describes his film, "Ultimately this movie is two people in a room."[29] Such strong disdain for the typical fruits of an exotic foreign shoot return us to the question Rodley posed regarding why Cronenberg bothered to shoot part of the film on location in China.

Cronenberg's decision to film in China but deny the audience the visual delights such a production traditionally provides calls attention to the desire to see more of the tantalizingly glimpsed wonders. Based on the film's critical and commercial reception, it seems that most audiences and critics would have preferred to see the sights of China than Lone's stubble. Todd McCarthy, one of only a handful of critics to even mention the film's location shooting, ended his review with his disappointment over the lack of realism of the production despite the film's wide-ranging travels: "Lensed in China, Hungary and France, this is Cronenberg's first film shot outside Canada. Unfortunately, nothing manages to disguise the feel of artifice that surrounds the entire production."[30] As McCarthy implies, Cronenberg might as well have stayed home.

In the discussion of the transitional period of film history at the conclusion of chapter 2, I suggest that the unique power of cinema, particularly regarding later fictional narrative films, arises from its ability to lend realism to narrative while narrative helps to make sense of the reality captured on film. Tom Gunning describes this operation in terms of how the filmic image's capacity for showing defines its unique way of telling.[31] In the example of *M. Butterfly*, Cronenberg's refusal to show China in a more conventional fashion led critics to view the film's narrative as incredible. As the relative success of Bertolucci's *The Last Emperor* (1987) suggests, when it comes to films shot on location in China, audiences prefer to be brought closer to China, not distanced from it. The critical and commercial failure of *M. Butterfly* suggests just how deeply ingrained are the conventions of making, promoting, and seeing films shot on location in faraway places. It is even more fitting, given the critical concerns of this study, that the narrative turns on stereotypes and false knowledge of Asians and Asia. The political critique of Hwang's play hinges on an inability or refusal to distinguish between fact and fiction—that is, between Gallimard's fantasy of the perfect Oriental woman and the reality of his relationship with Song. Cronenberg's decision to subordinate the landscape of China denies audience members the materials with which to spin their own fantasies of being in China with Gallimard. However, by withholding the possibility of knowing China through spectacular cinematic images and thus denying audiences the power and pleasures that such visions offer, the film lays bare the assumptions that come with filming on location in China. Thus, in its "failure," the film illuminates a more than century-old tradition of knowing China through film.

Notes

1. Max J. Herzberg, foreword to Sarah M. Mullen, *A Guide to the Discussion of the Screen Version of Pearl Buck's Prize-Winning Novel* The Good Earth (Newark, N.J.: Educational and Recreational Guides, 1937), 3, *The Good Earth* Production File, Margaret Herrick Library, Academy of Motion Picture Arts and Sciences, Beverly Hills, Calif.

2. The fact that "on location" referred to China as well as to an ersatz Chinese farming community meticulously staged in Chatsworth, California, highlights the constructed nature of authenticity in this example.

3. Jeffrey Ruoff, "The Filmic Fourth Dimension: Cinema as Audiovisual Vehicle," in *Virtual Voyages: Cinema and Travel,* ed. Jeffrey Ruoff (Durham: Duke University Press, 2006), 1.

4. The use of "Far East" to refer to Asia presumes that Europe is at the center of the world. My use of this somewhat outdated yet still relatively common term here and throughout this work is intended as a critique of this perspective and its construction of geographical distance and cultural difference.

5. Edward W. Said, *Orientalism* (New York: Random House, 1978), 12.

6. Ibid., 55. Geographers have taken up the term *imaginative geographies* to refer to the register of representation and to the cultural production of space and place; a number of scholars working in this field trace the genealogy of this term to Said's work. As one introductory textbook puts it, "Imaginative geographies [are] representations of place, space and landscape that structure people's understandings of the world, and in turn help to shape their actions. In the work of Edward Said, the term refers to the projection of images of identity and difference on to geographical space in a way that sustains unequal relationships of power" (Felix Driver, "Imaginative Geographies," in *Introducing Human Geographies,* ed. Paul Cloke, Philip Crang and Mark Goodwin, 2nd ed. [London: Hodder Arnold, 2005], 140).

7. The adjective *American* technically refers to all of North and South America, but following common usage in the United States, I use the term here specifically in reference to the United States.

8. Said, *Orientalism,* 1–2.

9. Lisa Lowe, *Immigrant Acts: On Asian American Cultural Politics* (Durham: Duke University Press, 1996), 178 n. 7. John R. Eperjesi describes his book *The Imperialist Imaginary* as a response to the question of whether Said's work can "help us understand the history of U.S. expansion into Asia and the Pacific" (*The Imperialist Imaginary: Visions of Asia and the Pacific in American Culture* [Lebanon, N.H.: University Press of New England, 2005], 18–19).

10. For discussions of U.S. orientalism and East Asia, see Gary Y. Okihiro, *Margins and Mainstreams: Asians in American History and Culture* (Seattle: University of Washington Press, 1994); Malini Johar Schueller, *U.S. Orientalisms: Race, Nation, and Gender in Literature, 1790–1890* (Ann Arbor: University of Michigan Press, 1998); John Kuo Wei Tchen, *New York before Chinatown: Orientalism and the Shaping of American Culture, 1776–1882* (Baltimore: John Hopkins University Press, 1999); Mae M. Ngai, "American Orientalism," *Reviews in American History* 28 (September 2000): 408–15; Christina Klein, *Cold War Orientalism: Asia in the Middlebrow Imagination, 1945–1961* (Berkeley: University of California Press, 2003); Mari Yoshihara, *Embracing the East: White Women and American Orientalism* (Oxford: Oxford University Press, 2003); Karen Leong, *The China Mystique: Pearl S. Buck, Anna May Wong, Mayling Soong, and the Transformation of American Orientalism* (Berkeley: University of California Press, 2005); Colleen Lye, *America's Asia: Racial Form and American Literature, 1893–1945* (Princeton: Princeton University Press, 2005); Eperjesi, *Imperialist Imaginary.*

11. See Okihiro, *Margins and Mainstreams;* David Palumbo-Liu, *Asian/American: Historical Crossings of a Racial Frontier* (Stanford: Stanford University Press, 1999).

12. Lowe, *Immigrant Acts,* 4.

13. See esp. Lisa Lowe, *Critical Terrains: French and British Orientalisms* (Ithaca: Cornell University Press, 1991); Edward W. Said, *Culture and Imperialism* (New York: Vintage, 1994).

14. Homi K. Bhabha, *The Location of Culture* (London: Routledge, 1994), 148.

15. Ibid., 147, 145.

16. Ibid., 145.

17. Lowe, *Immigrant Acts,* 5.

18. *BLT Genesis,* directed by Evan J. Leong (Arowana Films/MTV Films, 2003).

19. Eugene Franklin Wong, *On Visual Media Racism: Asians in the American Motion Pictures* (New York: Arno, 1978), 56–57, 73. *Heathen Chinese and the Sunday School Teachers* intimates improper interracial contact. *The Chinese Rubbernecks* is a comic scene featuring Chinese laundrymen, and *The Yellow Peril* plays on the reference to the nineteenth-century fear of hordes of invading Asians to describe an accident-prone Chinese servant. All three films were produced by the American Mutoscope and Biograph Company.

20. The excitement surrounding the film resulted in an impressive grassroots campaign to spread the word and encourage Asian Americans to support the film. In advance of the film's release, volunteers on Team BLT put up posters, handed out postcards, and otherwise helped to promote the film. Community organizations in various cities bought out screenings of the film on opening weekend, and Asian American students at universities around the country organized group outings to go see the film. See Oliver Wang and Hua Hsu, "Taking on Tomorrow," review of *Better Luck Tomorrow, PopMatters,* April 11, 2003, http://www.popmatters.com/pm/review/better-luck-tomorrow/ (accessed September 27, 2008).

21. Book-length studies include Dorothy B. Jones, *The Portrayal of China and India on the American Screen, 1896–1955* (Cambridge: MIT Press, 1955); Wong, *On Visual Media Racism;* Gina Marchetti, *Romance and the "Yellow Peril": Race, Sex, and Discursive Strategies in Hollywood Fiction* (Berkeley: University of California

Press, 1993); James S. Moy, *Marginal Sights: Staging the Chinese in America* (Iowa City: University of Iowa Press, 1993); Darrell Y. Hamamoto, *Monitored Peril: Asian Americans and the Politics of TV Representation* (Minneapolis: University of Minnesota Press, 1994); Matthew Bernstein and Gaylyn Studlar, eds., *Visions of the East: Orientalism in Film* (New Brunswick: Rutgers University Press, 1997); Robert G. Lee, *Orientals: Asian Americans in Popular Culture* (Philadelphia: Temple University Press, 1999); Sheng-Mei Ma, *The Deathly Embrace: Orientalism and Asian American Identity* (Minneapolis: University of Minnesota Press, 2000); Peter X. Feng, ed., *Screening Asian Americans* (New Brunswick: Rutgers University Press, 2002); Hye Seung Chung, *Hollywood Asian: Philip Ahn and the Politics of Cross-Ethnic Performance* (Philadelphia: Temple University Press, 2006). Asian American cultural producers have long challenged cinematic stereotypes of Asians through their work. A few examples of documentary films that critique popular stereotypes are *Slaying the Dragon* (Deborah Gee, 1988); *Picturing Oriental Girls: A (Re)Educational Videotape* (Valerie Soe, 1992); and *Hollywood Chinese* (Arthur Dong, 2007). See also Russell Leong, ed., *Moving the Image: Independent Asian Pacific American Media Arts* (Los Angeles: UCLA Asian American Studies Center, 1991); Darrell K. Hamamoto and Sandra Liu, eds., *Countervisions: Asian American Film Criticism* (Philadelphia: Temple University Press, 2000); Peter X. Feng, *Identities in Motion: Asian American Film and Video* (Durham: Duke University Press, 2002).

22. Said, *Orientalism*, 22.

23. Kandice Chuh and Karen Shimakawa, "Introduction: Mapping Studies in the Asian Diaspora," in *Orientations: Mapping Studies in the Asian Diaspora*, ed. Kandice Chuh and Karen Shimakawa (Durham: Duke University Press, 2001), 4. See also Okihiro, *Margins and Mainstreams;* Lowe, *Immigrant Acts;* Palumbo-Liu, *Asian/American.*

24. James Clifford, *Routes: Travel and Translation in the Late Twentieth Century* (Cambridge: Harvard University Press, 1997), 2, 11.

25. Ibid., 6–7.

26. Dean MacCannell, *The Tourist: A New Theory of the Leisure Class* (New York: Schocken, 1976).

27. I recognize the specificity of U.S.-Hawaiian relations and the experiences of indigenous peoples of the Pacific Islands. However, I include discussions of films of and travels to Hawai'i in my examination of early cinematic visions of Asia because many of the travelers I examine stopped in Hawai'i en route to Asia or on their way back to the U.S. mainland. Turn-of-the-century debates about U.S. overseas imperialism also often included Hawai'i as well as Asian countries, despite very different histories and circumstances.

28. Jennifer Lynn Peterson, "World Pictures: Travelogue Films and the Lure of the Exotic, 1890–1920" (Ph.D. diss., University of Chicago, 1999), 6, 175.

29. See esp. Lowe, *Critical Terrains;* Ali Behdad, *Belated Travelers: Orientalism in the Age of Colonial Dissolution* (Durham: Duke University Press, 1994); Inderpal Grewal, *Home and Harem: Nation, Gender, Empire, and the Cultures of Travel* (Durham: Duke University Press, 1996). For related analyses of the rhetorics of travel, see Mary Louise Pratt, *Imperial Eyes: Travel Writing and Transculturation* (London: Routledge, 1992); Caren Kaplan, *Questions of Travel: Postmodern Discourses of Displacement* (Durham: Duke University Press, 1996); Clifford, *Routes.*

30. See Stephen Kern, *The Culture of Time and Space, 1880–1918* (Cambridge: Harvard University Press, 1983); Wolfgang Schivelbusch, *The Railway Journey: The Industrialization of Time and Space in the Nineteenth Century* (Berkeley: University of California Press, 1986); Lynne Kirby, *Parallel Tracks: The Railroad and the Cinema* (Durham: Duke University Press, 1997). Cinema's ability to bring the distant near also brings to mind Walter Benjamin's important essay, "The Work of Art in the Age of Mechanical Reproduction," in which he remarks on "the desire of contemporary masses to bring things 'closer' spatially and humanly, which is just as ardent as their bent toward overcoming the uniqueness of every reality by accepting its reproduction" (in Benjamin, *Illuminations: Essays and Reflections,* ed. and intro. Hannah Arendt, trans. Harry Zohn [New York: Schocken, 1968], 223).

31. Alison Landsberg, *Prosthetic Memory: The Transformation of American Remembrance in the Age of Mass Culture* (New York: Columbia University Press, 2004), 12.

32. See Anne Friedberg, *Window Shopping: Cinema and the Postmodern* (Berkeley: University of California Press, 1993); Tom Gunning, "The World as Object Lesson: Cinema Audiences, Visual Culture and the St. Louis World's Fair, 1904," *Film History* 6 (Winter 1994): 422–44; Tom Gunning, "The Whole World within Reach: Travel Images without Borders," in *Cinéma sans Frontières, 1896–1918,* ed. Roland Cosandey and François Albera (Lausanne: Payot, 1995), 21–36; Fatimah Tobing Rony, *The Third Eye: Race, Cinema, and Ethnographic Spectacle* (Durham: Duke University Press, 1996); Lauren Rabinovitz, *For the Love of Pleasure: Women, Movies, and Culture in Turn-of-the-Century Chicago* (New Brunswick: Rutgers University Press, 1998); Vanessa R. Schwartz, *Spectacular Realities: Early Mass Culture in Fin-de-Siècle Paris* (Berkeley: University of California Press, 1998).

33. Friedberg, *Window Shopping,* 2–3.

34. Ruoff, "Filmic Fourth Dimension," 1.

35. Susan Sontag, *On Photography* (New York: Dell, 1973), 89.

36. Frith cited in Carol Armstrong, *Scenes in a Library: Reading the Photograph in the Book, 1843–1875* (Cambridge: MIT Press, 1998), 285.

37. Steve Clark, introduction to *Travel Writing and Empire: Postcolonial Theory in Transit,* ed. Steve Clark (London: Zed, 1999), 1. In the prehistory of cinema, the use of photography as evidence is perhaps most famously associated with Eadweard Muybridge, who captured in detail the movements of a race horse, purportedly to settle a bet made by Leland Stanford.

38. Armstrong, *Scenes,* 295–96.

39. In this era of digital imaging, the "simple truthfulness" of the camera is no longer taken for granted. However, as a number of scholars have pointed out, things were not always so simple in analog times, even if these technologies were eventually associated with nature and truth. See James Lastra's discussion of perception and representation in *Sound Technology and the American Cinema: Perception, Representation, Modernity* (New York: Columbia University Press, 2000), esp. chaps. 1–2; W. J. T. Mitchell, *The Reconfigured Eye: Digital Truth in the Post-Photographic Era* (Cambridge: MIT Press, 1992).

40. Stephen Prince, "True Lies: Perceptual Realism, Digital Images, and Film Theory," *Film Quarterly* 49 (Spring 1996): 27–37, offers a brief overview of this di-

vision and then suggests that it has become increasingly irrelevant in the age of photorealistic computer-generated imaging technologies.

41. Ellen Strain, *Public Places, Private Journeys: Ethnography, Entertainments, and the Tourist Gaze* (New Brunswick: Rutgers University Press, 2003), has argued that exotic scenes of distant lands have often functioned to show off technological advances in cinema to their greatest effect.

42. Said, *Orientalism,* 22.

43. Ruth Vasey, *The World According to Hollywood, 1918–1939* (Madison: University of Wisconsin Press, 1997), 210.

44. Ibid., 115–20.

45. Hays cited in ibid., 50.

46. In recent years, location shooting has been increasingly associated with lowering production costs in a practice known as "runaway production." In these instances, the location is usually unrelated to the setting of the narrative since its appeal is in factors such as lower wages, tax incentives, and minimal regulation of labor. In these cases, the fact of shooting on location is not highlighted in the publicity and marketing of the film. The ideological implications of this type of location shooting obviously differ substantially from the kind of location work at issue in this book. See Toby Miller, Nitin Govil, John McMurria, Ting Wang, Richard Maxwell, *Global Hollywood 2* (London: British Film Institute, 2005), 126–70; Greg Elmer and Mike Gasher, eds., *Contracting out Hollywood: Runaway Productions and Foreign Location Shooting* (Lanham, Md.: Rowman and Littlefield, 2005).

47. James Duncan and Derek Gregory, introduction to *Writes of Passage: Reading Travel Writing,* ed. James Duncan and Derek Gregory (London: Routledge, 1999), 5.

48. In terms of fictional films of the war, the substitution of a wide variety of locales for Vietnam—including Georgia, Alabama, Mexico, the Philippines, and Thailand—resulted in part from the lack of diplomatic relations between the United States and Vietnam after the war and indicated the generic "jungle" mise-en-scène of many of these films. The impact of the American war in Vietnam on U.S. national identity is so enormous yet so specific that an analysis of the subject exceeds the parameters of this study. For example, the unique authenticity of images captured on location functions quite differently when it comes to Vietnam; many Americans saw images of Vietnam on a regular basis while the war was ongoing, but on their television sets rather than on the silver screen. In addition, representations of Vietnam by Americans who were there, including personal accounts by veterans and the professional accounts of war correspondents, are too numerous to count.

49. Duncan and Gregory, introduction, 4.

50. Palumbo-Liu uses the formulation *Asian/American* to signify "both the distinction installed between 'Asian' and 'American' and a dynamic, unsettled, and inclusive movement" (*Asian/American,* 1).

51. Janet Staiger, *Perverse Spectators: The Practices of Film Reception* (New York: New York University Press, 2000), 1, 7. See also Janet Staiger, *Interpreting Films: Studies in the Historical Reception of American Cinema* (Princeton: Princeton University Press, 1992).

52. Barbara Klinger, *Melodrama and Meaning: History, Culture, and the Films of Douglas Sirk* (Bloomington: Indiana University Press, 1994), xvi.

53. Staiger, *Perverse Spectators*, 1.

54. Klinger, *Melodrama*, xx.

55. Jean-Louis Comolli, "Machines of the Visible," in *The Cinematic Apparatus*, ed. Teresa de Lauretis and Stephen Heath (New York: St. Martin's, 1980), 122–23.

56. Ibid., 122.

57. Kristin Whissel, *Picturing American Modernity: Traffic, Technology, and the Silent Cinema* (Durham: Duke University Press, 2008), constitutes an important addition to the scholarship in this area.

58. Rémy de Gourmont, "Epilogues: Cinematograph," in *French Film Theory and Criticism, Volume One*, 1907–29, ed. Richard Abel (Princeton: Princeton University Press, 1988), 48.

59. Ibid., 49–50.

60. Julius W. Pratt, *Expansionists of 1898: The Acquisition of Hawaii and the Spanish Islands* (Baltimore: Johns Hopkins Press, 1936), 326.

61. Charles Musser, *The Emergence of Cinema: The American Screen to 1907* (New York: Scribner's, 1990), 261.

62. Klein, *Cold War Orientalism*, 9.

63. The term *American Century* derives from an editorial written by Henry Luce, the founder and publisher of *Time* and *Life* magazines, that appeared in *Life* on February 17, 1941, 61–65. Luce, the China-born son of missionary parents, argued that Americans needed to enter into the Second World War as part of accepting their responsibilities and obligations as the predominant power in the world.

64. E. Burton Holmes, *The World Is Mine* (Culver City, Calif.: Murray and Gee, 1953), 199.

65. Tom Gunning, "The Cinema of Attractions: Early Film, Its Spectator, and the Avant-Garde," in *Early Cinema: Space, Frame, Narrative*, ed. Thomas Elsaesser (London: British Film Institute, 1990), 57.

66. Karen Leong, *China Mystique*, 1–2.

67. Mary Louise Pratt uses the term *anti-conquest* to refer to "strategies of representation whereby European bourgeois subjects seek to secure their innocence in the same moment as they assert European hegemony" (*Imperial Eyes*, 7). Klein also uses this term in her analysis of Cold War orientalism, which "legitimated U.S. expansion while denying its coercive or imperial nature" (*Cold War Orientalism*, 13).

CHAPTER ONE

1. E. Burton Holmes, *The World Is Mine* (Culver City, Calif.: Murray and Gee, 1953), ix–x.

2. Ibid., 199.

3. Edward W. Said, *Culture and Imperialism* (New York: Vintage, 1994), 12.

4. Arthur M. Schlesinger Jr., "Burton Holmes," in E. Burton Holmes, *Peking (The World 100 Years Ago)*, ed. Fred L. Israel (Philadelphia: Chelsea House, 1998), 24–25.

5. Holmes, *World Is Mine,* 199.

6. Charles Musser, *The Emergence of Cinema: The American Screen to 1907* (New York: Scribner's, 1990), 15–16.

7. Rick Altman, *Silent Film Sound* (New York: Columbia University Press, 2004), 71.

8. Said, *Culture and Imperialism,* 68.

9. Holmes's manager, Louis Francis Brown, sometimes presented the Burton Holmes Lectures to audiences.

10. Holmes, *World Is Mine,* 85, 86.

11. Holmes lectured repeatedly on the country over the course of his career. For a listing of Holmes's lectures and travelogues organized by year, see http://www.burtonholmes.org (accessed June 3, 2007).

12. Holmes, *World Is Mine,* 86.

13. Ibid., 135, 137.

14. Irving Wallace, "Everybody's Rover Boy," in E. Burton Holmes, *The Man Who Photographed the World: Burton Holmes Travelogues, 1886–1938,* ed. Genoa S. Caldwell (New York: Abrams, 1977), 16. In *The World Is Mine,* Holmes refers to slides hand-colored in Yokohama, not Tokyo (138).

15. Holmes, *World Is Mine,* 139.

16. See, for example, Tom Gunning, "The World as Object Lesson: Cinema Audiences, Visual Culture and the St. Louis World's Fair, 1904," *Film History* 6 (Winter 1994): 422–44; Lauren Rabinovitz, "The Fair View: Female Spectators and the 1893 Chicago World's Columbian Exposition," in *The Image in Dispute: Art and Cinema in the Age of Photography,* ed. Dudley Andrew (Austin: University of Texas Press, 1997), 87–116; Anne Friedberg, *Window Shopping: Cinema and the Postmodern* (Berkeley: University of California Press, 1993); Fatimah Tobing Rony, *The Third Eye: Race, Cinema, and Ethnographic Spectacle* (Durham: Duke University Press, 1996).

17. Rabinovitz, "Fair View," 89.

18. Holmes's first public presentation, "Through Europe with a Kodak," based on his 1890 visit to Europe, was a benefit for the Chicago Camera Club, of which he was serving as secretary. See X. Theodore Barber, "The Roots of Travel Cinema: John L. Stoddard, E. Burton Holmes, and the Nineteenth-Century Illustrated Travel Lecture," *Film History* 5 (March 1993): 79.

19. Holmes, *World Is Mine,* 142.

20. "Can Not Beat Santa," *Washington Post,* December 18, 1898, 29.

21. John L. Stoddard, *John L. Stoddard's Lectures* (Boston: Balch, 1898), 3:7.

22. Ibid., 8.

23. For a useful comparison of Stoddard's and Holmes's careers, see Barber, "Roots."

24. E. Burton Holmes, *Burton Holmes Travelogues,* vol. 1, *Into Morocco, Fez, the Moorish Empire* (New York: McClure, 1910), n.p.

25. Ibid.

26. Altman, *Silent Film Sound,* 56, 59.

27. E. Burton Holmes, *Burton Holmes Travelogues,* vol. 9, *Down the Amur, Peking, the Forbidden City* (New York: McClure, 1910), 159.

28. Amy Kaplan, *The Anarchy of Empire in the Making of U.S. Culture* (Cambridge: Harvard University Press, 2002), 1.

29. Holmes, *World Is Mine*, 123.

30. E. Burton Holmes, *Burton Holmes Travelogues*, vol. 10, *Seoul—The Capital of Korea, Japan—The Country, Japan—The Cities* (New York: McClure, 1910), 65.

31. Oscar B. Depue, "My First Fifty Years in Motion Pictures," in *A Technological History of Motion Pictures and Television*, ed. Raymond Fielding (Berkeley: University of California Press, 1967), 60. This essay offers fascinating details about Depue's early work with Holmes and his many ingenious solutions to the challenges of early motion picture work.

32. Ibid., 60.

33. Burton Holmes Lectures program, 1899–1900, cited in Charles Musser with Carol Nelson, *High-Class Moving Pictures: Lyman H. Howe and the Forgotten Era of Traveling Exhibition, 1880–1920* (Princeton: Princeton University Press, 1991), 125.

34. Ibid.

35. The "invitation lecture" was a means of introducing Holmes to a new public by inviting audience members to attend one lecture free of charge in the hopes that they and their friends would then purchase tickets to the coming series of lectures.

36. "Burton Holmes' Lecture," *Washington Post*, December 29, 1898, 9.

37. Ibid.

38. "Burton Holmes' Lecture Course," *Washington Post*, January 15, 1899, 24.

39. Marion Mills Miller, ed., *Great Debates in American History: From the Debates in the British Parliament on the Colonial Stamp Act (1764–1765) to the Debates in Congress at the Close of the Taft Administration (1912–1913)*, vol. 3, *Foreign Relations*, part 2 (New York: Current Literature, 1913), 270.

40. E. Burton Holmes, *Burton Holmes Travelogues*, vol. 5, *The Hawaiian Islands, the Edge of China, Manila* (New York: McClure, 1910), 5–6, 10.

41. John R. Eperjesi, *The Imperialist Imaginary: Visions of Asia and the Pacific in American Culture* (Hanover, N.H.: Dartmouth College Press, 2005), 2.

42. The images are of various shapes and sizes, placed on the page in a way that often forces the text to work itself around the edges of the image. At times, parts of the frame of an image fade away to invisibility, so that a building's roof, for example, protrudes into the lines of text while its grounds remain firmly enclosed within a rectangular border. In other instances, the scene is artfully blended into the page so that all its edges gradually fade into the background.

43. Holmes, *Burton Holmes Travelogues*, 5:6–7.

44. Ibid., 91–92.

45. Holmes cited in Irving Wallace, "The Great Globe Trotter," in Holmes, *Peking*, 14.

46. Ibid., 13.

47. Schlesinger, "Burton Holmes," 25.

48. Fred Israel, "The World 100 Years Ago," in Holmes, *Peking*, 28.

49. Holmes, *Burton Holmes Travelogues*, 5:14.

50. Ibid., 29.

51. Ibid., 24, 52.

52. Ibid., 23.

53. Ibid., 52.

54. Ibid., 67.

55. Ibid., 68.

56. Ibid., 31–32.

57. Amy Kaplan, "The Birth of an Empire," *PMLA* 114 (October 1999): 1069.

58. "Burton Holmes on Hawaii," *Washington Post,* January 19, 1899, 2.

59. Depue, "My First Fifty Years," 61.

60. Holmes, *Burton Holmes Travelogues,* 5:112.

61. "Burton Holmes on Hawaii," 2.

62. The struggle for Hawaiian sovereignty continues in the present. See Haunani-Kay Trask, *From a Native Daughter: Colonialism and Sovereignty in Hawai'i,* rev. ed. (Honolulu: University of Hawai'i Press, 1999); Noenoe K. Silva, *Aloha Betrayed: Native Hawaiian Resistance to American Colonialism* (Durham: Duke University Press, 2004).

63. Julius W. Pratt, *Expansionists of 1898: The Acquisition of Hawaii and the Spanish Islands* (Baltimore: Johns Hopkins Press, 1936).

64. Harry P. Mawson and J. W. Buel, comps., *Leslie's Official History of the Spanish-American War; a Pictorial and Descriptive Record of the Cuban Rebellion, the Causes That Involved the United States, and a Complete Narrative of Our Conflict with Spain on Land and Sea; Supplemented with Fullest Information Respecting Cuba, Porto Rico, the Philippines, and Hawaii* (Washington, D.C.: War Records Office, 1899), 608.

65. The reference to Filipinos who were fighting against U.S. forces as "insurrectionists" or "insurgents" presumes the legitimacy of the U.S. claim to the Philippines. My use of these terms is meant to reflect the historical perspective of the texts under discussion. From another perspective, these same Filipinos are known as nationalists and freedom fighters.

66. "Passengers on the Lucania," *New York Times,* April 29, 1899, 3.

67. "Maurice Grau Decorated," *New York Times,* August 27, 1899, 16.

68. "Says Otis Is in Bad Health," *Chicago Daily Tribune,* September 1, 1899, 1.

69. Advertisement, *Washington Post,* December 17, 1899, 31.

70. Holmes, *Burton Holmes Travelogues,* 5:227.

71. Ibid., 236.

72. Ibid., 227.

73. Ibid., 267, 227.

74. Ibid., 253, 255–56.

75. "Holmes Talks of Luzon," *Chicago Daily Tribune,* October 27, 1899, 5.

76. Ibid.

77. "Says Otis Is in Bad Health," 1.

78. Burton Holmes Lectures, Supplementary Series Delivered by Louis Francis Brown, 1900–1901, 3, Burton Holmes Historical Collection, Seattle.

79. "Holmes' Lecture on Manila," *Washington Post,* December 27, 1899, 2.

80. The published lecture does not include any images of carabao, though reviews of the lecture in 1899–1900 suggest that two films of this subject were shown. The book version of the lecture depicts instead an image from a filmstrip of soldiers titled "Ninth Infantry on the Bridge of Spain," a photograph of "General Lawton's Villa," and an image of "Calle Nozaleda," perhaps the street where Holmes saw the carabao.

81. Holmes, *Burton Holmes Travelogues,* 5:268–69.

82. Ibid., 289–90.

83. Ibid., 293.

84. Ibid., 299–300.

85. Ibid., 309.

86. Ibid., 315.

87. Ibid., 316.

88. "Lecture by Two Authors," *Chicago Daily Tribune*, October 22, 1899, 38.

89. Burton Holmes Lectures program, 1899–1900, cited in Musser with Nelson, *High-Class Moving Pictures*.

90. Holmes, *Burton Holmes Travelogues*, 5:321.

91. Ibid.

92. Ibid.

93. Ibid.

94. "Cutting Manila Wires," *Boston Daily Globe*, January 21, 1900, 21.

95. Holmes, *Burton Holmes Travelogues*, 5:322.

96. Ibid., 335.

97. He returned about a decade and a half later and gave another lecture on the Philippines during the 1913–14 season.

98. Holmes, *Burton Holmes Travelogues*, 5:336.

99. Ibid., 9:210. Holmes may have been traveling in China with Senator Albert Beveridge. A brief news item regarding Beveridge's mid-August 1901 visit to Peking states that "E. Burton Holmes is with the Beveridge party" ("Government Meets Defeat," *Washington Post*, August 14, 1901, 3), but Holmes does not mention Beveridge in his lecture.

100. Holmes, *Burton Holmes Travelogues*, 9:228.

101. Ibid., 248.

102. Ibid., 256–57.

103. Ibid., 267.

104. "Forbidden City's Wonders," *Washington Post*, March 12, 1902, 10.

105. "News of the Theater," *Chicago Daily Tribune*, December 13, 1901, 4.

106. More than a century later, the Forbidden City is a museum open to all who pay the price of entry, which suggests some of the enormous changes that have taken place in China over the course of the twentieth century.

107. Holmes, *Burton Holmes Travelogues*, 9:239.

108. Ibid., 278.

109. Ibid., 289.

110. Ibid., 303.

111. Ibid., 306–8.

112. Edward W. Said, *Orientalism* (New York: Random House, 1978), 20.

113. Ibid.

114. Charles Musser, "The Travel Genre in 1903–1904: Moving towards Fictional Narrative," in *Early Cinema: Space, Frame, Narrative*, ed. Thomas Elsaesser (London: British Film Institute, 1990), 127.

115. Altman, *Silent Film Sound*, 69.

116. Ibid. See also Musser, "Travel Genre."

117. Altman, *Silent Film Sound*, 69–70.

118. Carol Armstrong, *Scenes in a Library: Reading the Photograph in the Book, 1843–1875* (Cambridge: MIT Press, 1998), 334.

CHAPTER 2

1. Charles Musser, *The Emergence of Cinema: The American Screen to 1907* (New York: Scribner's, 1990), 4.

2. Tom Gunning, "The Cinema of Attractions: Early Film, Its Spectator, and the Avant-Garde," in *Early Cinema: Space, Frame, Narrative,* ed. Thomas Elsaesser (London: British Film Institute, 1990), 57.

3. According to Lynne Kirby, "Early film production up to about 1904 was overwhelmingly dominated by actualities. Most actualities were travel and scenic films, meaning everything from train journeys through various parts of the world to sights of all kinds photographed in exotic or remote locales" (*Parallel Tracks: The Railroad and Silent Cinema* [Durham: Duke University Press, 1997], 19). See also Jennifer Lynn Peterson, "World Pictures: Travelogue Films and the Lure of the Exotic, 1890–1920" (Ph.D. diss., University of Chicago, 1999).

4. Charles Musser with Carol Nelson, *High-Class Moving Pictures: Lyman H. Howe and the Forgotten Era of Traveling Exhibition, 1880–1920* (Princeton: Princeton University Press, 1991), 181.

5. Ella Shohat, "Imaging Terra Incognita: The Disciplinary Gaze of Empire," *Public Culture* 3 (Spring 1991): 41.

6. Two hundred reels of film by Holmes dating from 1898 to 1952 were discovered in 2004. The Burton Holmes Historical Collection has since donated the films to the George Eastman House, where efforts are under way to restore and preserve the material. Whether any turn-of-the-century films have survived is not yet clear. The press release announcing the discovery of the films is available at http://www.burtonholmesfilms.com/rediscovery/release.html (accessed June 3, 2007).

7. For more information about the Edison and Biograph films available at the Library of Congress, see Kemp Niver, *Early Motion Pictures: The Paper Print Collection in the Library of Congress* (Washington, D.C.: Library of Congress, 1985).

8. Much of the following section on the early history of the Edison company is based on Charles Musser, *Edison Motion Pictures, 1890–1900: An Annotated Filmography* (Washington, D.C.: Smithsonian Institution Press, 1997); Charles Musser, *Before the Nickelodeon: Edwin S. Porter and the Edison Manufacturing Company* (Berkeley: University of California Press, 1991).

9. Musser notes, "Japanese performers, almost exclusively male acrobats and female dancers, were a significant presence on the New York stage in the mid 1890s" (*Edison Motion Pictures,* 153).

10. The film *Robetta and Doretto [no. 2]* can be viewed at the Library of Congress's American Memory archive at the site Inventing Entertainment: The Motion Pictures and Sound Recordings of the Edison Companies at http://memory.loc.gov/ammem/edhtml/edhome.html (accessed Sept. 13, 2003).

11. Musser, *Before the Nickelodeon,* 66.

12. At the end of the Boxer Uprising, Biograph filmmakers visited Li Hung Chang in China and presented him with a Parlor Mutoscope. They then filmed him viewing a film of his visit to New York City on his new Mutoscope.

13. Musser, *Before the Nickelodeon,* 93.

14. Kirby, *Parallel Tracks*, 22. See also Musser, *Emergence of Cinema*, 234.

15. Charles Musser, "Before the Rapid Firing Kinetograph: Edison Film Production, Representation, and Exploitation in the 1890s," in Musser, *Edison Motion Pictures*, 33.

16. *Edison Films Complete Catalogue*, March 1900, 14, in Charles Musser, ed., *Motion Picture Catalogs by American Producers and Distributors, 1894–1908: A Microfilm Edition* (Frederick, Md.: University Publications of America, 1985).

17. Ibid.

18. James Duncan and Derek Gregory, introduction to *Writes of Passage: Reading Travel Writing*, ed. James Duncan and Derek Gregory (London: Routledge, 1999), 4.

19. John Haskell Kemble, "The Big Four at Sea: The History of the Occidental and Oriental Steamship Company," *Huntington Library Quarterly* 3 (April 1940): 350–53.

20. Ibid., 353.

21. Ibid. Kemble refers to these passengers as "Orientals" or "Asiatics" without distinguishing them by national origins, but it would be reasonable to assume that the majority of them were Chinese. However, according to the Smithsonian Institution, the SS *Gaelic,* one of the Occidental and Oriental Steamship Company's ships, also brought the first wave of Korean immigrants to Hawai'i on January 13, 1903 ("2003 Korean American Centennial Celebration Curriculum Guide," http://www.apa.si.edu/Curriculum%20Guide-Final/index.htm [accessed June 18, 2006]).

22. Kemble, "Big Four at Sea," 353.

23. Gorham and Company to West Orange Laboratory, May 17, 1898, Thomas Edison Papers, Document File Series—1898: (D-98-02) Edison, T. A.—General (TAED D9802), http://edison.rutgers.edu/NamesSearch/DocDetImage.php3 (accessed August 6, 2007).

24. The list of Edison companies on the Edison Papers Web site indicates that the Continental Commerce Company's exclusive rights as sales and exhibition agent for Edison's kinetoscope and kinetoscope films in Europe were enlarged to include Africa and Asia in 1894. However, in 1897, Edison brought suit against the company, by then called Maguire and Baucus, for infringing on his motion picture patents. See "The Edison Papers: Edison Companies," http://edison.rutgers.edu/list.htm#movie (accessed August 6, 2007).

25. Kristen Whissel, "The Gender of Empire: American Modernity, Masculinity, and Edison's War Actualities," in *A Feminist Reader in Early Cinema*, ed. Jennifer M. Bean and Diane Negra (Durham: Duke University Press, 2002), 143.

26. On the attractions of China and Japan for white women in the United States in the late nineteenth and early twentieth centuries, see Mari Yoshihara, *Embracing the East: White Women and American Orientalism* (Oxford: Oxford University Press, 2003).

27. *Catalogue of Edison-Lalande Batteries, Kinetoscopes, Edison X-Ray Apparatus, Edison Cautery Transformers, Edison Electro-Medical Appliances,* 1898, 31, in Musser, *Motion Picture Catalogs*.

28. John Kuo Wei Tchen, *New York before Chinatown: Orientalism and the Shaping of American Culture, 1776–1882* (Baltimore: John Hopkins University Press, 1999), 99.

29. Ibid.

30. For further discussions of representations of Asians in nineteenth-century U.S. culture, see James Moy, *Marginal Sights: Staging the Chinese in America* (Iowa City: University of Iowa Press, 1993); Philip P. Choy, Lorraine Dong, and Marlon K. Hom, eds., *Coming Man: Nineteenth Century American Perceptions of the Chinese* (Seattle: University of Washington Press, 1994); Robert G. Lee, *Orientals: Asian Americans in Popular Culture* (Philadelphia: Temple University Press, 1999); Tchen, *New York before Chinatown;* Yoshihara, *Embracing the East.*

31. Three Edison actuality films from this period depict Chinese in the United States but do so from such a great distance that the racial identity of the film's subjects would not be evident if not for the titles and descriptions: *Arrest in Chinatown, San Francisco, Cal.* (1897), *Chinese Procession, no. 12* (1898), and *Parade of Chinese* (1898).

32. According to Alison Griffiths, the term *ethnographic film* did not come into wide use until after the Second World War. However, in her study of early films, she uses the phrase to refer to "a generalized and dispersed set of practices, a way of using the cinematic medium to express ideas about racial and cultural difference" (*Wondrous Difference: Cinema, Anthropology, and Turn-of-the-Century Visual Culture* [New York: Columbia University Press, 2002], xxix). Similarly, in this instance, I use *ethnographic film* to refer not to a genre of film but to a specific way of looking at and filming Others that highlights and hierarchizes racial and cultural difference.

33. Griffiths, *Wondrous Difference,* 75.

34. Ibid., 226.

35. *The Phonoscope,* July 1898, 14, cited in Musser, *Edison Motion Pictures,* 405.

36. Griffiths, *Wondrous Difference,* 226.

37. *Edison Films,* March 1900, 15, in Musser, *Motion Picture Catalogs.*

38. *The Phonoscope,* July 1898, 14, cited in Musser, *Edison Motion Pictures,* 405.

39. Tom Gunning, "'The Whole World within Reach': Travel Images without Borders," in *Cinéma sans Frontières, 1896–1918,* ed. Roland Cosandey and François Albera (Lausanne: Payot, 1995), 33–34.

40. Ibid., 33.

41. Alison Griffiths offers a different interpretation of these films, emphasizing their performative aspects and arguing that the expectation of monetary reward for diving shows "a glimpse of native subjectivity" (*Wondrous Difference,* 184–86), whereas I view the diving more as a tourist ritual that has the effect of turning subjects into objects. However, we share the belief that the viewers of the film are implicated in the monetary exchange depicted in the film.

42. One well-known example is the debate that followed the publication of Ben Singer's "Manhattan Nickelodeons: New Data on Audiences and Exhibitors," *Cinema Journal* 34 (Spring 1995): 5–35. The films I examine in this chapter predate the nickelodeon era, but the discussion indicates the challenges of researching audiences for and the reception of early cinema. See Robert Allen, "Manhattan Myopia; or Oh! Iowa!" *Cinema Journal* 35 (Spring 1996): 75–103; Ben Singer, "New York, Just Like I Pictured It . . . ," *Cinema Journal* 35 (Spring 1996): 104–28; William Uricchio and Roberta E. Pearson, "Manhattan's Nickelodeons New York? New York! William Uricchio and Roberta E. Pearson Comment on the Singer-Allen Exchange," *Cinema Journal* 36 (Summer 1997): 98–102. For extended analyses of the

reception of early cinema and the problems inherent in studying this topic, see Miriam Hansen, *Babel and Babylon: Spectatorship in American Silent Film* (Cambridge: Harvard University Press, 1991); Janet Staiger, *Interpreting Films: Studies in the Historical Reception of American Cinema* (Princeton: Princeton University Press, 1992).

43. *New York Clipper,* April 30, 1898, 153, cited in Musser, *Edison Motion Pictures,* 397.

44. See Raymond Fielding, "Hale's Tours: Ultrarealism in the Pre–1910 Motion Picture," in *Film before Griffith,* ed. John Fell (Berkeley: University of California Press, 1983), 116–30.

45. On the *maréorama* and *cinéorama,* see Anne Friedberg, *Window Shopping: Cinema and the Postmodern* (Berkeley: University of California Press, 1993), 84–86; Emmanuelle Toulet, "Cinema at the Universal Exposition, Paris, 1900," *Persistence of Vision* 9 (1991): 10–36.

46. *The Phonoscope,* August 1898, 15, cited in Musser, *Edison Motion Pictures,* 399.

47. *Edison Films,* March 1900, 15, cited in ibid., 401.

48. *The Phonoscope,* August 1898, 15, cited in ibid., 403.

49. *The Phonoscope,* August 1898, 14, cited in ibid., 407.

50. *The Phonoscope,* July 1898, 14, cited in ibid., 406.

51. Cited in Griffiths, *Wondrous Difference,* 262.

52. Edward W. Said, *Orientalism* (New York: Random House, 1978), 12.

53. David Palumbo-Liu, *Asian/American: Historical Crossings of a Racial Frontier* (Stanford: Stanford University Press, 1999), 2–3, 17.

54. Kirby, *Parallel Tracks,* 36. Another way of approaching the question of perception is via Jonathan Crary, *Techniques of the Observer: On Vision and Modernity in the Nineteenth Century* (Cambridge: MIT Press, 1990). Wolfgang Schivelbusch, *The Railway Journey: The Industrialization of Time and Space in the Nineteenth Century* (Berkeley: University of California Press, 1986), has been influential in studies of railroads and early film.

55. Kirby, *Parallel Tracks,* 7–8.

56. For an overview of the complicated international negotiations over railway concessions in China, see Clarence B. Davis, "Railway Imperialism in China, 1895–1939," in *Railway Imperialism,* ed. Clarence B. Davis and Kenneth E. Wilburn Jr., with Ronald E. Robinson (New York: Greenwood, 1991), 155–74.

57. Musser, *Emergence of Cinema,* 261.

58. Kristen Whissel, "Uncle Tom, Goldilocks, and the Rough Riders: Early Cinema's Encounter with Empire," *Screen* 40 (Winter 1999): 389, 390.

59. Philip Rosen, "Document and Documentary: On the Persistence of Historical Concepts," in *Theorizing Documentary,* ed. Michael Renov (New York: Routledge, 1993), 73; also published as "Document and Documentary: On the Persistence of Historical Concepts," in Rosen, *Change Mummified: Cinema, Historicity, Theory* (Minneapolis: University of Minnesota Press, 2001), chap. 6.

60. Rosen, "Document and Documentary," 74.

61. *New York Journal and Advertiser,* April 26, 1898, 16, cited in Musser, *Before the Nickelodeon,* 131.

62. Musser, *Before the Nickelodeon*, 135.

63. Whissel, "Uncle Tom," 387.

64. *American Mutoscope and Biograph Company Picture Catalogue*, November 1902, 135, in Musser, *Motion Picture Catalogs*, 135.

65. Ibid., 136.

66. Ibid., 181.

67. Whissel, "Gender of Empire," 143.

68. *Edison Films Complete Catalogue*, July 1901, 16, in Musser, *Motion Picture Catalogs*.

69. Ibid.

70. *American Mutoscope and Biograph Company Picture Catalogue*, November 1902, 155–56, in Musser, *Motion Picture Catalogs*.

71. Ibid., 138.

72. Ibid., 139.

73. This conclusion is based on my review of a number of sources, including Niver, *Early Motion Pictures;* Musser, *Emergence of Cinema*.

74. According to Jay Leyda, *Congress of Nations* was an imitation of the Méliès film *La Chine contre les Allies* (1900) (*Dianying: Electric Shadows: An Account of Films and the Film Audience in China* [Cambridge: MIT Press, 1972], 3–7). I have not seen the Méliès film, but it was a common practice at the time for companies to produce their own versions of popular films or to even dupe them and claim them as their own, so it would not be surprising if Blackton and Smith modeled their film after the Méliès version. Leyda also discusses a number of other reenactments of incidents from the Boxer Uprising and films of Peking during and after the uprising. *Congress of Nations* may be viewed online at the Library of Congress's American Memory archive at the site Inventing Entertainment at http://memory.loc.gov/ammem/edhtml/edhome.html (accessed September 13, 2003).

75. *Edison Films*, July 1901, 81, cited in Musser, *Edison Motion Pictures*, 640.

76. *New York Clipper*, November 17, 1900, 852, cited in ibid. The situation in China was often referred to as "the Chinese question," though historically, the term has also been applied to issues regarding Chinese immigrants in the United States.

77. William Basil Courtney, "History of Vitagraph," *Motion Picture News*, March 21, 1925, 1221, cited in Leyda, *Dianying*, 6.

78. American Film Institute Catalog Online, http://afi.chadwyck.com (accessed October 14, 2003).

79. Ibid.

80. *Biograph Picture Catalogue*, November 1902, 164, in Musser, *Motion Picture Catalogs*.

81. The Library of Congress has created an online site documenting films of the Spanish-American War and Philippine-American War as part of its American Memory project at http://memory.loc.gov/ammem/sawhtml/sawsp1.html (accessed September 21, 2003).

82. David Levy, "Re-Constituted Newsreels, Re-Enactments, and the American Narrative Film," in *Cinema 1900/1906: An Analytical Study by the National*

Film Archive (London) and the International Federation of Film Archives, comp. Roger Holman (Brussels: Fiaf, 1982), 249.

83. Kristen Whissel, "Placing the Spectator on the Scene of History: The Battle Re-Enactment at the Turn of the Century, from Buffalo Bill's Wild West to the Early Cinema," *Historical Journal of Film, Radio, and Television* 22 (August 2002): 239.

84. Alison Griffiths, "'Shivers down Your Spine': Panoramas and the Origins of the Cinematic Reenactment," *Screen* 44 (Spring 2003): 11.

85. Ibid., 12.

86. Rosen, "Document and Documentary," 75.

87. *Biograph Bulletin,* August 29, 1903, reprinted in Kemp Niver, comp., *Biograph Bulletins, 1896–1908* (Los Angeles: Locare, 1971), 90.

88. Musser, *Emergence of Cinema,* 342.

89. Charles Musser, "The Travel Genre in 1903–1904: Moving towards Fictional Narrative," in *Early Cinema: Space, Frame, Narrative,* ed. Thomas Elsaesser (London: British Film Institute, 1990), 124–25.

90. Amy Kaplan, "The Birth of an Empire," *PMLA* 114 (October 1999): 1073.

91. Charlie Keil, "Steel Engines and Cardboard Rockets: The Status of Fiction and Nonfiction in Early Cinema," *Persistence of Vision* 9 (1991): 43.

92. Tom Gunning, *D. W. Griffith and the Origins of American Narrative Film: The Early Years at Biograph* (Urbana: University of Illinois Press, 1991), 18.

93. Gunning, "Cinema of Attractions," 56.

94. Eileen Bowser, *The Transformation of Cinema: 1907–1915* (Berkeley: University of California Press, 1990), xi. Other works devoted to this period include Gunning, *D. W. Griffith;* Charlie Keil, *Early American Cinema in Transition: Story, Style, and Filmmaking, 1907–1913* (Madison: University of Wisconsin Press, 2002); Charlie Keil and Shelley Stamp, eds., *American Cinema's Transitional Era: Audiences, Institutions, Practices* (Berkeley: University of California Press, 2004). See also David Bordwell, Janet Staiger, and Kristin Thompson, *The Classical Hollywood Cinema: Film Style and Mode of Production to 1960* (New York: Columbia University Press, 1985), esp. "Part Three: The Formulation of the Classical Style: 1908–28."

95. In *The American Soldier in Love and War,* the first scene, the home of the soldier's sweetheart, is also shot on a stage, but the artificiality of the domestic interior appears much less jarring than that of the outdoor scenes representing the Philippines, at least to contemporary eyes. Anne Friedberg offers a detailed, shot-by-shot analysis of *European Rest Cure* and makes the point that the foreign is "presented in very clumsy faux-virtual landscapes" while "'home' is presented with more realistic detail." She argues that the film thus offers an "antitravel message" that asserts the superiority of cinema "as a more spectacular and fluid form of virtual mobility" (*Window Shopping,* 100). *European Rest Cure* may be viewed online at the Library of Congress' American Memory archive at the Inventing Entertainment site at http://memory.loc.gov/ammem/edhtml/edhome.html (accessed December 8, 2003).

96. The 1906 film *The Policeman's Tour of the World* (Tour du Monde d'un Policier), produced by the French company Pathé and inspired by Jules Verne's 1872 novel *Around the World in Eighty Days,* similarly mixes actuality films with staged footage, but according to a different logic than the distinction between the foreign and the familiar. For an analysis of the film, including its use of actuality

footage, see Philip Rosen, "Disjunction and Ideology in a Preclassical Film: A Policeman's Tour of the World," *Wide Angle* 12 (1990): 20–36.

97. Gunning, *D. W. Griffith*, 138.

98. Ibid., 140, 216.

99. Ibid., 140–41.

100. Keil, *Early American Cinema*, 131.

101. Musser, *Before the Nickelodeon*, 66.

102. *Edison Films Complete Catalogue*, March 1900, 14, in Musser, *Motion Picture Catalogs*.

CHAPTER 3

1. Pearl S. Buck, *My Several Worlds: A Personal Record* (New York: Day, 1954). Both the similarity and contrast between *My Several Worlds* and the title of Burton Holmes's autobiography, *The World Is Mine,* are worth noting.

2. Karen J. Leong, *The China Mystique: Pearl S. Buck, Anna May Wong, Mayling Soong, and the Transformation of American Orientalism* (Berkeley: University of California Press, 2005), 1.

3. Ibid.

4. Ibid., 5.

5. Ibid., 43.

6. A handful of book-length studies have been devoted to the representation of Asians in mainstream U.S. film, including Dorothy B. Jones, *The Portrayal of China and India on the American Screen, 1896–1955* (Cambridge: MIT Press, 1955); Eugene Franklin Wong, *On Visual Media Racism: Asians in the American Motion Pictures* (New York: Arno, 1978); Gina Marchetti, *Romance and the "Yellow Peril": Race, Sex, and Discursive Strategies in Hollywood Fiction* (Berkeley: University of California Press, 1993). See also Jun Xing, *Asian America through the Lens: History, Representations, and Identity* (Walnut Creek, Calif.: Altamira, 1998); Peter X. Feng, ed. *Screening Asian Americans* (New Brunswick: Rutgers University Press, 2002). The following works consider Asians in mainstream film in the context of a broader examination of representations in various media, including literature and theater: James S. Moy, *Marginal Sights: Staging the Chinese in America* (Iowa City: University of Iowa Press, 1993); Robert G. Lee, *Orientals: Asian Americans in Popular Culture* (Philadelphia: Temple University Press, 1999); David Palumbo-Liu, *Asian/American: Historical Crossings of a Racial Frontier* (Stanford: Stanford University Press, 1999); Sheng-Mei Ma, *The Deathly Embrace: Orientalism and Asian American Identity* (Minneapolis: University of Minnesota Press, 2000). Finally, the American Film Institute's online catalog of U.S. films, available through many university libraries or to members of the AFI through its Web site, allows users to search the database by subject or keywords, including *China* and *Chinese*.

7. Hayakawa's character was originally identified as Japanese, but protests from the Japanese government led the studio to change the character into a "Burmese" ivory king. Only the intertitles of the film were modified; no efforts were made to correlate the character's dress, furnishings, or other traits with his new ethnic identity.

8. Oland is better known for his portrayal of the detective Charlie Chan,

based on a character created by Earl Derr Biggers and inspired by the real-life Chinese American detective Chang Apana of the Honolulu Police Force. In the first few Charlie Chan films, Chan was a relatively minor character played by Asian actors. Oland took the first of his sixteen turns in the title role in *Charlie Chan Carries On* (Hamilton McFadden, 1931).

9. Jones, *Portrayal*, 19.

10. Ibid. Despite the more sympathetic attitude toward China and the Chinese of *Oil for the Lamps of China*, which told the story of an employee of an American oil company in China, the country and its people serve primarily as a backdrop for the actions of the (white) American characters. Today, the American Film Institute categorizes many of these kinds of films under the subject heading "Americans in Foreign Countries," a descriptive turn of phrase that precisely pinpoints their narrative focus.

11. Jones, *Portrayal*, 20. For a detailed history of representations of Asians in U.S. films from the turn of the century to the 1970s, see Wong, *On Visual Media Racism*.

12. Jones, *Portrayal*, 26.

13. Peter Conn, *Pearl S. Buck: A Cultural Biography* (Cambridge: Cambridge University Press, 1996), 34. Obviously there were members of Chinese communities in the United States who were intimately familiar with Chinese culture and fluent in Chinese but they did not serve as an institutionalized source for the dissemination of knowledge about China.

14. James C. Thomson Jr., Peter W. Staley, and John Curtis Perry, *Sentimental Imperialists: The American Experience in East Asia* (New York: Harper and Row, 1981), 45.

15. Conn, *Pearl S. Buck*, 113.

16. Ibid., 123.

17. Ibid., 141.

18. Harold R. Isaacs, *Scratches on Our Minds: American Images of China and India* (Westport, Conn.: Greenwood, 1958), 155. Conn puts the number of U.S. ticket sales at the slightly higher figure of more than twenty-five million (*Pearl S. Buck*, 192).

19. Isaacs, *Scratches*, 155. *The Good Earth* was selected for Oprah Winfrey's Book Club in September 2004, suggesting the book's continuing appeal.

20. James C. Thomson Jr., "Pearl S. Buck and the American Quest for China," in *The Several Worlds of Pearl S. Buck*, ed. Elizabeth J. Lipscomb, Frances E. Webb, and Peter Conn (Westport, Conn.: Greenwood, 1994), 14.

21. "'The Good Earth' and Other Recent Works of Fiction," *New York Times*, March 31, 1931, 60. Lafcadio Hearn (1850–1904) was a writer who developed a reputation as an interpreter of Japanese culture to the West, especially the "traditional" aspects of culture he viewed as threatened by the efforts to modernize and Westernize during the Meiji period. He traveled to Japan in 1890, married a Japanese woman, and eventually became a Japanese citizen. His most well known work is a collection of lectures, *Japan: An Attempt at Interpretation* (1904).

22. For a discussion of Chinese reactions to *The Good Earth*, see Liu Haiping, "Pearl S. Buck's Reception in China Reconsidered," in *Several Worlds*, ed. Lipscomb, Webb, and Conn, 55–70.

23. Younghill Kang, review of *The Good Earth*, *New Republic*, July 1, 1931, ex-

cerpted in "Critical Excerpts," in Pearl S. Buck, *The Good Earth,* intro. and ed. Peter Conn (New York: Simon and Schuster, 1994), 368.

24. Editorial comment *New Republic,* July 1, 1931, excerpted in ibid.

25. Kiang Kang-hu, "A Chinese Scholar's View of Mrs. Buck's Novels," *New York Times,* January 15, 1933, BR2.

26. Pearl S. Buck, "Mrs. Buck Replies to Her Chinese Critic," *New York Times,* January 15, 1933, BR2.

27. Ibid.

28. Ibid.

29. Louis van den Ecker, "A Veteran's View of Hollywood Authenticity," *Hollywood Quarterly* 4 (Summer 1950): 323–31.

30. Ibid., 323.

31. Ruth Vasey, *The World According to Hollywood, 1918–1939* (Madison: University of Wisconsin Press, 1997), 20.

32. Ibid.

33. Van den Ecker, "Veteran's View," 326.

34. Ibid., 324.

35. Ibid., 328–29.

36. Ibid., 328.

37. Ibid., 329.

38. Ibid. In a slightly different context, the conflict between the notions of realism held by technical advisers and those of Hollywood filmmakers is a recurring theme in the history of the incorporation of new technologies into Hollywood. See James Lastra, *Sound Technology and the American Cinema: Perception, Representation, Modernity* (New York: Columbia University Press, 2000), chap. 5.

39. Van den Ecker, "Veteran's View," 330.

40. Vivian Sobchack, "'Surge and Splendor': A Phenomenology of the Hollywood Historical Epic," *Representations* 29 (Winter 1990): 31.

41. Ibid., 47.

42. Edward Maeder, comp., *Hollywood and History: Costume Design in Film* (New York: Thames and Hudson, 1987), 69, 15, cited in Sobchack, "'Surge and Splendor,'" 47.

43. Van den Ecker, "Veteran's View," 323.

44. Vasey, *World,* 153.

45. Ibid.

46. Chinese students who had seen *Shanghai Express* in Germany and the United States contacted Beh Chuan Peng, a member of the Chinese Film Censorship Committee, about the film. Peng then complained to Willys Peck, the American consul general in Nanking (Eric Smoodin, *Regarding Frank Capra: Audience, Celebrity, and American Film Studies, 1930–1960* [Durham: Duke University Press, 2004], 60).

47. Ibid., 62.

48. Ibid., 75.

49. Vasey, *World,* 49.

50. Charles G. Clarke, "China Photographically Ideal," *American Cinematographer,* September 1934, 202.

51. Jay Leyda, *Dianying: Electric Shadows: An Account of Films and the Film Audience in China* (Cambridge: MIT Press, 1972), 110.

52. Clarke, "China Photographically Ideal," 202, 211.

53. The *American Film Institute Catalog of Feature Films* entry for *The Good Earth* cites *Film Daily* and *Hollywood Reporter* news items from January 31, 1934, stating that MGM had been denied permission by the Chinese government to film in China, a decision that was apparently reversed after the establishment of the formal agreement between MGM and the government ("The Good Earth," http://afi.chadwyck.com [accessed November 13, 2003]).

54. Vasey, *World,* 189. For a discussion of negotiations among the Chinese government, the U.S. State Department, and MGM regarding the making of *The Good Earth,* see Hye Seung Chung, *Hollywood Asian: Philip Ahn and the Politics of Cross-Ethnic Performance* (Philadelphia: Temple University Press, 2006), 87–104.

55. Jones, *Portrayal,* 44.

56. "Details of Agreement with M-G-M Made Public," *Central News Agency* (China), April 24, 1937, cited in ibid., 44–45.

57. Near the conclusion of production, Tu was replaced by Huang Chao-Chin without explanation.

58. Vasey, *World,* 105.

59. Conn, *Pearl S. Buck,* 146.

60. Pearl S. Buck to David Lloyd, May 7, 1932, cited in ibid., 146–47.

61. The *American Film Institute Catalog of Feature Films* entry for *The Good Earth* states that Buck was hired as a technical consultant, but I have found only one example of direct correspondence between Buck and MGM regarding the production. Various individuals in China and in California other than Buck were listed as technical advisers to the film, including Bessie Ochs, an American living in China, and Jimmy Lee, a Chinese student at USC. General Tu was also sometimes listed as a technical adviser or consultant in stories about the production of the film ("The Good Earth," http://afi.chadwyck.com [accessed November 13, 2003]).

62. Pearl S. Buck to J. Robert Rubin, August 24, 1932, 1. *The Good Earth* Story Files, Folder 2, MGM Collection, Cinema-Television Library, University of Southern California, Los Angeles. This is the only correspondence between Buck and the studio in the files. In later years, Buck claimed that she had no involvement in the making of the film.

63. Ibid., 2.

64. "The Good Earth," http://afi.chadwyck.com (accessed November 13, 2003).

65. George Hill to Ben Piazza, November 6, 1933, *Good Earth* Story Files.

66. "The Good Earth," http://afi.chadwyck.com (accessed November 13, 2003).

67. Chung, *Hollywood Asian,* xiii.

68. Cari Beauchamp, *Without Lying Down: Frances Marion and the Powerful Women of Early Hollywood* (Berkeley: University of California Press, 1998), 319–20. George Hill died in California of a self-inflicted gunshot wound in August 1934, before production on *The Good Earth* was completed. Victor Fleming was hired to take over the production but was forced to leave for health reasons. Sidney Franklin completed the film and was credited as its director.

69. For an account of Anna May Wong's life and career, see Karen Leong, *China Mystique,* chap. 3. Biographies of Anna May Wong include Anthony B.

Chan, *Perpetually Cool: The Many Lives of Anna May Wong (1905–1961)* (Lanham, Md.: Scarecrow, 2003); Graham Russell Hodges, *Anna May Wong: From Laundryman's Daughter to Hollywood Legend* (New York: Palgrave Macmillan, 2004).

70. Barbara Klinger, "Digressions at the Cinema: Reception and Mass Culture," *Cinema Journal* 28 (Summer 1989): 3.

71. Ibid., 5.

72. Ibid., 11.

73. Ibid., 12.

74. Ibid., 13.

75. Ibid., 15.

76. Ibid.

77. "*The Good Earth:* With M.G.M. on Location," *Town and Sportsman,* June 1934, 26, *The Good Earth* Production File, Margaret Herrick Library, Academy of Motion Picture Arts and Sciences, Beverly Hills, Calif.

78. Ibid.

79. Ibid.

80. John Schwarzkopf, "On Location with *The Good Earth,*" *Motion Picture,* October 1936, 40, *Good Earth* Production File.

81. Ibid., 41.

82. Ibid.

83. "The Good Earth," *Movie Classic,* October 1936, 2, *Good Earth* Production File.

84. *The Good Earth Program, Good Earth* Production File.

85. For an analysis of race, cinema, and ethnographic villages, see Fatimah Tobing Rony, *The Third Eye: Race, Cinema, and Ethnographic Spectacle* (Durham: Duke University Press, 1996). Mae M. Ngai considers not only how the Other was represented but also the role of the Other in such representations in her examination of the case of the Chinese village at the 1893 World's Columbian Exposition in Chicago, which was produced and financed by Chinese American entrepreneurs ("Transnationalism and the Transformation of the 'Other': Response to the Presidential Address," *American Quarterly* 57 [March 2005]: 59–65).

86. However, this is not to suggest that discriminatory practices in casting are no longer an issue. See the introduction for a discussion of the challenges facing actors of Asian descent in the contemporary U.S. film and television industries.

87. Alicia Annas, "The Photogenic Formula: Hairstyles and Makeup in Historical Films," in *Hollywood and History,* comp. Maeder, 58.

88. Schwarzkopf, "On Location with *The Good Earth,*" 40.

89. "Intensive Location Work Starts upon 'The Good Earth,'" 2, *Good Earth* Production File.

90. Schwarzkopf, "On Location with *The Good Earth,*" 65.

91. Glenn Chaffin, "2000 Chinese in New Film Spectacle," *Page Four,* ca. 1937, 3, *Good Earth* Production File.

92. Charles L. Leong, "Mandarins in Hollywood," in *Moving the Image: Independent Asian Pacific American Media Arts,* ed. Russell Leong (Los Angeles: UCLA Asian American Studies Center and Visual Communications, 1991), 125. Paul Muni also reportedly shaved his head for the role rather than wear a prosthetic device. His decision was understood as an indication of his commitment to an authentic portrayal of the character.

93. Ibid.

94. Ibid., 128.

95. Ibid., 129.

96. Ibid., 129, 131.

97. Ibid., 131.

98. Ibid.

99. *The Chinese Digest* 3 (March 1937) was devoted to *The Good Earth* (Karen Leong, *China Mystique,* 54). In Frank Chin's 1991 novel, *Donald Duk* (Minneapolis: Coffee House, 1991), the production of *The Good Earth* is acknowledged but also criticized as part of the history of Chinese American communities in California. The reference occurs when the twelve-year-old title character's father, King, has an exchange with the Frog Twins, two elderly inhabitants of San Francisco's Chinatown, about Asian actors in the movies. King tells the twins, "I know, I know, you were in *The Good Earth,* girls. I hate that movie. I know you're in the Screen Actors Guild. I hate Oriental actors. So don't talk about acting. . . . I wish Pearl Buck was alive and walk into my restaurant so I can cut out her heart and liver. That's how much I hate that movie" (135).

100. Pearl S. Buck to Emma Edmunds White, February 5, 1937, cited in Conn, *Pearl S. Buck,* 196.

101. Max J. Herzberg, foreword to Sarah M. Mullen, *A Guide to the Discussion of the Screen Version of Pearl Buck's Prize-Winning Novel* The Good Earth (Newark, N.J.: Educational and Recreational Guides, 1937), 3, *Good Earth* Production File.

102. William Lewin, *Photoplay Appreciation in American High Schools* (New York: Appleton-Century, 1934).

103. Max J. Herzberg, introduction to *A Study Guide to Victor Hugo's* Les Miserables, *Photoplay Studies,* April 1935, 3. The price of the guides, which were available through mail order, was relatively reasonable: fifteen cents for a single guide, with the price per guide decreasing with the number of guides requested to as low as three cents each when between 100 and 999 were ordered. The guides were also available by subscription at one dollar each for up to 10 subscriptions or seventy cents each for between 11 and 99 subscriptions.

104. Ibid., 4.

105. "Miniature Stills for Notebooks: *The Good Earth*—Series 3" (Newark, N.J.: Educational and Research Guides, 1937), n.p., *Good Earth* Production File. This scene is not included in the final film, which only shows Wang Lung standing before the Great Mistress as O-lan is brought to him.

106. Mullen, *Guide,* 26.

107. For example, *Study Guide to* The Good Earth (New York: Commission on Human Relations, Progressive Education Association, 1939), *Good Earth* Production File, focuses on the status of women, the famine sequence, and the locust sequence, and the material targets high school and college students and teachers.

108. Isaacs, *Scratches,* 157.

109. Thomson, "Pearl S. Buck," 13.

110. "Ballyhoo," *The Good Earth* press book, *Good Earth* Production File. The studio placed Chinese in quotation marks ("Chinese" girls) since actual Chinese women were used, whenever possible, but if none were available the studio recommended using white women dressed in Chinese clothing.

111. Conn, *Pearl S. Buck*, 131.
112. Karen Leong, *China Mystique*, 56.

CHAPTER 4

1. James A. Michener, *The World Is My Home: A Memoir* (New York: Random House, 1992), 464. Christina Klein notes, however, that the United States "was hardly 'isolationist' fifty years before [Michener] began writing: the turn of the twentieth century marked the peak of U.S. territorial imperialism in the Pacific and the Caribbean" (*Cold War Orientalism: Asia in the Middlebrow Imagination, 1945–1961* [Berkeley: University of California Press, 2003]), 120).
2. E. Burton Holmes, *The World Is Mine* (Culver City, Calif.: Murray and Gee, 1953), 199.
3. Irving Wallace, "Everybody's Rover Boy," in E. Burton Holmes, *The Man Who Photographed the World: Burton Holmes Travelogues, 1886–1938*, ed. Genoa S. Caldwell (New York: Abrams, 1977), 12.
4. Klein, *Cold War Orientalism*, 5.
5. Michener, *World*, 250.
6. Holmes, *World*, 90.
7. E. Burton Holmes, *Burton Holmes Travelogues*, vol. 10, *Seoul—The Capital of Korea, Japan—The Country, Japan—The Cities* (New York: McClure, 1910), 293.
8. "How to Tell Japs from Chinese," *Life*, December 22, 1941, 81–82.
9. See Clayton R. Koppes and Gregory D. Black, *Hollywood Goes to War: How Politics, Profits, and Propaganda Shaped World War II Movies* (New York: Free Press, 1987).
10. John W. Dower, *War without Mercy: Race and Power in the Pacific War* (New York: Pantheon, 1986), 28.
11. Ibid., 23.
12. Klein, *Cold War Orientalism*, 9.
13. See, for example, Edwin Schallert, "Tokyo Movie Hectic Thrill to U.S. Cast," *Los Angeles Times*, October 15, 1950, part IV, pp. 1, 4, *Tokyo File 212* Production File, Margaret Herrick Library, Academy of Motion Picture Arts and Sciences, Beverly Hills, Calif. The film *Tokyo Joe* (Stuart Heisler, 1949) was, according to a December 10, 1948, *Hollywood Reporter* article, the first American production allowed to film on location in Japan by the U.S. Army authorities after the Second World War. However, the article indicates that the second unit team shot background footage in Japan, which suggests that the main filming took place elsewhere ("Tokyo Joe," http://www.afi.chadwyck.com [accessed May 14, 2005]).
14. Schallert, "Tokyo Movie," 4. Immediately after *Tokyo File 212*, Breakston produced two other low-budget films shot on location in Japan, *Oriental Evil* (1952) and *Geisha Girl* (1952).
15. A. H. Weiler, "Random Notes about People and Pictures," *New York Times*, April 23, 1950, X5, *Tokyo File 212* Production File.
16. Ibid.
17. Marly also played opposite Humphrey Bogart in *Tokyo Joe*.
18. Schallert, "Tokyo Movie," 4.

19. Patricia Clary, "Film Alert on Reds," *Los Angeles Evening Herald and Express,* July 20, 1950, B10, *Tokyo File 212* Production File.

20. Ibid.

21. Most scholars today believe that the Tanaka Memorial, a text outlining Japan's imperial ambitions and supposedly submitted by the prime minister to the emperor in 1927, was an anti-Japanese hoax (Dower, *War without Mercy,* 22).

22. "Tokyo File 212," *Variety,* April 25, 1951, 14, *Tokyo File 212* Production File.

23. "Tokyo File 212," *Box Office,* May 5, 1951, 1255, *Tokyo File 212* Production File.

24. A.W., "The Screen in Review," *New York Times,* June 1, 1951, 20, *Tokyo File 212* Production File.

25. Tom Gunning, "The Cinema of Attractions: Early Film, Its Spectator, and the Avant-Garde" in *Early Cinema: Space, Frame, Narrative,* ed. Thomas Elsaesser (London: British Film Institute, 1990), 57.

26. Ibid., 61.

27. Although one possible strategy of narration is to withhold information until a later moment in the plot of the film, the end of the encounter scene is so abrupt and the content of the conversation is revealed so soon thereafter that this example does not appear to be a deliberate use of restricted narration.

28. J. D. Spiro, "Hollywood Dossier: Gable Form Own Company but Keep Metro Ties—Race Prejudice in Reverse New Slant No Fooling," *New York Times,* October 1, 1950, 113.

29. J. D. Spiro, "Produced in Occupied Japan," *New York Times,* November 12, 1950, 100, *Tokyo File 212* Production File.

30. John W. Dower, *Embracing Defeat: Japan in the Wake of World War II* (New York: Norton, 1999), 211–12.

31. Klein, *Cold War Orientalism,* 9.

32. Ibid., 9–10.

33. *Three Stripes in the Sun* was based on "A Reporter at Large—The Gentle Wolfhound," by E. J. Kahn Jr., which originally appeared in the *New Yorker,* May 9, 1953. *Navy Wife* was adapted from the 1953 novel *Mother, Sir!* by Tats Blain, which was based on her experiences as the first American woman to join her military husband in occupied Japan. *Joe Butterfly,* which many reviewers saw as another version of *The Teahouse of the August Moon,* is set in Tokyo just after the Japanese surrender. It follows the efforts of a group of U.S. soldiers, including Audie Murphy as Private Woodley, to publish the first postwar issue of *Yank: The Army Weekly,* the well-known U.S. Army magazine. They are aided in their efforts by Japanese interpreter and all-around facilitator Joe Butterfly, played by Burgess Meredith.

34. "Vern Sneider, the Writer of a Book on Okinawa," *New York Times,* May 3, 1981, http://nytimes.com/1981/05/03/obituaries/vern-sneider-the-writer-of-a-book-on-okinawa.html?scp=/&sq="Vern Sneider"&st=cse (accessed March 1, 2008).

35. In his autobiography, Brando writes bluntly of the film, "It was a horrible picture and I was miscast" (Marlon Brando with Robert Lindsey, *Brando: Songs My Mother Taught Me* [New York: Random House, 1994], 236).

36. John Patrick, *The Teahouse of the August Moon* (New York: Putnam's, 1952), 8.

37. Cecil Smith, "Author at Loss over Success of 'Teahouse,'" *Los Angeles Times,* November 27, 1955, part IV, p. 4.

38. Ibid.

39. Ibid.

40. Patrick, *Teahouse,* 172.

41. Philip K. Scheuer, "Rains Came to 'Teahouse' in Japan, but NO Feuds," *Los Angeles Times,* June 24, 1956, part IV, p. 2, *The Teahouse of the August Moon* Production File, Margaret Herrick Library, Academy of Motion Picture Arts and Sciences, Beverly Hills, Calif.

42. Ibid.

43. "Teahouse Tattle," *MGM Press Book Teahouse of August Moon, Teahouse* Production File.

44. Bob Thomas, *Marlon: Portrait of the Rebel as an Artist* (New York: Random House, 1973), n.p., cited by Mario Beguiristain in the program notes for Marlon Brando: Portrait of an Actor, Los Angeles County Museum of Art, April 17, 1976, 1, *Teahouse* Production File.

45. Thomas C. Ryan, "Banzai Brando," *Collier's,* December 2, 1956, n.p., *Teahouse* Production File.

46. Ibid.

47. Ibid.

48. Ray Falk, "Bivouac at an Okinawa 'Teahouse" in Japan," *New York Times,* June 10, 1956, 125.

49. Lowell E. Redelings, "'Teahouse' a Hit, MGM Comedy Applauded," *Hollywood Citizen-News,* November 21, 1956, *Teahouse* Production File.

50. John L. Scott, "'Teahouse' Film Opens at Brilliant Premiere," *Los Angeles Times,* November 21, 1956, *Teahouse* Production File.

51. Falk, "Bivouac," 125.

52. Bosley Crowther, "Okinawan Farce," *New York Times,* December 2, 1956, *Teahouse* Production File.

53. Ibid. Crowther refers to the film, however, as *The Magnificent Seven,* which is what John Sturges titled his 1960 film that was based on the Kurosawa film.

54. Ibid. Although I cannot pursue this question here, the standard for authentic representations of Japan and the Japanese, at least for a few metropolitan film critics, had been considerably affected by the recent release of Japanese films in the United States. Fans of Kurosawa's *Rashomon* (1950) might have recognized, for example, Machiko Kyo in *The Teahouse of the August Moon.* In a dramatic and compelling performance, she played the violated wife in Kurosawa's film, while in *Teahouse* she was cast as the considerably less convincing Lotus Blossom, the giggling geisha who is given as a gift to Fisby.

55. "There's Nothing There but Village Will Be on Map" (MGM press book), *Teahouse* Production File.

56. Dower, *War without Mercy,* 45.

57. The following consideration of the production history of *Sayonara* is intended to complement the many existing scholarly analyses of the film. For an examination of *Sayonara* in terms of interracial romances between Asians and Caucasians in Hollywood films, see Gina Marchetti, *Romance and the "Yellow Peril": Race, Sex, and Discursive Strategies in Hollywood Fiction* (Berkeley: University of California Press, 1993), 125–43. Robert G. Lee discusses the film in "The Cold War

Origins of the Model Minority Myth," in *Orientals: Asian Americans in Popular Culture* (Philadelphia: Temple University Press, 1999), 145–79. Caroline Chung Simpson references both the novel and the film in her discussion of Japanese war brides in *An Absent Presence: Japanese Americans in Postwar American Culture, 1945–1960* (Durham: Duke University Press, 2001), 149–85.

58. Warner Brothers Studios, production notes on *Sayonara*, n.d., 1, *Sayonara* Production File, Margaret Herrick Library, Academy of Motion Picture Arts and Sciences, Beverly Hills, Calif.

59. Joshua Logan, *Movie Stars, Real People, and Me* (New York: Delacorte, 1978), 93.

60. Marchetti, *Romance and the "Yellow Peril,"* 126.

61. James Michener, *Sayonara* (New York: Random House, 1954), 243.

62. Caroline Chung Simpson compares the ending of the novel to that of the film in her essay on Japanese war brides and the resettlement of Japanese Americans in the United States after the Second World War. She also notes that in 1955, Michener married a Japanese American woman he met in Japan, Mari Yoriko Sabusawa ("'Out of an Obscure Place': Japanese War Brides and Cultural Pluralism in the 1950s," *differences* 10 [Fall 1998]: 47–81; also published in Simpson, *Absent Presence,* chap. 5).

63. Warner Brothers Studios, production notes on *Sayonara*, 2.

64. For a study of the effects of immigration and antimiscegenation legislation on notions of race, gender, and nation in the United States, see Susan Koshy, *Sexual Naturalization: Asian Americans and Miscegenation* (Stanford: Stanford University Press, 2004).

65. Logan, *Movie Stars,* 96.

66. Significant similarities exist between Karen Leong's conception of the "China mystique" and what Klein calls "Cold War orientalism," but they focus on different historical periods with only some overlap in the years immediately following the Second World War.

67. Klein, *Cold War Orientalism,* 11.

68. Logan, *Movie Stars,* 97. Ironically, many reviewers persisted in describing *Sayonara* as a *Madame Butterfly*–type story.

69. Ibid., 109.

70. Cited in Joan Cohen, "Program Notes: Sayonara," Los Angeles County Museum of Art, April 29, 1976, 1, *Sayonara* Production File.

71. Warner Brothers Studios, production notes on *Sayonara*, 6.

72. Ellsworth Fredricks, "The Photography of 'Sayonara,'" *American Cinematographer,* November 1957, 723.

73. Ibid., 722.

74. Ibid.

75. Technirama was a widescreen cinema system developed in the mid-1950s that utilized a double-frame negative to create a greater horizontal expanse of screen (ibid., 723).

76. Philip K. Scheuer, "'Sayonara' Features Two Love Stories," *Los Angeles Times,* November 17, 1957, F1, F3.

77. Bosley Crowther, "Screen: Brando Stars in 'Sayonara,'" *New York Times,* December 6, 1957, 39.

78. Ruth Waterbury, "'Sayonara' Tender, Romantic Story," *L.A. Examiner,* December 26, 1957, *Sayonara* Production File.

79. Ibid.

80. Logan, *Movie Stars*, 94.

81. Ibid., 94–95.

82. As popular as *Sayonara* was, David Lean's *The Bridge on the River Kwai*, about British soldiers in a Japanese prisoner of war camp, won the year's Oscar for best picture, and Lean won for best director, even though *Sayonara* was nominated in both categories. The view of the Japanese as brutal aggressors clearly still resonated with U.S. audiences.

83. Lee, *Orientals*, 162–63. These scenes may have been filmed in the royal gardens in Kyoto.

84. Simpson, "'Out of an Obscure Place,'" 48–49.

85. Simpson, *Absent Presence*, 11.

86. Warner Brothers Studios, production notes on *Sayonara*, 3.

87. Philip K. Scheuer, "'Sayonara' Filming Loaded with High Drama, Intrigue," *Los Angeles Times*, January 19, 1958, E2.

88. Dorothy Manners, "Miiko Becomes Star in Her First Film!" *L.A. Examiner*, December 1, 1957, 9, 11, *Sayonara* Production File.

89. John L. Scott, "Fortune Bolt Puts Miiko in Top Film Spot," *Los Angeles Times*, May 5, 1957, *Sayonara* Production File.

90. Liza Wilson, "Brando's Cinderella," *L.A. Examiner*, March 2, 1958, 6, *Sayonara* Production File.

91. For a critique of the U.S. institution of citizenship with regard to the material history of Asians in the United States, see Lisa Lowe, *Immigrant Acts: On Asian American Cultural Politics* (Durham: Duke University Press, 1996).

92. In 1988, President Ronald Reagan publicly apologized for the wrongful wartime relocation and internment of Japanese Americans during the Second World War and signed into law a measure providing restitution to surviving internees.

93. Bob Thomas, "Asia Journey Stirs Brando," *Los Angeles Mirror-News*, June 21, 1956, part I, p. 2, Marlon Brando Files, Margaret Herrick Library, Academy of Motion Picture Arts and Sciences, Beverly Hills, Calif.

94. Ibid. *House of Bamboo* (Samuel Fuller, 1955) was a remake of an earlier film noir, *The Street with No Name* (William Keighley, 1948), and depicts an American crime ring in Tokyo composed entirely of ex-cons who had been drafted by the U.S. Army and then dishonorably discharged. It was shot on location in Tokyo, Yokohama, and the Japanese countryside. During its opening weekend in Japan, the film was reportedly preceded by an onscreen apology requesting that the audience be "immensely generous at many mistakes . . . which could not be avoided because the picture was edited in Hollywood." Still, the audience greeted the film with jeers, and the review of the film that ran in Tokyo's largest evening paper described it as "strictly a commercial item trying to sell exoticism to an American audience, using Japan as a stage and a Japanese actress, Shirley Yamaguchi, as the female lead. Its manner of completely ignoring Japanese habits, geography and sentiment make us feel quite awkward" ("'Bamboo House' Doesn't Bamboozle Japanese," *Hollywood Citizen-News*, August 30, 1955, *Bamboo House* Production File, Margaret Herrick Library, Academy of Motion Picture Arts and Sciences, Beverly Hills, Calif.).

95. Thomas, "Asia Journey."

96. Paramount Pictures, "Production Notes and Synopsis: 'My Geisha' (A Steve Parker Production for Paramount)," n.d., 3, *My Geisha* Production File,

Margaret Herrick Library, Academy of Motion Picture Arts and Sciences, Beverly Hills, Calif.

97. There are conflicting accounts of the elder Parker's vocation and length of stay in Japan. One version has him in Japan from 1937 to 1939 working for the U.S. State Department, while another dates the beginning of the family's time in Japan to 1936, when the father was sent to work as an engineer for General Electric on a Japanese hydroelectric project. See Art Seidenbaum, "Show Business Gets in 'Peace Corps' Act," *Los Angeles Times,* March 10, 1963, 13; Bob Thomas, "Star's Mate Tells Why He Became Producer in Japan," *Hollywood Citizen-News,* August 25, 1959, Steve Parker File, Margaret Herrick Library, Academy of Motion Picture Arts and Sciences, Beverly Hills, Calif.

98. Seidenbaum, "Show Business," 13.

99. Paramount Pictures, "Production Notes and Synopsis," 4.

100. Dick Williams, "Movie Stars Best Envoys to Asia, Declares Parker," *L.A. Mirror,* August 2, 1961, Parker File.

101. "Cardiff Jabs Japan for Deterring Prod'n There of Paramount's 'Geisha,'" *Daily Variety,* May 18, 1961, 3, Parker File.

102. "'Geisha' Producer Parker Challenges Director Cardiff's Raps at Japan," *Daily Variety,* May 23, 1961, 1, 9, Parker File.

103. Paramount Pictures, "Production Notes and Synopsis," 1.

104. Jon Whitcomb, "Operation Kimono," *Cosmopolitan,* June 1961, 15, *My Geisha* Production File.

105. Ibid., 14.

106. Paramount Pictures, "Production Notes and Synopsis," 7.

107. Bosley Crowther, "Comedy Set in Japan Opens at 2 Theatres," *New York Times,* March 4, 1961, 16.

108. In this sense, Paul's nostalgia might be compared to what Renato Rosaldo has called "imperialist nostalgia," the phenomenon of yearning, on the part of the agents of colonialism, for the culture they have destroyed (*Culture and Truth: The Remaking of Social Analysis* [Boston: Beacon, 1989], 68).

109. Whitcomb, "Operation Kimono," 16.

110. Lee Belser, "Geisha 'Most Difficult' Role for Shirley MacLaine," *L.A. Mirror,* May 30, 1961, *My Geisha* Production File.

111. Paramount Pictures, "Production Notes and Synopsis," 3.

112. Whitcomb, "Operation Kimono," 14.

113. Thomas, "Star's Mate."

114. Whitcomb, "Operation Kimono," 15.

115. Ibid.

116. Ibid.

117. Holmes, *World Is Mine,* 86.

118. Whitcomb, "Operation Kimono," 17.

CONCLUSION

1. David Henry Hwang, *M. Butterfly* (New York: Plume, 1988), 99. David Cronenberg is a Canadian film director, but the film was based on an Asian American text and produced by a U.S. company.

2. Susan Koshy begins her study of Asian-white miscegenation and the racialized constitution of U.S. national identity with John Luther Long's short story "Madame Butterfly" (1898). She focuses in particular on the critique of U.S. imperialism in the John Luther Long short story "Madame Butterfly" as compared to other, more popular, versions of the same narrative (*Sexual Naturalization: Asian Americans and Miscegenation* [Stanford: Stanford University Press, 2004], 29–49).

3. Hwang's play was inspired by a short notice in the *New York Times* about an espionage case involving a French diplomat and a Chinese opera singer. For an account of the Boursicot-Shi affair, based on extensive interviews with Bernard Boursicot, see Joyce Wadler, *Liaison: The Gripping Real Story of the Diplomat Spy and the Chinese Opera Star Whose Affair Inspired* M. Butterfly (New York: Bantam, 1993). Shi Pei-Pu was interviewed in the fall of 1993 by Barbara Walters on *20/20*. Like Hwang, I am less interested in the actual details of the affair than in the dramatic possibilities offered by the situation. There is, however, one notable element of the Boursicot-Shi affair from which the play departs: Shi lived publicly as a man while avowing his true identity as a woman to Boursicot, while in *M. Butterfly,* Song appears as a woman until the scene of his unveiling.

4. Cronenberg made his name as a director with a particular brand of visceral horror. His films prior to *M. Butterfly* include *Shivers* (1975), *Scanners* (1982), *Videodrome* (1982), *The Fly* (1986), *Dead Ringers* (1988), and *Naked Lunch* (1991).

5. Brian D. Johnson, "A Director's Obsession," *MacLean's,* September 13, 1993, 41.

6. In Hwang's play, for example, *Madama Butterfly* is Gallimard's favorite opera, while in the film, he is unfamiliar with the opera and must have the plot explained to him by a fellow audience member. Thus, in the play, Gallimard may be said to be living out a lifelong fantasy, while in the film his relationship with Song does not so closely parallel the familiar story. Dorinne Kondo discusses the film's relation to the play in her interview with Hwang in *About Face: Performing Race in Fashion and Theater* (New York: Routledge, 1997), 211–26.

7. Teresa de Lauretis points out that most of the scenes that take place in Paris were actually shot in Hungary, and some of the scenes set in Beijing were filmed in Toronto ("Popular Culture, Private and Public Fantasies: Femininity and Fetishism in David Cronenberg's 'M. Butterfly,'" *Signs* 24 [Winter 1999]: 312). I focus, however, on the scenes that both take place in China and were shot in China.

8. See, for example, Rey Chow, "The Dream of a Butterfly," in *Ethics after Idealism: Theory-Culture-Ethnicity-Reading* (Bloomington: Indiana University Press, 1998), 74–97; de Lauretis, "Popular Culture."

9. Janet Staiger, *Perverse Spectators: The Practices of Film Reception* (New York: New York University Press, 2000), 163.

10. Janet Maslin, "Seduction and the Impossible Dream," *New York Times,* October 1, 1993, C3.

11. John Simon, "Misadaptations," *National Review,* November 1, 1993, 72.

12. Richard Corliss, "Betrayal in Beijing," *Time,* October 4, 1993, 85.

13. Todd McCarthy, "'Butterfly' Goes Nowhere," *Variety,* September 20, 1993, 26.

14. Terry Pristin, "'M. Butterfly' Is Forced to Face Glare of the Spotlight," *Los Angeles Times,* October 11, 1993, F6.

15. Chris Rodley, introduction to David Cronenberg, *Cronenberg on Cronenberg,* ed. Chris Rodley, rev. ed. (London: Faber and Faber, 1992), xxiii.

16. Cronenberg, *Cronenberg on Cronenberg,* 178.

17. Burton Holmes Lectures program, 1899–1900, cited in Charles Musser with Carol Nelson, *High-Class Moving Pictures: Lyman H. Howe and the Forgotten Era of Traveling Exhibition, 1880–1920* (Princeton: Princeton University Press, 1991), 125.

18. Cronenberg, *Cronenberg on Cronenberg,* 178.

19. Hwang, *M. Butterfly,* 99.

20. For a discussion of films and videos made by Asian American producers documenting their travels to Asia, see Peter X. Feng, *Identities in Motion: Asian American Film and Video* (Durham: Duke University Press, 2002), 103–47.

21. Edward W. Said, *Orientalism* (New York: Random House, 1978), 20.

22. Cronenberg, *Cronenberg on Cronenberg,* 178.

23. Chow, "Dream," 78.

24. For an analysis of the two films together, see Leighton Grist, "'It's Only a Piece of Meat': Gender Ambiguity, Sexuality, and Politics in 'The Crying Game' and 'M. Butterfly,'" *Cinema Journal* 42 (Summer 2003): 3–28.

25. Rodley, introduction, xxiii.

26. Rodley, *Cronenberg on Cronenberg,* 177.

27. Cronenberg, ibid.

28. Ibid., 178.

29. Ibid.

30. McCarthy, "'Butterfly' Goes Nowhere," 26.

31. Tom Gunning, *D. W. Griffith and the Origins of American Narrative Film: The Early Years at Biograph* (Urbana: University of Illinois Press, 1991), 18.

Selected Bibliography

Abel, Richard. *The Red Rooster Scare: Making Cinema American, 1900–1910*. Berkeley: University of California Press, 1999.

Abel, Richard, ed. *French Film Theory and Criticism*. Vol. 1, 1907–39. Princeton: Princeton University Press, 1988.

Allen, Robert C., and Douglas Gomery. *Film History: Theory and Practice*. New York: McGraw-Hill, 1985.

Alloula, Malek. *The Colonial Harem*. Trans. Myrna Godzich and Wlad Godzich. Minneapolis: University of Minnesota Press, 1986.

Altman, Rick. *Silent Film Sound*. New York: Columbia University Press, 2004.

Anderson, Benedict. *Imagined Communities: Reflections on the Origins and Spread of Nationalism*. Rev. ed. London: Verso, 1983.

Andrew, Dudley, ed. *The Image in Dispute: Art and Cinema in the Age of Photography*. Austin: University of Texas Press, 1997.

Appadurai, Arjun. *Modernity at Large: Cultural Dimensions of Globalization*. Minneapolis: University of Minnesota Press, 1996.

Armstrong, Carol. *Scenes in a Library: Reading the Photograph in the Book, 1843–1875*. Cambridge: MIT Press, 1998.

Bal, Mieke. "Telling, Showing, Showing Off." *Critical Inquiry* 18 (Spring 1992): 556–94.

Balázs, Béla. *Theory of Film: Character and Growth of a New Art*. Trans. Edith Bone. New York: Dover, 1970.

Barber, X. Theodore. "The Roots of Travel Cinema: John L. Stoddard, E. Burton Holmes, and the Nineteenth-Century Illustrated Travel Lecture." *Film History* 5 (March 1993): 68–84.

Barnouw, Erik. *Documentary: A History of the Non-Fiction Film*. Rev. ed. Oxford: Oxford University Press, 1974.

Barsam, Richard Meyer. *Nonfiction Film: A Critical History*. New York: Dutton, 1973.

Barthes, Roland. *Camera Lucida: Reflections on Photography*. Trans. Richard Howard. New York: Hill and Wang, 1981.

Barthes, Roland. "L'Effet de Réel." In *Oeuvres Complètes*, 2: 479–84. Paris: Seuil, 1994.

Barthes, Roland. *Image—Music—Text*. Trans. Stephen Heath. New York: Hill and Wang, 1977.

Barthes, Roland. *Mythologies*. Paris: Seuil, 1957.

Bate, David. "The Occidental Tourist: Photography and Colonizing Vision." *Afterimage* 19 (Summer 1992): 11–13.

Baudrillard, Jean. *Simulations*. Trans. Paul Foss, Paul Patton, and Philip Beitchman. New York: Semiotext(e), 1983.

Bazin, André. *What Is Cinema*. Vol. 1. Trans. Hugh Gray. Berkeley: University of California Press, 1967.

Beauchamp, Cari. *Without Lying Down: Frances Marion and the Powerful Women of Early Hollywood*. Berkeley: University of California Press, 1998.

Bean, Jennifer M., and Diane Negra, eds. *A Feminist Reader in Early Cinema*. Durham: Duke University Press, 2002.

Behdad, Ali. *Belated Travelers: Orientalism in the Age of Colonial Dissolution*. Durham: Duke University Press, 1994.

Benjamin, Roger. "Matisse in Morocco: A Colonizing Esthetic?" *Art in America* 78 (November 1990): 156–65, 211, 213.

Benjamin, Walter. *Charles Baudelaire: A Lyric Poet in the Era of High Capitalism*. Trans. Harry Zohn. London: NLB, 1973.

Benjamin, Walter. *Illuminations*. Ed. Hannah Arendt. Trans. Harry Zohn. New York: Schocken, 1969.

Benjamin, Walter. "Lettre de Paris (II): Peinture et Photographie." *La Quinzaine Littéraire*, September 1–15, 1993, 14–15.

Benjamin, Walter. *One Way Street and Other Writings*. Trans. Edmund Jephcott and Kingsley Shorter. London: NLB, 1979.

Benjamin, Walter. *Reflections*. Ed. Peter Demetz. Trans. Edmund Jephcott. New York: Schocken, 1978.

Berlant, Lauren. *The Queen of America Goes to Washington City: Essays on Sex and Citizenship*. Durham: Duke University Press, 1997.

Berman, Marshall. *All That Is Solid Melts into Air: The Experience of Modernity*. New York: Simon and Schuster, 1982.

Bernardi, Daniel, ed. *The Birth of Whiteness: Race and the Emergence of U.S. Cinema*. New Brunswick: Rutgers University Press, 1996.

Bernstein, Matthew, and Gaylyn Studlar, eds. *Visions of the East: Orientalism in Film*. New Brunswick: Rutgers University Press, 1997.

Bhabha, Homi K. *The Location of Culture*. New York: Routledge, 1994.

Bhabha, Homi K., ed. *Nation and Narration*. New York: Routledge, 1990.

Bloch, Ernst, Georg Lukács, Bertolt Brecht, Walter Benjamin, and Theodor Adorno. *Aesthetics and Politics*. Ed. and trans. Ronald Taylor. London: Verso, 1977.

Bolton, Richard, ed. *The Contest of Meaning: Critical Histories of Photography*. Cambridge: MIT Press, 1989.

Boorstin, Daniel J. *The Image: A Guide to Pseudo-Events in America*. New York: Vintage, 1961.

Bordwell, David, Janet Staiger, and Kristin Thompson. *The Classical Hollywood Cinema: Film Style and Mode of Production to 1960*. New York: Columbia University Press, 1985.

Bowser, Eileen. *The Transformation of Cinema: 1907–1915*. Berkeley: University of California Press, 1990.

Brando, Marlon, with Robert Lindsey. *Brando: Songs My Mother Taught Me*. New York: Random House, 1994.

Brinkley, Alan. *The Unfinished Nation: A Concise History of the American People*. New York: McGraw-Hill, 1993.

Browne, Nick. "Orientalism as an Ideological Form: American Film Theory in the Silent Period." *Wide Angle* 11 (October 1989): 23–31.

Brownlow, Kevin. *Behind the Mask of Innocence: Sex, Violence, Prejudice, Crime: Films of Social Conscience in the Silent Era.* Berkeley: University of California Press, 1990.

Buck, Pearl S. *The Good Earth.* Intro. and ed. Peter Conn. New York: Simon and Schuster, 1994.

Buck, Pearl S. *My Several Worlds: A Personal Record.* New York: Day, 1954.

Burch, Noël. *Life to Those Shadows.* Trans. and ed. Ben Brewster. London: British Film Institute, 1990.

Carroll, Noel. "From Real to Reel: Entangled in Nonfiction Film." *Philosophic Exchange* 14 (Winter 1983): 5–45.

Cartwright, Lisa. *Screening the Body: Tracing Medicine's Visual Culture.* Minneapolis: University of Minnesota Press, 1995.

Cavell, Stanley. *The World Viewed: Reflections on the Ontology of Film.* Cambridge: Harvard University Press, 1971.

Chan, Anthony B. *Perpetually Cool: The Many Lives of Anna May Wong (1905–1961).* Lanham, Md.: Scarecrow, 2003.

Chan, Sucheng. *Asian Americans: An Interpretive History.* Boston: Twayne, 1991.

Chanan, Michael. *The Dream That Kicks: The Prehistory and Early Years of Cinema in Britain.* London: Routledge and Kegan Paul, 1980.

Charney, Leo, and Vanessa R. Schwartz, eds. *Cinema and the Invention of Modern Life.* Berkeley: University of California Press, 1995.

Cheng, Anne Anlin. "Race and Fantasy in Modern America: Subjective Dissimulation/Racial Assimilation." In *Multiculturalism and Representation: Selected Essays,* ed. John Rieder and Larry E. Smith, 175–97. Honolulu: University of Hawai'i Press, 1996.

Cheung, Hye Seung. *Hollywood Asian: Philip Ahn and the Politics of Cross-Ethnic Performance.* Philadelphia: Temple University Press, 2006.

Chin, Frank. *Donald Duk.* Minneapolis: Coffee House, 1991.

Chow, Rey. *Ethics after Idealism: Theory—Culture—Ethnicity—Reading.* Bloomington: Indiana University Press, 1998.

Chow, Rey. *Primitive Passions: Visuality, Sexuality, Ethnography, and Contemporary Chinese Cinema.* New York: Columbia University Press, 1995.

Chow, Rey. *Women and Chinese Modernity: The Politics of Reading between West and East.* Minneapolis: University of Minnesota Press, 1991.

Chow, Rey. *Writing Diaspora: Tactics of Intervention in Contemporary Cultural Studies.* Bloomington: Indiana University Press, 1993.

Choy, Philip P., Lorraine Dong, and Marlon K. Hom, eds. *Coming Man: Nineteenth Century American Perceptions of the Chinese.* Seattle: University of Washington Press, 1994.

Christie, Ian. *The Last Machine: Early Cinema and the Birth of the Modern World.* London: British Film Institute, 1994.

Chuh, Kandice. *Imagine Otherwise: On Asian Americanist Critique.* Durham: Duke University Press, 2003.

Chuh, Kandice, and Karen Shimakawa, eds. *Orientations: Mapping Studies in the Asian Diaspora.* Durham: Duke University Press, 2001.

Clark, Steve, ed. *Travel Writing and Empire: Postcolonial Theory in Transit.* London: Zed, 1999.

Clarke, Charles G. "China Photographically Ideal." *American Cinematographer,* September 1934, 202, 211–12.

Clifford, James. *The Predicament of Culture: Twentieth-Century Ethnography, Literature, and Art.* Cambridge: Harvard University Press, 1988.

Clifford, James. *Routes: Travel and Translation in the Late Twentieth Century.* Cambridge: Harvard University Press, 1997.

Clifford, James, and George E. Marcus, eds. *Writing Culture: The Poetics and Politics of Ethnography.* Berkeley: University of California Press, 1986.

Cloke, Paul, Philip Crang, and Mark Goodwin, eds. *Introducing Human Geographies.* New York: Oxford University Press, 1999.

Coe, Brian. *The History of Movie Photography.* London: Ash and Grant, 1981.

Collins, Jim, Hilary Radner, and Ava Preacher Collins, eds. *Film Theory Goes to the Movies.* New York: Routledge, 1993.

Conn, Peter. *Pearl S. Buck: A Cultural Biography.* Cambridge: Cambridge University Press, 1996.

Coombes, Annie E., and Steve Edwards. "Site Unseen: Photography in the Colonial Empire: Images of Subconscious Eroticism." *Art History* 12 (December 1989): 510–16.

Cosandey, Roland, and François Albera, eds. *Cinéma sans Frontières, 1896–1918: Images across Borders.* Lausanne: Payot, 1995.

Cotkin, George. *Reluctant Modernism: American Thought and Culture, 1880–1900.* New York: Twayne, 1992.

Crary, Jonathan. *Techniques of the Observer: On Vision and Modernity in the Nineteenth Century.* Cambridge: MIT Press, 1990.

Crawford, Peter Ian, and David Turton, eds. *Film as Ethnography.* Manchester: Manchester University Press, 1992.

Cronenberg, David. *Cronenberg on Cronenberg.* Ed. Chris Rodley. London: Faber and Faber, 1992.

Dalle Vacche, Angela. *The Body in the Mirror: Shapes of History in Italian Cinema.* Princeton: Princeton University Press, 1992.

Davis, Clarence B. and Kenneth E. Wilburn Jr., with Ronald E. Robinson, eds. *Railway Imperialism.* New York: Greenwood, 1991.

De Lauretis, Teresa. *Alice Doesn't: Feminism, Semiotics, Cinema.* Bloomington: Indiana University Press, 1982.

De Lauretis, Teresa. "Popular Culture, Private and Public Fantasies: Femininity and Fetishism in David Cronenberg's 'M. Butterfly.'" *Signs* 24 (Winter 1999): 303–34.

De Lauretis, Teresa, and Stephen Heath, eds. *The Cinematic Apparatus.* New York: St. Martin's, 1980.

Depue, Oscar. "My First Fifty Years in Motion Pictures." In *A Technological History of Motion Pictures and Television,* ed. Raymond Fielding, 60–64. Berkeley: University of California Press, 1967.

Dittmar, Linda, and Gene Michaud, eds. *From Hanoi to Hollywood: The Vietnam War in American Film.* New Brunswick: Rutgers University Press, 1990.

Dower, John W. *Embracing Defeat: Japan in the Wake of World War II.* New York: Norton, 1999.

Dower, John W. *War without Mercy: Race and Power in the Pacific War.* New York: Pantheon, 1986.

Duncan, James, and Derek Gregory, eds. *Writes of Passage: Reading Travel Writing.* London: Routledge, 1999.

During, Simon, ed. *The Cultural Studies Reader.* London: Routledge, 1993.

Dyer, Richard. *The Matter of Images: Essays on Representations.* London: Routledge, 1993.

Elsaesser, Thomas, with Adam Barker, eds. *Early Cinema: Space, Frame, Narrative.* London: British Film Institute, 1990.

Eng, David L. "In the Shadows of a Diva: Committing Homosexuality in David Henry Hwang's *M. Butterfly.*" In *Asian American Sexualities: Dimensions of the Gay and Lesbian Experience,* ed. Russell Leong, 131–52. New York: Routledge, 1996.

Eng, David L. "Out Here and Over There: Queerness and Diaspora in Asian American Studies." *Social Text* 52–53 (Fall–Winter 1997): 31–52.

Eng, David L. *Racial Castration: Managing Masculinity in Asian America.* Durham: Duke University Press, 2001.

Eng, David L, and Alice Y. Hom, eds. *Q and A: Queer in Asian America.* Philadelphia: Temple University Press, 1998.

Eperjesi, John R. *The Imperialist Imaginary: Visions of Asia and the Pacific in American Culture.* Hanover, N.H.: University Press of New England, 2005.

Fabian, Johannes. *Time and the Other: How Anthropology Makes Its Object.* New York: Columbia University Press, 1983.

Fabian, Rainer, and Hans-Christian Adam. *Masters of Early Travel Photography.* New York: Vendome, 1981.

Fanon, Frantz. *Black Skin, White Masks.* Trans. Charles Lam Markmann. New York: Grove Weidenfeld, 1967.

Fell, John L., ed. *Film before Griffith.* Berkeley: University of California Press, 1983.

Fell, John L., et al. *Before Hollywood: Turn-of-the-Century American Film.* New York: Hudson Hills Press, 1987.

Feng, Peter X. *Identities in Motion: Asian American Film and Video.* Durham: Duke University Press, 2002.

Feng, Peter X, ed. *Screening Asian Americans.* New Brunswick: Rutgers University Press, 2002.

Ferguson, Kathy E., and Phyllis Turnbull. *Oh, Say, Can You See? The Semiotics of the Military in Hawai'i.* Minneapolis: University of Minnesota Press, 1999.

Fredricks, Ellsworth. "The Photography of 'Sayonara.'" *American Cinematographer,* November 1957, 722–23, 742–44.

Friedberg, Anne. *Window Shopping: Cinema and the Postmodern.* Berkeley: University of California Press, 1993.

Friedman, Lester D., ed. *Unspeakable Images: Ethnicity and the American Cinema.* Urbana: University of Illinois Press, 1991.

Fullerton, John, ed. *Celebrating 1895: The Centenary of Cinema.* Sydney: Libbey, 1998.

Gaines, Jane. "White Privilege and Looking Relations: Race and Gender in Feminist Film Theory." *Screen* 29 (Autumn 1988): 12–27.

Garber, Marjorie. "The Occidental Tourist: *M. Butterfly* and the Scandal of Transvestism." In *Nationalisms and Sexualities,* ed. Andrew Parker, Mary Russo, Doris Sommer, and Patricia Yaeger, 121–46. New York: Routledge, 1991.

Gardner, Lloyd C. *Imperial America: American Foreign Policy since 1898.* New York: Harcourt Brace Jovanovich, 1976.

Gates, Henry Louis, Jr., ed. *"Race," Writing, and Difference.* Chicago: University of Chicago Press, 1986.

Genthe, Arnold, and John Kuo Wei Tchen. *Genthe's Photographs of San Francisco's Old Chinatown.* New York: Dover, 1984.

Gérard, Fabien S. *Ombres Jaunes: Journal de Tournage, le Dernier Empereur de Bernardo Bertolucci.* Paris: Seuil, 1987.

Gilman, Sander L. *Difference and Pathology: Stereotypes of Sexuality, Race, and Madness.* Ithaca: Cornell University Press, 1985.

Goldberg, David Theo, ed. *Anatomy of Racism.* Minneapolis: University of Minnesota Press, 1990.

Gong, Stephen. "Zen Warrior of the Celluloid (Silent) Years: The Art of Sessue Hayakawa." *Bridge* 8 (Winter 1982–83): 37–41.

Gramsci, Antonio. *Selections from the Prison Notebooks.* Ed. and trans. Quintin Hoare and Geoffrey Nowell Smith. New York: International, 1971.

Greenhalgh, Paul. *Ephemeral Vistas: The Expositions Universelles, Great Exhibitions, and Worlds Fairs, 1851–1939.* Manchester: Manchester University Press, 1988.

Gregory, Derek. *Geographical Imaginations.* Cambridge: Blackwell, 1994.

Grewal, Inderpal. *Home and Harem: Nation, Gender, Empire, and the Cultures of Travel.* Durham: Duke University Press, 1996.

Griffiths, Alison. "'Shivers Down Your Spine': Panoramas and the Origins of the Cinematic Reenactment." *Screen* 44 (Spring 2003): 1–37.

Griffiths, Alison. *Wondrous Difference: Cinema, Anthropology, and Turn-of-the-Century Visual Culture.* New York: Columbia University Press, 2002.

Grossberg, Lawrence, Cary Nelson, and Paula Treichler, eds. *Cultural Studies.* New York: Routledge, 1992.

Gunning, Tom. *D. W. Griffith and the Origins of American Narrative Film: The Early Years at Biograph.* Urbana: University of Illinois Press, 1991.

Gunning, Tom. "The Whole World within Reach: Travel Images without Borders." In *Cinéma sans Frontières, 1896–1918,* ed. Roland Cosandey and François Albera, 21–36. Lausanne: Payot, 1995.

Gunning, Tom. "The World as Object Lesson: Cinema Audiences, Visual Culture and the St. Louis World's Fair, 1904." *Film History* 6 (Winter 1994): 422–44.

Hall, Stuart. "Cultural Identity and Cinematic Representation." *Framework* 36 (1989): 68–81.

Hall, Stuart. "The Emergence of Cultural Studies and the Crisis of the Humanities." *October* 53 (Summer 1990): 11–23.

Hall, Stuart. "New Ethnicities." In *Black Film/British Cinema,* ed. Kobena Mercer, 27–31. London: Institute of Contemporary Arts, 1988.

Hamamoto, Darrell K. *Monitored Peril: Asian Americans and the Politics of Representation.* Minneapolis: University of Minnesota Press, 1994.

Hamamoto, Darrell K., and Sandra Liu, eds. *Countervisions: Asian American Film Criticism.* Philadelphia: Temple University Press, 2000.

Hansen, Miriam. *Babel and Babylon: Spectatorship in American Silent Film.* Cambridge: Harvard University Press, 1991.

Hansen, Miriam. "Benjamin, Cinema, and Experience: 'The Blue Flower in the Land of Technology.'" *New German Critique* 40 (Winter 1987): 179–224.

Haraway, Donna. *Simians, Cyborgs, and Women: The Reinvention of Nature.* New York: Routledge, 1991.

Harris, Neil. "All the World a Melting Pot? Japan at American Fairs, 1876–1904." In *Mutual Images: Essays in American-Japanese Relations,* ed. Akira Iriye, 24–54. Cambridge: Harvard University Press, 1976.

Heath, Stephen. *Questions of Cinema.* Bloomington: Indiana University Press, 1981.

Hendler, Jane. *Best-Sellers and Their Film Adaptations in Postwar America:* From Here to Eternity, Sayonara, Giant, Auntie Mame, Peyton Place. New York: Lang, 2001.

Hertogs, Daan, and Nico de Klerk. *Nonfiction from the Teens.* Amsterdam: Stichting Nederlands Filmmuseum, 1994.

Hobsbawm, E. J. *The Age of Empire, 1875–1914.* New York: Pantheon, 1987.

Hodges, Graham Russell. *Anna May Wong: From Laundryman's Daughter to Hollywood Legend.* New York: Palgrave Macmillan, 2004.

Hoganson, Kristin. *Fighting for American Manhood: How Gender Politics Provoked the Spanish-American and Philippine-American Wars.* New Haven: Yale University Press, 1998.

Holman, Roger, comp. *Cinema 1900/1906: An Analytical Study by the National Film Archive (London) and the International Federation of Film Archives.* Brussels: Fiaf, 1982.

Holmes, E. Burton. *Burton Holmes Travelogues.* Vols. 1–12. New York: McClure, 1910.

Holmes, E. Burton. *Burton Holmes Travelogues: The Greatest Traveler of His Time, 1892–1952.* Ed. Genoa Caldwell. Cologne: Taschen, 2006.

Holmes, E. Burton. *The Man Who Photographed the World: Burton Holmes Travelogues, 1886–1938.* Ed. Genoa S. Caldwell. New York: Abrams, 1977.

Holmes, E. Burton. *Peking (The World 100 Years Ago).* Ed. Fred L. Israel. Philadelphia: Chelsea House, 1998.

Holmes, E. Burton. *The World Is Mine.* Culver City, Calif.: Murray and Gee, 1953.

Horkheimer, Max, and Theodor Adorno. *Dialectic of Enlightenment.* Trans. John Cumming. New York: Continuum, 1993.

Hwang, David Henry. *M. Butterfly.* New York: Plume, 1988.

Isaacs, Harold R. *Scratches on Our Minds: American Images of China and India.* Westport, Conn.: Greenwood, 1958.

Jacobs, Lewis. *The Rise of the American Film: A Critical History.* New York: Teachers College Press, 1939.

Jacobs, Lewis, ed. *The Documentary Tradition.* 2nd ed. New York: Norton, 1979.

James, C. L. R. *Beyond a Boundary.* Durham: Duke University Press, 1993.

Jameson, Fredric. *The Geopolitical Aesthetic: Cinema and Space in the World System.* Bloomington: Indiana University Press, 1992.

Jameson, Fredric. "On 'Cultural Studies.'" *Social Text* 34 (1993): 17–52.

Jameson, Fredric. *Postmodernism; or, The Cultural Logic of Late Capitalism.* Durham: Duke University Press, 1991.

Jones, Dorothy B. *The Portrayal of China and India on the American Screen,*

1896–1955. Cambridge: Center for International Studies, Massachusetts Institute of Technology, 1955.

Jones, Howard Mumford. *The Age of Energy: Varieties of American Experience, 1865–1915*. New York: Viking, 1971.

Jordan, Pierre-L. *Cinéma: Premier Contact—Premier Regard*. Marseille: Musées de Marseille—Images en Manoeuvres Éditions, 1992.

Kaes, Anton. "German Cultural History and the Study of Film: Ten Theses and a Postscript." *New German Critique* 65 (Spring–Summer 1995): 47–58.

Kaplan, Amy. *The Anarchy of Empire in the Making of U.S. Culture*. Cambridge: Harvard University Press, 2002.

Kaplan, Amy. "The Birth of Empire." *PMLA* 114 (October 1999): 1068–79.

Kaplan, Amy, and Donald Pease, eds. *Cultures of United States Imperialism*. Durham: Duke University Press, 1993.

Kaplan, Caren. *Questions of Travel: Postmodern Discourses of Displacement*. Durham: Duke University Press, 1996.

Kaplan, E. Ann. *Looking for the Other: Feminism, Film, and the Imperial Gaze*. New York: Routledge, 1997.

Kasson, John F. *Amusing the Million: Coney Island at the Turn of the Century*. New York: Hill and Wang, 1978.

Keil, Charlie. *Early American Cinema in Transition: Story, Style, and Filmmaking, 1907–1913*. Madison: University of Wisconsin Press, 2001.

Keil, Charlie. "Steel Engines and Cardboard Rockets: The Status of Fiction and Nonfiction in Early Cinema." *Persistence of Vision* 9 (1991): 37–45.

Keil, Charlie, and Shelley Stamp, eds. *American Cinema's Transitional Era: Audiences, Institutions, Practices*. Berkeley: University of California Press, 2004.

Kemble, John Haskell. "The Big Four at Sea: The History of the Occidental and Oriental Steamship Company." *Huntington Library Quarterly* 3 (April 1940): 339–57.

Kenseth, Joy, ed. *The Age of the Marvelous*. Hanover, N.H.: Hood Museum of Art, Dartmouth College, 1991.

Kern, Stephen. *The Culture of Time and Space, 1880–1918*. Cambridge: Harvard University Press, 1983.

Kincaid, Jamaica. *A Small Place*. New York: Penguin, 1988.

King, Anthony D., ed. *Culture, Globalization, and the World-System: Contemporary Conditions for the Representation of Identity*. Minneapolis: University of Minnesota Press, 1997.

Kirby, Lynne. *Parallel Tracks: The Railroad and the Cinema*. Durham: Duke University Press, 1997.

Klein, Christina. *Cold War Orientalism: Asia in the Middlebrow Imagination, 1945–1961*. Berkeley: University of California Press, 2003.

Klinger, Barbara. "Digressions at the Cinema: Reception and Mass Culture." *Cinema Journal* 28 (Summer 1989): 3–19.

Klinger, Barbara. *Melodrama and Meaning: History, Culture, and the Films of Douglas Sirk*. Bloomington: Indiana University Press, 1994.

Kondo, Dorinne K. *About Face: Performing Race in Fashion and Theater*. New York: Routledge, 1997.

Kondo, Dorinne K. "*M. Butterfly*: Orientalism, Gender, and a Critique of Essentialist Identity." *Cultural Critique* 16 (Fall 1990): 5–29.

Koppes, Clayton R., and Gregory D. Black. *Hollywood Goes to War: How Politics, Profits, and Propaganda Shaped World War II Movies.* New York: Free Press, 1987.

Koshy, Susan. *Sexual Naturalization: Asian Americans and Miscegenation.* Stanford: Stanford University Press, 2004.

Kowalewski, Michael, ed. *Temperamental Journeys: Essays on the Modern Literature of Travel.* Athens: University of Georgia Press, 1992.

Kracauer, Siegfried. *Theory of Film: The Redemption of Physical Reality.* New York: Oxford University Press, 1960.

Landsberg, Alison. *Prosthetic Memory: The Transformation of American Remembrance in the Age of Mass Culture.* New York: Columbia University Press, 2004.

Lastra, James. *Sound Technology and the American Cinema: Perception, Representation, Modernity.* New York: Columbia University Press, 2000.

Lee, Josephine. *Performing Asian America: Race and Ethnicity on the Contemporary Stage.* Philadelphia: Temple University Press, 1997.

Lee, Josephine, Imogene L. Lim, and Yuko Matsukawa, eds. *Re/Collecting Early Asian America: Essays in Cultural History.* Philadelphia: Temple University Press, 2002.

Lee, Quentin. "Between the Oriental and the Transvestite." *Found Object* 8 (Fall 1993): 45–59.

Lee, Robert G. *Orientals: Asian Americans in Popular Culture.* Philadelphia: Temple University Press, 1999.

Leigh-Kile, Donna. "Glimpse of the Forbidden City: An International Film Company Goes behind the Red Doors." *Life,* April 1987, 36–40.

Leong, Karen J. *The China Mystique: Pearl S. Buck, Anna May Wong, Mayling Soong, and the Transformation of American Orientalism.* Berkeley: University of California Press, 2005.

Leong, Russell, ed. *Moving the Image: Independent Asian Pacific American Media Arts.* Los Angeles: UCLA Asian American Studies Center and Visual Communications, 1991.

Leyda, Jay. *Dianying: Electric Shadows: An Account of Films and the Film Audience in China.* Cambridge: MIT Press, 1972.

Li, David Leiwei. *Imagining the Nation: Asian American Literature and Cultural Consent.* Stanford: Stanford University Press, 1998.

Lipscomb, Elizabeth J., Frances E. Webb, and Peter Conn, eds. *The Several Worlds of Pearl S. Buck.* Westport, Conn.: Greenwood, 1994.

Logan, Joshua. *Movie Stars, Real People, and Me.* New York: Delacorte, 1978.

Long, John Luther. *Madame Butterfly, Purple Eyes, a Gentleman of Japan, and a Lady, Kito, Glory.* New York: Century, 1902.

Loo, Chalsa. "*M. Butterfly:* A Feminist Perspective." In *Bearing Dreams, Shaping Visions: Asian Pacific American Perspectives,* ed. Linda A. Revilla, Gail M. Nomura, Shawn Wong, and Shirley Hune, 177–84. Pullman: Washington State University Press, 1993.

Low, Gail Ching-Liang. *White Skins, Black Masks: Representation and Colonialism.* London: Routledge, 1996.

Lowe, Lisa. *Critical Terrains: French and British Orientalisms.* Ithaca: Cornell University Press, 1991.

Lowe, Lisa. *Immigrant Acts: On Asian American Cultural Politics.* Durham: Duke University Press, 1996.

Lubiano, Wahneema. "But Compared to What? Reading Realism, Representation, and Essentialism in *School Daze, Do the Right Thing,* and the Spike Lee Discourse." *Black American Literature Forum* 25 (Summer 1991): 253–82.

Luce, Henry. "The American Century." *Life,* February 17, 1941, 61–65.

Lye, Colleen. *America's Asia: Racial Form and American Literature, 1893–1945.* Princeton: Princeton University Press, 2005.

Lye, Colleen. "*M. Butterfly* and the Rhetoric of Antiessentialism: Minority Discourse in an International Frame." In *The Ethnic Canon: Histories, Institutions, and Interventions,* ed. David Palumbo-Liu, 260–89. Minneapolis: University of Minnesota Press, 1995.

Lynch, Lawrence. *Jules Verne.* New York: Twayne, 1992.

Ma, Sheng-Mei. *The Deathly Embrace: Orientalism and Asian American Identity.* Minneapolis: University of Minnesota Press, 2000.

MacCannell, Dean. *The Tourist: A New Theory of the Leisure Class.* New York: Schocken, 1976.

MacDougall, David. *Transcultural Cinema.* Ed. and intro. Lucien Taylor. Princeton: Princeton University Press, 1998.

Maeder, Edward, comp. *Hollywood and History: Costume Design in Film.* New York: Thames and Hudson, 1987.

Marchetti, Gina. *Romance and the "Yellow Peril": Race, Sex, and Discursive Strategies in Hollywood Fiction.* Berkeley: University of California Press, 1993.

Mast, Gerald, ed. *The Movies in Our Midst: Documents in the Cultural History of Film in America.* Chicago: University of Chicago Press, 1982.

Mast, Gerald, and Marshall Cohen, eds. *Film Theory and Criticism: Introductory Readings.* New York: Oxford University Press, 1974.

Mawson, Harry P., and J. W. Buel, comps. *Leslie's Official History of the Spanish-American War: A Pictorial and Descriptive Record of the Cuban Rebellion, the Causes That Involved the United States, and a Complete Narrative of Our Conflict with Spain on Land and Sea; Supplemented with Fullest Information Respecting Cuba, Porto Rico, the Philippines, and Hawaii.* Washington, D.C.: War Records Office, 1899.

May, Lary. *Screening Out the Past: The Birth of Mass Culture and the Motion Picture Industry.* Chicago: University of Chicago Press, 1980.

Mayne, Judith. *Cinema and Spectatorship.* London: Routledge, 1993.

McClintock, Anne. *Imperial Leather: Race, Gender, and Sexuality in the Colonial Contest.* New York: Routledge, 1995.

Memmi, Albert. *Portrait du Colonisé Précédé du Portrait du Colonisateur.* Paris: Corréa, 1957.

Metz, Christian. *The Imaginary Signifier: Psychoanalysis and the Cinema.* Trans. Celia Britton, Annwyl Williams, Ben Brewster, and Alfred Guzzetti. Bloomington: Indiana University Press, 1977.

Michener, James A. *Sayonara.* New York: Random House, 1953.

Michener, James A. *The World Is My Home: A Memoir.* New York: Random House, 1992.

Miller, Marion Mills, ed. *Great Debates in American History: From the Debates in the British Parliament on the Colonial Stamp Act (1764–1765) to the Debates in Congress at the Close of the Taft Administration (1912–1913).* Vol. 3, Foreign Relations, part 2. New York: Current Literature, 1913.

Miller, Toby, Nitin Govil, John McMurria, Ting Wang, and Richard Maxwell. *Global Hollywood 2*. London: British Film Institute, 2005.

Mitchell, Timothy. *Colonising Egypt*. Berkeley: University of California Press, 1991.

Mitchell, William J. *The Reconfigured Eye: Visual Truth in the Post-Photographic Era*. Cambridge: MIT Press, 1992.

Miyoshi, Masao. "A Borderless World? From Colonialism to Transnationalism and the Decline of the Nation-State." *Critical Inquiry* 19 (Summer 1993): 726–51.

Morley, David, and Kuan-Hsing Chen, eds. *Stuart Hall: Critical Dialogues in Cultural Studies*. London: Routledge, 1996.

Morris, Meaghan. "At Henry Parkes Motel." *Cultural Studies* 2 (1988): 1–47.

Moy, James S. *Marginal Sights: Staging the Chinese in America*. Iowa City: University of Iowa Press, 1993.

Mullen, Sarah M. *A Guide to the Discussion of the Screen Version of Pearl Buck's Prize-Winning Novel* The Good Earth. Newark, N.J.: Educational and Recreational Guides, 1937.

Munsterberg, Hugo. *Film: A Psychological Study*. New York: Dover, 1970.

Musser, Charles. *Before the Nickelodeon: Edwin S. Porter and the Edison Manufacturing Company*. Berkeley: University of California Press, 1991.

Musser, Charles. *Edison Motion Pictures, 1890–1900: An Annotated Filmography*. Washington, D.C.: Smithsonian Institution Press, 1997.

Musser, Charles. *The Emergence of Cinema: The American Screen to 1907*. New York: Scribner's, 1990.

Musser, Charles, ed. *Motion Picture Catalogs by American Producers and Distributors, 1894–1908: A Microfilm Edition*. Frederick, Md.: University Publications of America, 1985.

Musser, Charles, and Carol Nelson. *High-Class Moving Pictures: Lyman H. Howe and the Forgotten Era of Traveling Exhibition, 1880–1920*. Princeton: Princeton University Press, 1991.

Naficy, Hamid. *The Making of Exile Cultures: Iranian Television in Los Angeles*. Minneapolis: University of Minnesota Press, 1993.

Naficy, Hamid, ed. *Home, Exile, Homeland: Film, Media, and the Politics of Place*. New York: Routledge, 1999.

Naremore, James, and Patrick Brantlinger, eds. *Modernity and Mass Culture*. Bloomington: Indiana University Press, 1991.

Neale, Steve. *Cinema and Technology: Image, Sound, Colour*. Bloomington: Indiana University Press, 1985.

Nelson, Cary, and Dilip Parameshwar Gaonkar, eds. *Disciplinarity and Dissent in Cultural Studies*. New York: Routledge, 1996.

Nelson, Cary, and Lawrence Grossberg, eds. *Marxism and the Interpretation of Culture*. Urbana: University of Illinois Press, 1988.

Ngai, Mae M. "American Orientalisms." *Reviews in American History* 28 (September 2000): 408–15.

Ngai, Mae M. "Transnationalism and the Transformation of the 'Other': Response to the Presidential Address." *American Quarterly* 57 (March 2005): 59–65.

Nguyen, Viet Thanh. *Race and Resistance: Literature and Politics in Asian America*. New York: Oxford University Press, 2002.

Nichols, Bill. *Representing Reality: Issues and Concepts in Documentary*. Bloomington: Indiana University Press, 1991.

Nichols, Bill, ed. *Movies and Methods*. Vol. 2. Berkeley: University of California Press, 1985.

Niver, Kemp. *Early Motion Pictures: The Paper Print Collection in the Library of Congress*. Washington, D.C.: Library of Congress, 1985.

Niver, Kemp, comp. *Biograph Bulletins, 1896–1908*. Ed. Bebe Bergsten. Los Angeles: Locare, 1971.

Nochlin, Linda. "The Imaginary Orient." *Art in America* 71 (May 1983): 119–30.

O'Barr, William M. *Culture and the Ad: Exploring Otherness in the World of Advertising*. Boulder, Colo.: Westview, 1994.

Okihiro, Gary Y. *Margins and Mainstreams: Asians in American History and Culture*. Seattle: University of Washington Press, 1994.

Omi, Michael, and Howard Winant. *Racial Formation in the United States: From the 1960s to the 1980s*. New York: Routledge, 1986.

Ong, Aihwa. *Flexible Citizenship: The Cultural Logics of Transnationality*. Durham: Duke University Press, 1999.

Ong, Paul, Edna Bonacich, and Lucie Cheng. *The New Asian Immigration in Los Angeles and Global Restructuring*. Philadelphia: Temple University Press, 1994.

Ono, Kent A., ed. *Asian American Studies after Critical Mass*. Malden, Mass.: Blackwell, 2005.

Orvell, Mike. *The Real Thing: Imitation and Authenticity in American Culture, 1880–1940*. Chapel Hill: University of North Carolina Press, 1989.

Palumbo-Liu, David. *Asian/American: Historical Crossings of a Racial Frontier*. Stanford: Stanford University Press, 1999.

Pao, Angela. "The Critic and the Butterfly: Sociocultural Contexts and the Reception of David Henry Hwang's *M. Butterfly*." *Amerasia Journal* 18 (1992): 1–16.

Parker, Andrew, Mary Russo, Doris Sommer, and Patricia Yeager. *Nationalisms and Sexualities*. New York: Routledge, 1992.

Patrick, John. *The Teahouse of the August Moon*. New York: Putnam's, 1952.

Peterson, Jennifer Lynn. "World Pictures: Travelogue Films and the Lure of the Exotic, 1890–1920." Ph.D. diss., University of Chicago, 1999.

Pieterse, Jan Nederveen. *White on Black: Images of Africa and Blacks in Western Popular Culture*. New Haven: Yale University Press, 1992.

Polan, Dana B. "'Above All Else to Make You See': Cinema and the Ideology of Spectacle." In *Postmodernism and Politics*, ed. Jonathan Arac, 55–69. Minneapolis: University of Minnesota Press, 1986.

Poole, Deborah. *Vision, Race, and Modernity: A Visual Economy of the Andean Image World*. Princeton: Princeton University Press, 1997.

Pratt, Julius W. *Expansionists of 1898: The Acquisition of Hawaii and the Spanish Islands*. Baltimore: Johns Hopkins Press, 1936.

Pratt, Mary Louise. *Imperial Eyes: Travel Writing and Transculturation*. London: Routledge, 1992.

Prince, Stephen. "True Lies: Perceptual Realism, Digital Images, and Film Theory." *Film Quarterly* 49 (Spring 1996): 27–37.

Rabinovitz, Lauren. *For the Love of Pleasure: Women, Movies and Culture in Turn-of-the-Century Chicago*. New Brunswick: Rutgers University Press, 1998.

Rafael, Vicente L. *White Love and Other Events in Filipino History*. Durham: Duke University Press, 2000.

Renov, Michael, ed. *Theorizing Documentary*. New York: Routledge, 1993.

Robbins, Bruce, ed. *The Phantom Public Sphere.* Minneapolis: University of Minnesota Press, 1993.

Roberts, Frances Markley. *Western Travellers to China.* Shanghai: Kelly and Walsh, 1932.

Rojek, Chris, and John Urry, eds. *Touring Cultures: Transformations of Travel and Theory.* London: Routledge, 1997.

Rony, Fatimah Tobing. "The Last Emperor." *Film Quarterly* 42 (Winter 1988): 47–52.

Rony, Fatimah Tobing. *The Third Eye: Race, Cinema, and Ethnographic Spectacle.* Durham: Duke University Press, 1996.

Root, Deborah. *Cannibal Culture: Art, Appropriation, and the Commodification of Difference.* Boulder, Colo.: Westview, 1996.

Rosaldo, Renato. *Culture and Truth: The Remaking of Social Analysis.* Boston: Beacon, 1989.

Rosen, Philip. *Change Mummified: Cinema, Historicity, Theory.* Minneapolis: University of Minnesota Press, 2001.

Rosen, Philip. "Disjunction and Ideology in a Preclassical Film: *A Policeman's Tour of the World.*" *Wide Angle* 12 (1990): 20–36.

Rosen, Philip, ed. *Narrative, Apparatus, Ideology: A Film Theory Reader.* New York: Columbia University Press, 1986.

Ruoff, Jeffrey, ed. *Virtual Voyages: Cinema and Travel.* Durham: Duke University Press, 2006.

Rutstein, Harry, and Joanne Kroll. *In the Footsteps of Marco Polo: A Twentieth-Century Odyssey.* New York: Viking, 1980.

Rydell, Robert W. *All the World's a Fair: Visions of Empire at American International Expositions, 1876–1916.* Chicago: University of Chicago Press, 1984.

Said, Edward W. *Culture and Imperialism.* New York: Vintage, 1994.

Said, Edward W. *Orientalism.* New York: Random House, 1978.

Savada, Elias, comp. *The American Film Institute Catalog of Motion Pictures Produced in the United States.* Vol. A, *Film Beginnings, 1893–1910.* Metuchen, N.J.: Scarecrow, 1995.

Savran, David, ed. *In Their Own Words: Contemporary American Playwrights.* New York: Theatre Communications, 1988.

Schivelbusch, Wolfgang. *The Railway Journey: The Industrialization of Time and Space in the Nineteenth Century.* Berkeley: University of California Press, 1986.

Schueller, Malini Johar. *U.S. Orientalisms: Race, Gender, and Nation in Literature, 1790–1890.* Ann Arbor: University of Michigan Press, 1998.

Schwartz, Vanessa R. *Spectacular Realities: Early Mass Culture in Fin-de-Siècle Paris.* Berkeley: University of California Press, 1998.

Scott, Joan W. "The Evidence of Experience." *Critical Inquiry* 17 (Summer 1991): 773–97.

Shimakawa, Karen. *National Abjection: The Asian American Body on Stage.* Durham: Duke University Press, 2002.

Shohat, Ella. "Imaging Terra Incognita: The Disciplinary Gaze of Empire." *Public Culture* 3 (Spring 1991): 41–70.

Shohat, Ella, and Robert Stam. *Unthinking Eurocentrism: Multiculturalism and the Media.* London: Routledge, 1994.

Silva, Noenoe K. *Aloha Betrayed: Native Hawaiian Resistance to American Colonialism.* Durham: Duke University Press, 2004.

Silverman, Debora. *Selling Culture: Bloomingdale's, Diana Vreeland, and the New Aristocracy of Taste in Reagan's America.* New York: Pantheon, 1986.

Silverman, Kaja. *Male Subjectivity at the Margins.* New York: Routledge, 1992.

Silverman, Kaja. *The Subject of Semiotics.* New York: Oxford University Press, 1983.

Simpson, Caroline Chung. *An Absent Presence: Japanese Americans in Postwar American Culture, 1945–1960.* Durham: Duke University Press, 2001.

Simpson, Caroline Chung. "'Out of an Obscure Place': Japanese War Brides and Cultural Pluralism in the 1950s." *differences* 10 (Fall 1998): 47–81.

Sklarew, Bruce H., Bonnie S. Kaufman, Ellen Handler Spitz, and Diane Borden, eds. *Bertolucci's* The Last Emperor: *Multiple Takes.* Detroit: Wayne State University Press, 1998.

Smoodin, Eric. *Regarding Frank Capra: Audience, Celebrity, and American Film Studies, 1930–1960.* Durham: Duke University Press, 2004.

Sobchack, Vivian. "'Surge and Splendor': A Phenomenology of the Hollywood Historical Epic." *Representations* 29 (Winter 1990): 24–49.

Sontag, Susan. *On Photography.* New York: Dell, 1973.

Spivak, Gayatri Chakravorty. *In Other Worlds: Essays in Cultural Politics.* New York and London: Routledge, 1988.

Spivak, Gayatri Chakravorty. *The Post-Colonial Critic: Interviews, Strategies, Dialogues.* Ed. Sarah Harasym. New York: Routledge, 1990.

Spivak, Gayatri Chakravorty. "Three Women's Texts and a Critique of Imperialism." *Critical Inquiry* 12 (Autumn 1985): 243–61.

Spurr, David. *The Rhetoric of Empire: Colonial Discourse in Journalism, Travel Writing, and Imperial Administration.* Durham: Duke University Press, 1993.

Staiger, Janet. *Interpreting Films: Studies in the Historical Reception of American Cinema.* Princeton: Princeton University Press, 1992.

Staiger, Janet. *Perverse Spectators: The Practices of Film Reception.* New York: New York University Press, 2000.

Stoddard, John L. *John L. Stoddard's Lectures.* Vol. 3. Boston: Balch, 1898.

Stoler, Ann Laura. *Race and the Education of Desire: Foucault's* History of Sexuality *and the Colonial Order of Things.* Durham: Duke University Press, 1995.

Strain, Ellen. *Public Places, Private Journeys: Ethnography, Entertainment, and the Tourist Gaze.* New Brunswick: Rutgers University Press, 2003.

Tagg, John. *The Burden of Representation: Essays on Photographies and Histories.* Amherst: University of Massachusetts Press, 1988.

Tajima, Renee. "Lotus Blossoms Don't Bleed: Images of Asian Women." In *Anthologies of Asian American Film and Video,* 28–33. New York: Third World Newsreel, 1984.

Takaki, Ronald. *Strangers from a Different Shore.* New York: Penguin, 1989.

Taylor, Lucien, ed. *Visualizing Theory: Selected Essays from V.A.R., 1990–1994.* New York: Routledge, 1994.

Tchen, John Kuo Wei. *New York before Chinatown: Orientalism and the Shaping of American Culture, 1776–1882.* Baltimore: Johns Hopkins University Press, 1999.

Thomas, Bob. *Marlon: Portrait of the Rebel as an Artist.* New York: Random House, 1973.

Thomson, James C., Jr., Peter W. Staley, and John Curtis Perry. *Sentimental Imperialists: The American Experience in East Asia.* New York: Harper and Row, 1981.

Thomson, John. *China and Its People in Early Photographs: An Unabridged Reprint of the Classic 1873/4 Work.* New York: Dover, 1982.

Tomlinson, John. *Globalization and Culture.* Chicago: University of Chicago Press, 1999.

Tonetti, Claretta Micheletti. *Bernardo Bertolucci: The Cinema of Ambiguity.* New York: Twayne, 1995.

Toulet, Emmanuelle. "Cinema at the Universal Exposition, Paris, 1900." *Persistence of Vision* 9 (1991): 10–36.

Trachtenberg, Alan. *The Incorporation of America: Culture and Society in the Gilded Age.* New York: Hill and Wang, 1982.

Trask, Haunani-Kay. *From a Native Daughter: Colonialism and Sovereignty in Hawai'i.* Rev. ed. Honolulu: University of Hawai'i Press, 1999.

Travel Photography. New York: Time-Life Books, 1972.

Trinh, T. Minh-Ha. *Woman, Native, Other: Writing Postcoloniality and Feminism.* Bloomington: Indiana University Press, 1989.

Trinh, T. Minh-Ha. *When the Moon Waxes Red: Representation, Gender, and Cultural Politics.* New York: Routledge, 1991.

Van den Ecker, Louis. "A Veteran's View of Hollywood Authenticity." *Hollywood Quarterly* 4 (Summer 1950): 323–31.

Vasey, Ruth. *The World According to Hollywood, 1918–1939.* Madison: University of Wisconsin Press, 1997.

Verne, Jules. *Around the World in Eighty Days.* Trans. George Makepeace Towle. 1873. Reprint, New York: Bantam, 1984.

Virilio, Paul. *War and Cinema: The Logistics of Perception.* London: Verso, 1989.

Wadler, Joyce. *Liaison: The Gripping Real Story of the Diplomat Spy and the Chinese Opera Star Whose Affair Inspired* M. Butterfly. New York: Bantam, 1993.

Weigman, Robyn. *American Anatomies: Theorizing Race and Gender.* Durham: Duke University Press, 1995.

Wetzel, Andreas. "Décrire l'Espagne: Référent et Réalité dans le Récit de Voyage Littéraire." *Stanford French Review* 11 (Fall 1987): 359–73.

Whissel, Kristen. *Picturing American Modernity: Traffic, Technology, and the Silent Cinema.* Durham: Duke University Press, 2008.

Whissel, Kristen. "Placing the Spectator on the Scene of History: The Battle Re-Enactment at the Turn of the Century, from Buffalo Bill's Wild West to the Early Cinema." *Historical Journal of Film, Radio, and Television* 22 (August 2002): 225–43.

Whissel, Kristen. "Uncle Tom, Goldilocks, and the Rough Riders: Early Cinema's Encounter with Empire." *Screen* 40 (Winter 1999): 384–404.

Williams, Linda. *Viewing Positions: Ways of Seeing Film.* New Brunswick: Rutgers University Press, 1995.

Willis, Sharon. *High Contrast: Race and Gender in Contemporary Hollywood Film.* Durham: Duke University Press, 1997.

Wilson, Rob, and Wimal Dissanayake, eds. *Global/Local: Cultural Production and the Transnational Imaginary.* Durham: Duke University Press, 1996.

Wong, Eugene Franklin. *On Visual Media Racism: Asians in the American Motion Pictures.* New York: Arno, 1978.

Wood, Frances. *Did Marco Polo Go to China?* London: Secker and Warburg, 1995.

Wood, Robin. *Hollywood from Vietnam to Reagan.* New York: Columbia University Press, 1986.

Xing, Jun. *Asian America through the Lens: History, Representations, and Identity.* Walnut Creek, Calif.: Altamira, 1998.

Yoshihara, Mari. *Embracing the East: White Women and American Orientalism.* New York: Oxford University Press, 2003.

Yoshimoto, Mitsuhiro. "The Difficulty of Being Radical: The Discipline of Film Studies and the Postcolonial World." *Boundary 2* 18 (Fall 1991): 242–57.

Young, Marilyn Blatt, ed. *American Expansionism: The Critical Issues.* Boston: Little, Brown, 1973.

Zhang, Longxi. "The Myth of the Other: China in the Eyes of the West." *Critical Inquiry* 15 (Autumn 1988): 108–31.

Zhang, Longxi. "The Tao and the Logos: Notes on Derrida's Critique of Logocentricism." *Critical Inquiry* 11 (March 1985): 385–98.

Index